GOVERNMENT AND PARLIAMENT

A Survey from the Inside

HERBERT MORRISON

P.C., C.H., M.P.

GOVERNMENT AND PARLIAMENT

A Survey from the Inside

GEOFFREY CUMBERLEGE

OXFORD UNIVERSITY PRESS

LONDON NEW YORK TORONTO

1954

Oxford University Press, Amen House, London E.C. 4

GLASGOW NEW YORK TORONTO MELBOURNE WELLINGTON
BOMBAY CALCUTTA MADRAS KARACHI CAPE TOWN IBADAN

Geoffrey Cumberlege, Publisher to the University

PRINTED IN GREAT BRITAIN

PREFACE

It was at Nuffield College, Oxford, that the idea of this book was born. I had been elected a Visiting Fellow in 1947, and in the autumn of that year I agreed to talk after dinner about the inside working of British government and in particular about the internal operations and life of Parliament. Usually these Nuffield after-dinner discussions are confined to members of the College, but on this occasion most of the teachers of Politics in the University were also present. I had visited universities before, either to take part in Union debates, to lecture, or to receive their kindly hospitality. My own education (for which I am grateful) was confined to that of the London elementary schools, and even at the time of this Nuffield seminar I was still a little university-shy—and this was a very friendly occasion. Since then, however, my visits to universities have increased and, consequent on the kindly facilities afforded me by the Warden and Fellows of Nuffield College, my visits to Oxford have been frequent, so that by now I am much more familiar with academic life.

Apparently the information given in my talk, and as a result of the questions and discussions, was considered to be interesting and valuable. All of us, I think, had a happy and interesting time. At the end of the evening some enthusiast said: 'Mr. Morrison, you really must write a book about all this. You have told us about a lot of things which have not yet reached the textbooks. As a co-ordinating Minister and Leader of the House of Commons you have just the kind of experience which fits you to write such a book.' There was general and cordial agreement among those present. I replied that I was a hard-worked Minister of the Crown and that it was impossible for me to write books, especially the by no means easy book which they had in mind, to which somebody, with an optimism which I did not find too pleasing, said: 'Well, you won't always be a Minister, you will get the sack at the hands of democracy some day; promise that you will do it then.' I told him that he was opening up a rather unwelcome prospect, but that I would certainly keep the idea in mind.

So some months after the General Election of 1951, when the United Kingdom parted with its Labour Government, I decided to try my hand at a volume which might be useful to the good and thoughtful citizen, students, and practitioners of public affairs, teachers, and perhaps even professors of Political Science. Well, here it is. Constitutional doctrine and practice arise in the course of this book, but it is not a book about the British Constitution as seen by the lawyer. It deals with the inside working of Government and Parliament and the relations between Government and Parliament, in the light of the experience of one who has been privileged to serve in four Governments and under three Prime Ministers, and who has been a Member of six Parliaments from the end of 1923, though with two interruptions.

I have not attempted to deal with every aspect of British government. For example, I make little reference to the important matter of financial control. To deal with this and many other matters would have made the book far too long. Moreover, much is already covered in the standard books. I have, therefore, concentrated on the less well known features, on recent developments and on proposals for change. I have, however, not confined myself to mere description. Where I felt it necessary I have not hesitated to express views on how particular institutions should operate or on the merits of recent changes and proposals. From these comments the reader will, no doubt, gather something of my political philosophy, and I think that my great love and admiration for British parliamentary democracy will clearly emerge.

This is not, however, a party political book; it seeks to be a genuine contribution to political studies. I have tried to be as objective as possible, but I have no doubt that many readers will find some of my views unacceptable and controversial, and I would ask them to be as tolerant as they can in reading these pages.

There are two general omissions which I should mention. First, I have not said a great deal about that fundamental characteristic of the British Constitution—the attitude and way of life of the British people, whether they be politicians or ordinary citizens. There was a time in our country, and not very long ago at that, when public life was ravaged by corruption and minorities were roughly treated. Nowadays, the standard of honesty in all walks of British public life must be as high as, if not higher than, almost any other country in the world. Equally important, respect for the law, for tradition, and for the rights of the other side are inherent in our way of life. What on paper appear to be the same institutions can work differently in different countries. Most of ours work as they do because that is how we feel they ought to work.

Second, this is a book about government at the centre—about Parliament and Ministers—and therefore I have had regretfully to leave out local government. I would, however, like to take this opportunity to affirm once again my belief that local government is an essential part of the British Constitution. It is not just an arrangement for administrative convenience, but part of our inheritance and British way of life.

In the first four chapters I deal with the Cabinet and Cabinet Committees, the size of Cabinets, the work of non-departmental Ministers, the idea of supervising Ministers—or what have come to be known as Overlords—and the position of Ministers outside the Cabinet, including Parliamentary Secretaries. A chapter is devoted to the Monarchy in our parliamentary democracy. And then we pass to a series of chapters on the relations between Government and Parliament and the internal working of both Houses. The manner in which the Labour Government changed the machinery for the organization of the legislative programme is described in Chapter XI. I have thought it well to include a chapter on Economic Planning, as this was an important development in organization and administration within the machinery of government. Similarly, there is a chapter on the socialization of industry, in which I am particularly concerned with public control and parliamentary accountability, for important questions in the relationship between Parliament and the public corporations are involved. Finally, in the chapter on Ministers and Civil Servants the relationship between Ministers and their officers is discussed, and some aspects of the staffing and administration of Government Departments are examined.

For a busy public man, it has been hard work to write this book. The Parliaments elected in 1950 and 1951, with their small majorities, have been something like prisoner-of-war camps, and there has been week-end speaking and other work to do. So it has been a matter of working for the most part during free week-ends, with a limited amount of labour during recesses when possible. I have been enormously aided by the secretarial and other facilities afforded to me by the Warden and Fellows of Nuffield College, and have found writing at an Oxford college a welcome change from previous experience. The expenses incurred by the College have been met out of money left to the College by Sir Gwilym Gibbon—a respected civil servant well known to me—for research into problems of government; most of the bequest is used to pay for the annual Gwilym Gibbon Research Fellow.

There are a number of people to whom I would wish to tender my thanks, and if by inadvertence (as I fear may be the case) I omit to mention some who ought to be mentioned, I ask forgiveness.

First and foremost I place my very good friend Mr. D. N. Chester, Fellow of Nuffield College. He encouraged me to go ahead and cheered and helped me when the tiring stage of cuts, insertion, rearranging, and rewriting was being passed through. No less did he engage in frank criticism and subject me to examination and even cross-examination from time to time, with a view to clarification.

Working with both of us, Miss Gweneth Gutch, Research Assistant at Nuffield, rendered aid of great value. In research, reading the manuscript, suggesting revisions, and preparing the index, Miss Gutch has eased my task considerably.

Mr. C. R. Attlee was good enough to read the earlier chapters and to give me his comments.

To my private secretary, Miss E. M. Donald, I tender my thanks for assistance with the manuscript, in collecting, guarding, and producing records and papers when required, and for most helpful secretarial assistance in many ways. Miss Rose Davy kindly read the proofs and made many useful suggestions.

I am indebted to my friends Mr. Hugh Gaitskell and Mr. Douglas Jay for their advice and assistance with the chapter on Economic Planning and Controls.

Professor K. C. Wheare and Mr. Max Beloff kindly read most of the chapters and gave me very useful comments and advice.

Mr. D. E. Butler and Mr. H. A. Clegg helped me similarly with certain parts of the book.

A number of distinguished civil servants and officers of both Houses of Parliament have been good enough to let me have their observations on the factual aspects of the manuscript.

To all these and others (including the excellent stenographers at Nuffield College) I extend sincere thanks, at the same time absolving them from any responsibility for the opinions expressed in this volume.

H. M.

HOUSE OF COMMONS, S.W. I

January 1954

CONTENTS

THE CABINET AND MINISTERS

CHAPTER I

At the Cabinet

No. 10 Downing Street is distinctly British. The British like dignified ceremony, but they do not like undue ostentation; and certainly there is nothing ostentatious about the outside of 10 Downing Street. This modest exterior is pleasing to the crowds of Londoners, Scots, Welsh, Irish, folk from provincial England, and people from the Commonwealth and foreign countries, who forgather opposite No. 10 and seem to have an uncanny knowledge of when Ministers are going to meet or when distinguished visitors are due to arrive.

They are a nice lot of people, this Downing Street crowd, quiet and orderly, though capable of a reasonable vocal enthusiasm on big occasions. I suspect that, as they stand there watching the comings and goings, looking at No. 10 where the Prime Minister works, at No. 11 which I know so well, for I worked there for over six years, and at No. 12 which is the Whips' Office, the sightseers probably find it pleasing that this nerve centre of Her Majesty's Government in the United Kingdom should be accommodated in these rather ordinary-looking houses.

Inside there is a quiet dignity. There are more rooms than the people outside would think, some of them larger than they imagine. There are commodious reception rooms and a dining-room of substantial size on the first floor at No. 10, with residential accommodation above. There is a fine large room on the first floor at No. 11 which I used for work and for Cabinet Committee meetings, with an excellent Secretary's room attached, and others used by the Chancellor of the Exchequer. On the ground floor of No. 10 there are a number of rooms, the principal of which is the holy of holies, the Cabinet Room, where vital debates and discussions take place and decisions are reached of great significance to our country and the world.

The Cabinet Room is not over-pretentious. It is painted white with touches of gold here and there. It is a longish room; at one end there are French windows from which one can look out at the pleasant garden of No. 10; at the other end are double doors opening into the Prime Minister's Private Secretaries' offices; and on the long side facing the fire-place are large windows through which one can see Horse Guards' Parade and the Admiralty. The entrance is by double doors from a hall which is reached by a corridor from the street entrance. When the Cabinet is to meet, the Ministers gather in this hallway and talk informally about the weather, or public opinion, or trouble in Parliament. This limited period of social concourse is pleasant and useful, for it leads to that good fellowship which is conducive to tolerance and good temper round the Cabinet table. It is here that Ministers not in the Cabinet await the summons until the item with which they are concerned is reached.

The Cabinet in Session

In a little while the Prime Minister or the Secretary to the Cabinet will appear and invite the Ministers to assemble round the long table covered with green baize. Each Cabinet Minister has his allotted place having some relationship to ministerial status. The Prime Minister is in the Chair with his back to the fire-place, facing Horse Guards' Parade.

An agenda and, probably, papers will already have been circulated. The relevant Cabinet Papers are indicated under each item and there may be references to earlier related documents. For most items there are papers, but sometimes a note will read, 'To be raised orally by . . .'.

Sometimes the Prime Minister or, with his agreement, other Ministers will raise matters of urgency not on the agenda, or mention the settlement of some problem that had arisen at a previous meeting.

The Prime Minister will call upon the Minister principally concerned with the first item on the agenda, unless convenience requires that the order of business be changed. The normal and most appropriate course is for that Minister to make his case. If there is general agreement a conclusion is expeditiously reached. But there may be criticism, alterations in the course proposed may be urged, there may even be outright opposition.

To describe the ministerial contributions as speeches would not be quite right. They are, or at any rate should be, to the point and in the nature of quiet, well-considered remarks, calculated to lead the Cabinet in the direction desired. They should not be in the nature of public meeting or parliamentary orations, though this has been known to happen. Personalities and bad temper are unusual and would certainly be discouraged, because it is very necessary for the Cabinet to be and to feel like a team, collectively concerned with the public interest. The number of Ministers taking part in a given discussion will depend on the subject before the Cabinet. Most items will only require the contributions of a few Ministers. But on exceptional matters of high and controversial policy, especially if about something new that may involve difficulty in Parliament or with public opinion, it may be that every Minister will indicate his point of view.

The contribution of the Prime Minister to the discussion is, of course, of particular importance, and weight is attached to the views of the Chairman of the Cabinet Committee concerned, if the item has been considered by a committee in advance, or if the matter is within his sphere as a co-ordinating Minister. The Prime Minister may indicate his views early in the discussion or else wait, until the other Ministers have spoken, to sum up and to indicate the course which he thinks the Cabinet wishes to follow or which should be followed. I have served under three Prime Ministers each of whom had his own technique. Largely it is a matter of personality.

How Decisions are Reached

So in due course we reach the point when what is called the Conclusion has to be reached. Now this is not done by voting, for the holding up of hands or the calling of 'Aye' and 'No' would not only be regarded as a breach of Cabinet decorum but would also be felt to symbolize and demonstrate, nakedly and unashamedly, a lack of Cabinet unity and solidarity which is always deprecated. In most cases the Prime Minister is able, with the assent of the Cabinet, to state that the general view would appear to be so and so, and that is duly recorded in the Conclusions as the decision reached. But there are occasions when it is necessary to 'collect the voices', that is to say, to go round the table and to get the views of Ministers for and against the proposition under consideration. Somebody is carefully noting the numbers each way and at the end the Prime Minister will declare the predominant view, avoiding the figures if he can. This, of course, is very near formal voting, but we protect tradition by somewhat regretfully collecting the voices and counting them as informally as we can.

In the exceptional case of the Cabinet being somewhat acutely divided and strong views being held on a matter of particular difficulty, the quality of the Prime Minister, and indeed others, is tested. Careful judgement is required to know whether the decision shall operate or whether the strength of feeling is such that not only would Cabinet unity be imperilled but also the success of the policy itself might be endangered. It may be right to let the decision stand and to go ahead, but it may be better to suggest that in view of the sharp division of opinion Ministers should think about the discussion and defer a final decision until a later meeting, if postponement be possible. Alternatively, the matter may be referred to a standing or specially constituted committee; or it may be arranged that the Prime Minister or other senior Minister should meet the principal disputants to promote the best, or a substantially agreed, settlement. The problem in any case is to secure the widest measure of agreement that is consistent with the public interest. It may well be necessary, however, to arrive at a clear-cut decision for or against a departmental Minister's view.

Often, before a matter reaches the Cabinet, formal or informal discussion will have taken place between Ministers departmentally concerned or those likely to be interested or troublesome to the initiating Minister. The Minister intending to bring a matter before the Cabinet may well consult the Prime Minister or other senior Minister to obtain advice or reach agreement, thus making the approval of his proposal easier or causing him to modify it. Such discussions may take place at officially organized inter-departmental meetings, possibly being convened by the initiating Department or by the Cabinet Secretariat which, among its responsibilities, has that of getting the ground cleared or prepared before the actual stage of Cabinet consideration, if that be possible. But such discussions will often take place informally, perhaps outside the Cabinet Room whilst Ministers are waiting for the Cabinet to commence, in a

Minister's room in Parliament, in a parliamentary corridor, or over a meal. The wise Minister will consider the possible snags and difficulties which lie ahead and seek to clear them out of the way to the greatest practicable extent before the crucial stage of Cabinet discussion is reached. If he or his civil servants have done this preliminary work well, the Cabinet consideration may be more or less formal and, in any case, his difficulties at the Cabinet table are more likely to be minimized.

However, unless the Minister or Ministers who are consulted fully understand the issues or have clear or intelligent convictions about them, they will be wise not finally to commit themselves, because arguments may come forward from other Ministers causing them to revise the provisional conclusion they had reached in discussion with the initiating Minister. Indeed, it is well in some cases for Ministers to make their agreement provisional and conditional upon what transpires in Cabinet, otherwise they may appear to be guilty of a breach of faith.

A Minister, in stating his case to the Cabinet, has a responsible and by no means always easy task. He must be conscious of possible objections to the course he proposes, though careful how far he anticipates them. However, he should not hide the real difficulties. He should state his case clearly and persuasively; he should know what he is talking about, for the chances are that he will be caught out if he is wrong on fact; he should not be over-long in stating his case or he will bore and annoy his colleagues. It is a possible fault not to say enough, but it is a more likely fault to talk too long. Much depends on the Minister's art of exposition and the confidence of his colleagues in his judgement.

Ministers are usually supplied with briefs by their civil servants not only on their own business but also on the business of other Ministers. Although it is legitimate in cases of technical complexity for it to be apparent that a Minister is relying on his brief, it is undesirable for this to be customary, otherwise it will again be clear that he is not the master of the business. Inevitably he will, from time to time, noticeably pick up points from his brief, but the reading of a brief in other than exceptional cases is undesirable and the Minister is likely to lose the interest and possibly the respect of his colleagues.

It is sometimes thought to be common for Permanent Secretaries or other senior civil servants to attend the Cabinet or Cabinet Committees. The fact is that in the case of the Cabinet this is very rare, and in the case of Cabinet Committees, other than the Legislation Committee, it is unusual. At the Legislation Committee Ministers can expound matters of policy but cannot be expected to be expert on the technical drafting and detail of Parliamentary Bills and delegated legislation. The parliamentary draftsmen concerned must in any case be there and the presence of other civil servants is often necessary to advise their Ministers. It is possible that false impressions about the attendance of civil servants at Cabinet and Cabinet Committee meetings are related to the exaggerated belief that civil servants and not Ministers run the Government. It is the general rule that the Prime Minister or the Chairman of the Cabinet Committee concerned has to give special permission for a Minister to bring a civil servant with him. This in itself shows that it is the exception rather than the rule. There have been occasions, however, when it has been thought appropriate for the Permanent Secretary of the Treasury to attend the Cabinet to assist the Chancellor of the Exchequer or possibly the Prime Minister. And there have been occasions when the Permanent Under-Secretary of State of the Foreign Office or other Foreign Office expert has attended to assist the Foreign Secretary when somewhat specialized information has been required. The Chiefs of Staff will be present when questions with military implications are before the Cabinet. But in general Ministers must, so to speak, stand on their own feet at Cabinet and Cabinet Committee meetings and be ready not only to expound their policies but also to stand up to cross-examination. This is a good thing, for it provides an incentive to Ministers to master their business and their Departments. It is legitimate now and again for a Minister to confess that he does not know the answer to a question, but if that becomes fairly habitual his reputation will suffer and he may indeed find himself replaced.

Cabinet Papers

Cabinet Papers play a most important part in the proceedings. There are rules about them which Ministers and the Cabinet

Secretariat must see are observed. During the Governments of 1945–51, for example, it was laid down that Papers were to be circulated not less than two clear days before the meeting at which they were to be considered. This timing is obviously important, and it is generally wise to circulate Papers, particularly long Papers, before the stipulated minimum time. Ministers have much reading to do and they are rightly quick to complain and to seek postponement if they have not been given reasonable time in which to master Papers. Another rule is that the Department or Departments directly or indirectly concerned shall have been consulted and given the opportunity to circulate Papers containing their own views. If a Minister concerned has not been consulted it is likely that the initiating Minister will be rapped over the knuckles and consideration postponed pending the necessary consultation. The Treasury in particular has to be consulted if expenditure, major economic policy, or additional staff or other establishment considerations are involved. There may be exceptional circumstances of urgency in which the rules have to be set aside, but that is not lightly done. The rules are sensible and conducive to the effective transaction of business. Unless they are observed, therefore, the Minister who is the author of the Paper may imperil the prospects of a decision being reached.

The Paper is prepared either by the Minister himself or, more usually, by civil servants under the direction of the Minister or Ministers concerned. The Minister will settle with his civil servants the line of argument to be used, and may well revise the draft Paper more than once. It is of great advantage if every effort is made to keep the Paper as short as possible. If, inevitably, the Paper is of some length, there is much to be said for part of it being embodied in an appendix or appendices. It may be convenient to indicate shortly what has happened before, to state the problem and the facts, to summarize the pros and cons, and finally to indicate the case for the course it is proposed should be taken as well as any formal recommendations. On exceptional occasions, a Minister may inevitably be hazy or undecided about what he wants done, but that is not a good thing. He should seek to set out clear and readily understandable recommendations—otherwise his reputation may suffer or he may even be told to go back and make up his mind what it is that he wants to do. The clarity of the language is important and also the honesty of the Paper in facing awkward facts. In short, a Cabinet Paper should be understandable, honest, persuasive, and clear. Obviously, therefore, the drafting of Cabinet Papers is worthy of the most careful attention.

Frequency of Cabinet Meetings

In the Labour Government of 1929–31 the Cabinet normally met once a week, and in those of 1945–51 twice a week. The War Cabinet of 1940–5 met twice a week in the ordinary way, but naturally there were many more special meetings than in peace-time, some of them late at night. The average length of meetings was about two hours, though in Mr. Churchill's War Government they were liable to last somewhat longer.

Parliamentary Business: Foreign Affairs

Each week, though not normally on the same day, there are two standing items of business, whether or not Papers relating to them have been circulated. One (when Parliament is sitting) is Parliamentary Business and the other is Foreign Affairs.

Under Parliamentary Business the Leader of the House of Commons indicates the matters requiring attention and the business it is proposed to take during the following week. The Leader of the House of Lords, as necessary, makes a similar report. Government speakers are settled, and also the line of argument if it has not already been finally determined.

Special and difficult issues may arise. It may be known that the Opposition intend to make a strong attack on some subject, and consideration has to be given to the policy and tactics involved. Or, more difficult and embarrassing, it may be that criticism or even defection is anticipated among the Government's own supporters. Difficulties can, of course, arise in the House of Lords. In all these matters the Government Whips play a big and useful part; it is therefore natural that the Chief Whip should attend when Parliamentary Business is under consideration.

At the formal Cabinet meetings with the Cabinet Secretariat present the cruder aspects of party electoral and parliamentary tactics and the internal problems of the party in power are not discussed more than is necessary. Certainly, the possibility of a dissolution would not be discussed. More direct aspects of party policy and strategy are better discussed either at a Cabinet without officers being present or possibly among a more limited circle of Ministers. Inevitably and rightly the reactions of public opinion to given matters of policy arise, for that is relevant to the democratic spirit of our parliamentary system and possible criticisms by the Opposition or the Government's supporters have to be taken into account. But, in full and formal Cabinet, these matters are not discussed more than is necessary, and then somewhat lightly. By far the greater part of discussion in a well-conducted Cabinet is directed to the determination of what is right, what is sound and sensible, and what is good for the nation. This is a sound moral principle and that is the main reason for it, but incidentally it is conducive to public respect. It is most likely to bring success in the parliamentary battle and is even better for party success in the country than if policy were settled by low-down considerations of party advantage.

Under the item of Foreign Affairs the Foreign Secretary is called upon for a report (if any) on foreign policy. Foreign Affairs may, of course, arise at any Cabinet meeting. It may be that an urgent unexpected difficulty has arisen with a foreign country, or that instructions must at once be given on the line of argument or voting at the United Nations, or one of its Committees, or at some international conference. A Minister other than the Foreign Secretary may wish to raise an urgent question, though he will be in a better position to do so if he has given notice to the Prime Minister and the Secretary of State.

The Cabinet Secretariat

There are one or two silent men on the right of the Prime Minister at the Cabinet table. They hear all but they do not speak unless asked for information. They have in front of them foolscap folio books with ruled lines. They are busy writing, writing, writing, all the time. These men are members of the Cabinet Secretariat (women are sometimes included among Committee Secretaries).

The Cabinet Secretariat was introduced by Mr. Lloyd

George in 1916, during the First World War. Sir Maurice Hankey, who was also Clerk of the Privy Council and Secretary to the Committee of Imperial Defence, was the first Secretary. The Secretariat has now become an important element in the organization of government. It serves not only the Cabinet but also its Committees and, at times, *ad hoc* meetings of selected Ministers to settle a particular matter which may be a subject of inter-departmental disagreement. Under the direction of the Prime Minister, or the Chairman of the Cabinet Committee concerned, it organizes the agenda paper. I say organizes, because a well-prepared agenda is not the mere listing of items of business to be transacted; the list has to be arranged in the most convenient order for the transaction of business. Ministers who are not members of the Cabinet, or the Cabinet Committee concerned, have to be invited at a time estimated to be appropriate and convenient in relation to the business for which they are attending.

The members of the Secretariat have many other duties including the circulation of periodical reports on the implementation of decisions. They must promote the smooth passage of business and obviate or remove possible or actual causes of friction between Departments. They do valuable work in promoting goodwill and co-operation. In fairness I must add that the departmental higher civil servants are generally energetic in seeking to avoid friction, not only between themselves inter-departmentally, but also between Ministers.

Recording of Cabinet Conclusions

One of the most delicate duties of the Cabinet Secretariat is the recording of what are called the Conclusions. But the Secretaries do not confine themselves to the recording of actual decisions. They also set out, for each item of business transacted, the subject and the identity of the Papers before the meeting and summarize the discussion. It is the summary of discussion that presents the most difficult task. Its length will vary according to how important and controversial is the business. The actual length requires judgement, but still more judgement is needed in summarizing what Ministers have said. Usually the only Ministers whose views are quoted by name are the Prime Minister, the Minister or Ministers initiating the business, or those directly concerned. A record of the general discussion does not attribute particular points of view to other individual Ministers, but the essentials of all the points of view expressed are summarized with much accuracy and fairness.

The reason for this considerable degree of anonymity is rather similar to the reasons for Cabinet secrecy. Fundamentally it is that in Cabinet the Ministers have one duty above all others: it is to speak the truth as they see it and pursue the public interest as they see it without fear. That has to be encouraged in every possible way. Thus a Minister who takes a line which he conscientiously believes to be right but which would be unpopular in certain quarters outside would perhaps be less likely to speak his mind if secrecy were not observed. Similarly, if the views of individual Ministers were recorded beyond a necessary minimum they might be tempted to speak over-much or evasively for the record. Moreover, the public interest requires secrecy. I have only to mention Budget leakages which could be exploited by private interests and discussions on Foreign Affairs, leakages about which could well prejudice our relations with foreign Powers and cause useful moves in foreign policy to fail. Every effort is made to preserve the secrecy of the record. Indeed, in matters of exceptional secrecy the Conclusions are not even circulated.

The highest compliment that I can pay the Cabinet Secretariat in respect of this part of their work is that their preliminary record, circulated with remarkable promptitude, is infrequently challenged. If a Minister does challenge it an amendment can be made by agreement, but if the amendment is important or disputed the matter may have to go to the Prime Minister.

Until the establishment of the Cabinet Secretariat, there was no record of Conclusions other than the report which the Prime Minister sent to the Sovereign. The proceedings, one gathers, were somewhat unorganized and desultory by modern standards. There must have been plenty of room for uncertainty and dispute about what the Cabinet had done. No doubt at the end of the meeting Ministers dispersed hoping that everybody knew and would remember what had been agreed upon. With all the complexities of modern government this way of transacting business would be quite impossible, or would, at any rate, lead to much confusion.

Selection of Cabinet Business

What business should go to the Cabinet and what should not? There are not, and cannot well be, any detailed standing orders or regulations about this. The responsibility is fairly placed on each Minister, subject, of course, to the right of the Prime Minister or the Cabinet to require a report, or of an individual Minister to raise the matter or ask for it to be placed on the agenda for consideration. With these reservations, it is for each Minister to decide what he ought to take to the Cabinet and what he ought not. The principal considerations which should be in his mind are these. Does what I propose to do raise new issues of government policy of sufficient importance to warrant Cabinet consideration? Will it involve substantial parliamentary or public controversy? Is it likely to cause embarrassment to the Government at home or abroad, or cause difficulty among ministerial supporters in Parliament? Is it likely that my intended line of action will be objected to by a sufficient number of my ministerial colleagues to warrant collective consideration? Is a major dispute with another Department involved? In short, is there going to be dispute about this or is there not, and if so what sort of dispute? Alternatively, is this my headache or is it the Government's headache?

On all this the Minister must form his own judgement. It is up to him to keep all these considerations in mind rather than to rely upon his civil servants, though no doubt they will give him advice about what they think is the right course. But the Minister must never forget that one of the main reasons for the existence of Ministers is that they are, or at any rate should be, more expert in political judgement and parliamentary and public reactions than are civil servants. If politics and parliamentary and public opinion did not matter, as most assuredly they do, possibly we could do without Ministers and the country could be run by civil servants. Let me say at once that I do not think that the bulk of the civil servants would like this. Indeed, such a responsibility would frighten most of them severely, and rightly so. It would be undemocratic, for one of the greatest of a Minister's duties is to be the protector of the rights of Parliament and of the people.

On the other hand, it would be a fault on the part of a Minister if he were so afraid of taking decisions himself that he too often went to the Cabinet to solve his difficulties for him. He would give an impression of weakness and of fear of responsibility. He would congest the Cabinet agenda. Many departmental decisions have serious consequences and may be controversial, but if the Minister is convinced that the decision is right, that no other decision can properly be taken, and that he can fight his way through, or that his colleagues will support him in the case of trouble ensuing, he can be quite confident in taking a decision on his own responsibility.

It will be seen, therefore, that the decision as to what should go to the Cabinet and what should not is one of importance and can be one of delicacy. But, in fact, Ministers do not often go wrong in this matter. Anyway, if they are in doubt they can always consult the Prime Minister or other appropriate senior colleague.

CHAPTER II

Cabinet Committees

SINCE I was Minister of Transport in the minority Labour Government of 1929–31 and a member of the Cabinet during its last five months, there has been not only a considerable development of the Cabinet Secretariat but also a substantial extension and much more systematic organization of Cabinet Committees.

Except for the Committee of Imperial Defence and *ad hoc* committees for particular subjects (e.g. unemployment), my recollection is that the Government of 1929–31 had only one Standing Committee. It was styled the Home Affairs Committee and its duties were, I think, confined to the examination of Bills about to be presented to Parliament, and did not include the shaping of the legislative programme which was very imperfectly dealt with by the Cabinet. Moreover, there was no Economic Section in existence (though an Economic Advisory Council was set up by that Government), no Central Statistical Office, no economic planners, and but little in the way of information services. There was little, indeed, of the extended apparatus which has been found necessary in the modern conditions of government, although it was badly needed at that time. In any case we did not possess and could not, in those parliamentary conditions, have got the powers necessary for the effective use of much of the machinery of government as it exists today. The amount of business done by the Cabinet was, of course, more limited. But most of it came direct to the Cabinet and there was little delegation to Committees. The life of a minority Government is indeed hard, especially when it is the victim of what Mr. Churchill described as a world economic blizzard, as that Government was. But life was made harder by the relatively primitive character of government organization at that time, having regard to the problems the Government was expected to face.

Cabinet Committees in War and Peace

In the last chapter we discussed the question of what should go to the Cabinet and what should not. Although the bulk of Government Business can be settled departmentally, decisions requiring collective deliberation are very numerous and much more considerable than they were. The field of government has extended, legislation has imposed upon Ministers a greatly increased number of duties, and the nation holds the Government responsible for a whole host of matters with which it would have thought it improper for government to be concerned 100 or even thirty years ago. In these circumstances the amount of business requiring collective deliberation and decision is in excess of what can properly be handled by the Cabinet. But it is not necessary that the Cabinet should deal with all these matters. Just as some questions are appropriate for departmental decision and others should go to the Cabinet, so some can go to Committees of the Cabinet for final decision, or at least can go there in the first place so that the issues can be sorted out before Cabinet consideration.

It may be held that delegation of work to Cabinet Committees impairs the doctrine of collective Cabinet responsibility. I hardly think so. Just as departmental Ministers must decide a host of things on their own responsibility, so also should Cabinet Committees. They are, after all, composed of Ministers and nearly always have a Cabinet Minister in the Chair. In any case they must keep in line with Cabinet policy and the Prime Minister or the Cabinet can pull them up if they go wrong.

It was an inevitable consequence of war conditions and particularly of the establishment of the small War Cabinets of Mr. Lloyd George in the First World War and of Mr. Churchill in the Second World War that a series of Cabinet Committees should be set up to relieve the War Cabinet of much work and leave it free to concentrate as far as possible on the prosecution of the war and on matters of exceptional importance.

Apart from *ad hoc* committees the Churchill War Cabinet had a group of committees dealing with a miscellany of matters, military, economic, administrative, and otherwise, which it was not essential to take to the Cabinet or which would go to the Cabinet after being sorted out in a committee. There was a

Defence (Operations) Committee and a Defence (Supply) Committee under the Chairmanship of the Prime Minister. The Lord President's Committee dealt with a variety of matters not within the terms of reference of other Committees; it evolved into what Mr. Churchill described in February 1942 as 'almost a parallel Cabinet concerned with home affairs'. The vast and difficult problem of shipping made it necessary to establish a committee to deal with this subject which included representatives of the providing and using Departments. There was a Civil Defence Committee. Towards the end of the war a Reconstruction Committee was established. This list is not exhaustive but it illustrates the sort of organization that existed. Such an organized system of Cabinet Committees had not been considered necessary in peace-time.

When the Labour Government was returned in 1945 it was necessary to give the most careful attention to Cabinet organization. We were confronted with a heavy legislative and administrative programme. Vast and complicated economic, industrial, and financial problems faced us. The country had given us a mandate, and indeed a direction, not to go back to things as they were in the years between the wars, but to go on to a new and better order of society. In these circumstances the Government was going to be very busy, and if we tried to do everything at Cabinet level we should be heading for a breakdown. Mr. Attlee, in consultation with myself as Deputy Prime Minister, surveyed the whole field of government and gave the matter the most careful consideration, taking into account the views he had urged in 1937 in his book, *The Labour Party in Perspective*. Other Ministers particularly concerned were also consulted, and the Secretaries to the Cabinet, Sir Edward Bridges and Sir Norman Brook, gave valuable advice and assistance. The Prime Minister, far from deciding to disband the Cabinet Committee system, determined to develop and elaborate it as a feature of peace-time government and to maintain a Cabinet Secretariat adequate for the proper servicing, not only of the Cabinet, but of the Cabinet Committees as well.

Post-war Cabinet Committee System

It will be useful to give a general picture of the Cabinet Committees which were established in the Labour Government, together with an indication of their scope. For the reasons given in Chapter III, it is undesirable during the lifetime of a Government to reveal the existence of Cabinet Committees, their terms of reference, or the names of their Chairmen. There are exceptions—for example, no secret was made of the existence of the Defence Committee under the Chairmanship of the Prime Minister, because it was the successor of the Committee of Imperial Defence, and because of its exceptional public importance. The Prime Minister also considered it right to announce that the Lord President was the Minister concerned with the co-ordination of the information services,[1] with the higher policy of the Central Office of Information, and (in association with the Postmaster-General) with certain matters connected with the British Broadcasting Corporation. The reason for this public announcement was that the office of Minister of Information had been abolished, that it was necessary to explain the new arrangements for the information services, and that, in view of the theoretical apprehension that the public information services might be used for party purposes, it was desirable to indicate the Minister who could be 'shot at' on the more important aspects of information policy. With these exceptions secrecy was maintained.

We will take the Standing Committees first. It is natural and proper that the Prime Minister should take a leading personal interest in defence matters, and Mr. Attlee presided over the Defence Committee of the Cabinet, both before and after the creation of a separate Minister of Defence. Defence and Foreign Affairs are inevitably related to each other and therefore the Foreign Secretary was a member. The Minister of Defence was a leading member and was appointed Deputy Chairman. Naturally the three Service Ministers—the First Lord of the Admiralty and the Secretaries of State for War and Air—were also members, as was the Minister of Supply by virtue of his responsibilities for the production of equipment and supplies for the Services. The Minister of Labour is also the Minister of National Service and the departmental Minister concerned with the supply of manpower, so it was appropriate that he should sit on the Defence Committee. The Chancellor of the Exchequer

[1] There was an Information Services Committee of the Cabinet of which the Lord President was Chairman.

was a member not only because of the large financial considerations involved but because of his senior position, and for this reason the Minister ranking as deputy to the Prime Minister was also included.

Normally the Chiefs of Staff—the First Sea Lord, the Chief of the Imperial General Staff, and the Chief of the Air Staff—were present and not only put in written reports but were frequently invited to take part in the discussion. They themselves also worked as a team in the Chiefs of Staff Committee transacting important business within their sphere and, in particular, preparing reports for the Prime Minister, the Minister of Defence, and the Defence Committee. The position of the Chiefs of Staff, therefore, was different from that of civil servants, who do not occupy such a prominent position in the deliberation of Cabinet Committees. Each of the three Service Departments has a civil servant as Permanent Under-Secretary, but the Chiefs of Staff have a separate principal status of their own. The First Sea Lord is, of course, a prominent member of the Board of Admiralty as is the C.I.G.S. a member of the Army Council and the C.A.S. a member of the Air Council. Each of the Chiefs of Staff frequently discussed important matters with his Service Minister, but he also had a direct relationship with the Prime Minister, the Minister of Defence, and at times with the Secretary of State for Foreign Affairs.

The Minister of Defence had separate meetings from time to time with the three Service Ministers and as necessary with the Minister of Supply.

A separate Committee for Civil Defence was constituted with the Home Secretary in the Chair.

The Lord President's Committee had referred to it questions of domestic policy not assigned to other Committees, including in the earlier period internal economic policy and the supervision of the general development of the nation's economy. It could be described as a sub-Cabinet or general purposes committee, and was, therefore, a committee of particular importance in the civil field. Its business ranged over a wide field of domestic affairs from matters of relatively small importance up to questions of considerable significance. It settled many issues of important policy and the agenda was usually heavy.

Until 1947 Mr. Arthur Greenwood was the member of the

Cabinet responsible for the co-ordination of the social services and a Social Services Committee functioned under him when he was Lord Privy Seal. Included among its duties were the supervision and co-ordination of schemes of National Insurance and Family Allowances. In 1947 the social services became one of the matters dealt with by the Lord President's Committee and the separate Committee was abolished.

When in September 1947 Sir Stafford Cripps became Minister for Economic Affairs, and soon after took with him the duties of that office to the Treasury as Chancellor of the Exchequer, it was plainly necessary and desirable to revise the Cabinet Committee arrangements for economic questions. Two committees were then established for this purpose; their work is further discussed in the chapter on Economic Planning. The Economic Policy Committee, presided over by the Prime Minister himself, dealt with high economic policy and generally supervised economic planning for both external and internal matters. This Committee had to face issues of great economic complexity and importance, and the Prime Minister was undoubtedly right in himself presiding over its deliberations.

The balance of payments, recurring difficulties about dollars and the Sterling Area, devaluation, labour problems, and fuel supplies—these were among the many heavy headaches with which the Prime Minister and his Committee had to wrestle. If Gladstone and Disraeli could have risen from their graves and attended our proceedings they would have been much surprised and even shocked at the matters dealt with and would have thought they had entered another world, which indeed would have been the case. They would have been no less surprised and possibly shocked had they been able to attend a meeting of the modern Cabinet or its other Committees.

The second economic committee was the Production Committee, which, under the Chairmanship of the Minister for Economic Affairs and, later, the Chancellor of the Exchequer, concerned itself with the supervision of production programmes designed to give effect to general economic planning and with certain questions of internal economic policy.

The crucial problem of making the best use of manpower, both from the view-point of the human beings involved and the requirements of economic policy and according to the progress of demobilization, made it necessary to appoint a Committee on Manpower, presided over until 1947 by the Foreign Secretary (for Mr. Bevin possessed a unique experience of these matters) and subsequently by the Minister of Labour.

There were two committees on legislation. The Legislation Committee, a fairly small body, which included the Lord Chancellor, the Law Officers, and the Chief Whip, examined draft Parliamentary Bills and important delegated legislation, and the general progress of the legislative programme during the Parliamentary Session. The Lord Privy Seal (Mr. Arthur Greenwood) presided over this Committee until 1947 and the Lord President from 1947 onwards. The other committee, the Chairman of which was the Lord President and Leader of the House of Commons, was the Future Legislation Committee, which had the task of shaping the legislative programme. I deal further with these Committees in the chapter on the Legislative Programme.

In view of the Government's programme it was necessary to establish a Committee on the Socialization of Industries for the supervision and co-ordination of schemes for socializing industries. The Lord President was Chairman. Its work is dealt with in Chapter XII.

The Prime Minister was Chairman of a Committee on India and Burma until it was abolished in 1947. A Colonial Affairs Committee was presided over by the Lord Privy Seal but this also was abolished in 1947. Subsequently the Prime Minister presided over a Commonwealth Affairs Committee, the function of which was to consider constitutional problems and other questions of policy affecting the Commonwealth and Empire. He was also Chairman of a Committee to consider major questions of policy concerning China and South-East Asia. The Foreign Secretary was in charge of a Committee concerned with Middle Eastern matters, and another to which were referred questions of administration of and policy towards liberated and ex-enemy countries.

The Machinery of Government Committee and the Information Services Committee met from time to time under the Chairmanship of the Lord President, and the same is true of the Civil Aviation Committee, presided over by the Secretary of State for Dominion Affairs (later Commonwealth Relations) and then by the Lord Privy Seal when Lord Addison was transferred from the Commonwealth Relations Office to be Lord Privy Seal.

Some of the above Committees appointed sub-Committees from time to time for particular matters, including problems connected with the reconversion of industry, the development of the export trade, the balanced redistribution of industry, and the problems of Development Areas.

Let us now look at the temporary or special committees. As examples of two important temporary committees I would mention the Housing Committee, which considered housing policy and programmes, and the Committee on the National Health Service, which examined its extensive organization and expenditure to assist the Ministers concerned with this important and comprehensive new service. The Prime Minister himself presided over both of these temporary committees.

Among the other important temporary committees dealing with home or economic affairs were the Committee on Food Supplies, under the Prime Minister, and the Fuel Committee, also under the Prime Minister, dealing with the fuel crisis of 1947 and settling plans to avoid a recurrence of trouble in the winter of 1947–8. In 1950–1 the Minister of Local Government and Planning presided over a Committee on the Distribution and Marketing of Meat, Fruit, and Vegetables in continuation of the work he had undertaken when Chancellor of the Duchy of Lancaster.

The Home Secretary was Chairman of the Civil Service Manpower Committee, concerned with fixing staff ceilings for Departments, and of the temporary Airfields Committee, which examined the future of existing airfields in the United Kingdom.

Composition

The Prime Minister gave careful consideration to the composition of the Committees. In the case of the Lord President's Committee dealing as it did with a wide variety of matters, he saw to it that it was broadly representative of the Government as a whole. He appointed to it leading members of the Cabinet (as did Mr. Churchill during the war) and a number of Ministers who were not members of the Cabinet. On the Committees dealing with more particular and less general matters he included the Ministers directly concerned, but frequently added other Ministers, and this had the value of bringing into the consultations the voices of Ministers above the battle. Ministers outside the Cabinet were extensively used even if their Departments were not directly or to a great extent concerned with the work of the Committee. This gave the Ministers outside the Cabinet an important share in collective discussions and the reaching of decisions; and to some extent eased the burden on members of the Cabinet. Committee Papers and Conclusions were circulated to all Ministers so that Cabinet and other full Ministers were kept informed.

Chairmen

Special attention was given by the Prime Minister to the choice of Chairmen of Committees. Normally he chose them from among members of the Cabinet. Although it was inevitable and proper that non-departmental Ministers should be extensively used it will have been noticed that the services of departmental Ministers were also utilized in some cases. For some of the less important Committees or sub-Committees composed of Parliamentary Secretaries and/or civil servants, Parliamentary Secretaries were appointed Chairmen, thus giving them valuable experience. The choice of Chairmen is affected by the general set-up of the Government and the suitability of Ministers and their availability for the work. For example, extensive changes had to be made when I ceased to be Lord President and became Secretary of State for Foreign Affairs in March 1951.

The work of co-ordination or the Chairmanship of a Cabinet Committee requires certain qualities. If such a Minister seeks to be a dictator or to act in the spirit of giving orders to departmental Ministers, or is impatient and irritable in listening to relevant arguments, he will not win that goodwill of his colleagues which is vital to the success of his work. His business is to be an understanding friend who is seeking to assist his colleagues in finding a way through the maze of conflicting considerations, for there is nearly always more than one side to a question. Whilst he needs to take trouble to understand the matters under consideration to the fullest practicable extent and whilst it is good that he should have a mind of his own he must remember that his business is to be a helpful conciliator and not an additional irritant. The confidence of the departmental Ministers in him is very important.

Meetings

Most of what I have said in the first chapter about the conduct of business by the Cabinet also applies to Cabinet Committees. There is, however, one important difference to bear in mind. The Cabinet is supreme and the Committees are subordinate to it. In some cases, therefore, the conclusions reached in a committee may still have to be confirmed by the Cabinet and in any case if any body of opinion in the Committee is not satisfied with the conclusion reached it may take it to the Cabinet. This does not happen often, otherwise the Committee system would be rather a waste of time.

As we have seen, the Cabinet Committees were of two sorts: standing committees and temporary committees for special purposes. Even a standing committee did not necessarily last for all time. So the membership and functions of all Cabinet Committees were and should be reviewed periodically, for there is great need to avoid getting into grooves, continuing committees when no longer needed and needlessly multiplying them. A well-considered plan of committees can facilitate the processes of government and save a good deal of irritating inter-departmental friction. Moreover, once an issue of policy is settled it does not need to come up again unless circumstances change or reconsideration is called for. On the other hand, too many committees can choke the machine, weary Ministers and officers, and hold up and weaken effective administration. Too many committees can be the enemies of decision.

Some of the standing committees met regularly, say once or even twice a week or fortnightly, but others were called as and when required. The terms of reference of a committee, after defining the subject or subjects with which the committee was to deal, authorized the committee to settle such matters on behalf of the Cabinet or to refer them to the Cabinet if it found that course desirable. In the case of special committees, they were sometimes required to report to the Cabinet and submit recommendations.

Just as it was within the discretion of a departmental Minister to decide matters on his own responsibility or to take the question to the Cabinet or a Cabinet Committee, so it was within the discretion of the Chairman of a Cabinet Committee or the Committee itself to refer a matter to the Cabinet or, as usually happened, itself to decide the question. A Minister who strongly dissented from a Cabinet Committee decision could require the matter to be taken to the Cabinet or to the Prime Minister, although this was not usually done other than for reasons of substance. The Cabinet Committee system relieved the Cabinet of a large amount of work; moreover, it enabled some matters requiring more detailed consideration than it was possible for the Cabinet to give to be more thoroughly examined and explored.

Official Committees and Working Parties

There were numerous committees or working parties of civil servants and service officers, sometimes working for particular Ministers but often sorting things out to present the facts and the views of the Departments in an orderly fashion and possibly make recommendations to Cabinet Committees. This advice helped us in our labours and saved a good deal of ministerial time. It was necessary, however, to be conscious of the same danger here as in the case of Cabinet Committees, namely, the possibility of multiplying them to such an extent that the machinery became clogged and officers were over-strained as the result of too many meetings and too much talk. It is just as dangerous to the efficiency of government for higher civil servants to be overstrained as it is for Ministers. It is proper, therefore, that the Cabinet Office should be under instructions, as they were under the Labour Government, systematically to review the hierarchy and number of official committees, and to report to the Prime Minister or other Minister concerned from time to time and in any case not less than once a year. Good government cannot live by talking alone: there are things to be done.

Servicing the Committees

As for the Cabinet so with Cabinet Committees: the excellent Cabinet Secretariat is a tower of strength. The Office serves the

Committees as well as the Cabinet, organizes the agenda and the business, and assists the Chairmen in many ways. The men of this office are always on the look-out for ways in which to facilitate the business and to lighten the burden of Ministers. They are responsible for drafting the conclusions of Committees in the same way as they are those of the Cabinet. In nearly all cases a secretary or secretaries from the Cabinet Office are appointed, but sometimes one of the secretaries is drawn from the office of the Chairman of the Committee or from one of the Departments principally concerned. This provides useful liaison and is conducive to the smoothness of operations.

CHAPTER III

Composition of the Cabinet: Overlords: Co-ordinators

Two controversies have emerged about the Cabinet and the machinery for central co-ordination. On the one hand, there is the question of what is the proper size of the Cabinet and, on the other, there is the controversy about the use of co-ordinating Ministers and Sir Winston Churchill's 'Overlords'. The two questions may be related, for the use of co-ordinating Ministers may enable a Prime Minister to keep the size of his Cabinet smaller. But it is better to look upon them as quite separate issues in the first instance.

In the matter of size there are really three possibilities. At one extreme there is the Cabinet composed of all, or substantially all, Ministers. This was the general pre-war pattern. Thus Mr. Neville Chamberlain's Cabinet in the spring of 1939 contained twenty-three members, and only the Minister of Pensions, the Postmaster-General, the First Commissioner of Works, the Paymaster-General, and the Law Officers of the Crown were excluded. I call this the 'full' Cabinet. At the other extreme there is the 'small' Cabinet composed of five or so Ministers. This is the size favoured by Mr. L. S. Amery, about which I shall have more to say later. It is exemplified by the War Cabinets of 1916–19 and 1939–45, though it should be noticed that neither Mr. Lloyd George nor Mr. Churchill found it possible or desirable to keep their Cabinets as low as five members—Mr. Churchill's War Cabinet usually had around eight Ministers. The third size falls roughly between these two extremes—about sixteen to eighteen members. This was the size adopted by Mr. Attlee and also by Sir Winston Churchill in his present Administration. It can be achieved only by leaving out a number of departmental Ministers.

General Considerations

In considering the size and composition of the Cabinet in normal peace-time conditions it is important to remember that members of the Cabinet serve in a dual capacity as leaders of the party in power and as heads of the more important Government Departments.

It is desirable that the membership of the Cabinet should be of a character which will command the general respect of and exercise authority among its parliamentary supporters. There is a tendency, therefore, for the leading and most influential members of the party to find a place, and even for the deliberate inclusion of members of varying political temperaments and approaches (provided there are fair prospects of their being able to work together), in order that the maximum goodwill of all the elements of the parliamentary party may be obtained. It must not be forgotten that our two-party system here, as in the case of the two-party system of the United States, is distinct from the many-party system—at times lack of system—of the parliamentary democracies of the continent of Europe. This inevitably and not unreasonably involves the existence of more than one temperament and approach within each of the two parties. In a sense the two great parties are each coalitions of opinion within themselves; this is noticeably the case as regards the Democratic and Republican Parties of the United States (where party discipline is somewhat loose), and although it is less noticeable in our Conservative and Labour Parties it is nevertheless true that within them are variations of political outlook. This is a factor which may or may not be disregarded in the composition of Cabinets. For example, in his third Cabinet Mr. Baldwin disregarded it in the case of Mr. Churchill, and Mr. Ramsay MacDonald disregarded it in his second Labour Government in the case of Mr. John Wheatley, but it is a consideration that has to be taken into account.

Departmental as well as personal considerations also arise. If, as I believe it should, the Cabinet is to contain the main departmental Ministers, it is virtually impossible to exclude certain Departments either because of their importance for government policy or because there would be considerable public outcry if they were omitted. Thus the Chancellor of the Exchequer, Foreign Secretary, and Home Secretary play such an important role in government policy that their presence is essential. The Minister of Defence also has obvious claims, as has the President of the Board of Trade and the Minister of

Labour. It would be insulting to omit Commonwealth Relations and the people of Scotland would feel very annoyed and unhappy if their Secretary of State were excluded. Apart from this consideration, however, the Scottish Office covers a wide field of domestic administration dealt with by other Departments for England and Wales only. Britain's obligations to the Colonial peoples also make it desirable to include the Colonial Secretary. The Leader of the House of Lords and the Lord Chancellor with his legal eminence also have strong claims. And as I will show later, there are considerable advantages in having available in the Cabinet two or three Ministers—in particular the Lord President of the Council and the Lord Privy Seal—who, not having heavy departmental responsibilities, are free to chair Cabinet Committees and undertake special work of an inter-departmental character. Including the Prime Minister this means a Cabinet of at least thirteen members. There are, however, other very strong claimants—Education, Housing and Local Government, Agriculture and Fisheries, Supply, Fuel and Power, Transport, and perhaps others. It is, therefore, very difficult to avoid a Cabinet of about sixteen to eighteen members and I am inclined to think this is about right in normal conditions, though not in wartime.

Provided Ministers do not talk needlessly long or for the sake of talking, I do not think such a number makes it impossible for business to be conducted expeditiously; much depends on the Prime Minister as Chairman. But if a Cabinet consists of more than twenty members concentration and businesslike discussion will in all probability become more difficult and it will not be easy to retain the spirit and atmosphere of a business committee.

Departmental Ministers Outside the Cabinet

Inclusion or non-inclusion of a Minister in the Cabinet presents a Prime Minister with a problem of some delicacy. It is natural that departmental Ministers should wish to be in the Cabinet and that the Departments themselves are happier if their Ministers are included. The standing and authority of the Minister and his Department are thereby increased, whereas if the Minister is left out, he and the Department feel that they are in the second class. But in recent years there has been a substantial growth in the number of Departments. In 1938, for example, the following Departments existing in 1953 had not been created: Defence, Food, Fuel and Power, Housing and Local Government, Materials, and Supply. When Mr. Attlee took office in July 1945 there were four Departments in existence which subsequently disappeared, viz. Burma, India, Aircraft Production (merged with Supply), and Information. Sir Winston Churchill continued this process of reduction by merging Civil Aviation with Transport and National Insurance with Pensions.

In spite of these reductions, if all full Ministers were included in the Cabinet we should still get Cabinets of nearly thirty members, which would clearly be too large for effective business. It is now the general rule, therefore, for the Ministers of the new (and some of the older) Departments to be left out, though they are called in to Cabinet meetings when matters affecting their Departments are under discussion and, as we have already seen, they have a place on Cabinet Committees. Moreover, although not receiving all Cabinet Papers and Foreign Office telegrams they are supplied with an extensive number of them and they receive the Cabinet Agenda and Conclusions. By this means they know most of what is going on and, if they think it right, can make a claim to be heard.

Though the practice of leaving the newer Departments out has been general, there is not and should not be any slavish rule about it, for—at particular times at any rate—they may be of equal or even more importance than some of the Departments included in the Cabinet; for example, the Ministry of Fuel and Power, the Ministry of Transport, and the Ministry of Supply are Departments of considerable economic significance. Indeed, the Minister of Fuel and Power, when the office was held by Mr. Emanuel Shinwell, was a member of Mr. Attlee's Cabinet until August 1947. Fuel and Power was of particular importance at that time as anybody who remembers the fuel crisis of 1947 will agree. Moreover, Mr. Shinwell was handling three big socialization Bills for the industries of coal-mining, electricity, and gas. It is likely, however, that Mr. Attlee in deciding to include him in the Cabinet was influenced by Mr. Shinwell's importance as a leading member of the Labour Party as much as by departmental considerations. On balance, the growth in the number of Departments of State has created a situation whereby it is likely that about ten Ministers in charge of Departments will be outside the Cabinet.

The Small Cabinet: super-Ministers

From time to time there is much discussion about the ideal size of the Cabinet. The most persistent suggestion for change is in favour of the small Cabinet of non-departmental or supervising Ministers. The case urged for this view is, I think, that the work of the departmental Minister is nowadays so heavy that he cannot give the time needed for those wide surveys of policy and the reading of numerous and sometimes long Cabinet Papers and Foreign Office telegrams that is necessary for the adequate discharge of Cabinet responsibilities; that as a consequence his contribution to Cabinet discussions tends to be inadequate, imperfect, animated unduly by departmental interests, and that he is, therefore, prone to be led to wrong rather than to right conclusions; and that such a Cabinet is likely to become sluggish and lacking in mental freshness. It is argued that in the small Cabinet of non-departmental Ministers discussion could be more thorough and intimate; that the members would have more time for thinking between Cabinets; that they could more thoroughly read and digest Cabinet Papers and other matter, from inside and outside sources, relevant to the business of government; that the work of co-ordinating or supervising Departments could be allocated among the members, and that thereby 'above the battle' views would be available on groups of related departmental problems, and impartial judgement pronounced after careful study and consultation with the Ministers concerned. It is also argued that in this way the functional element would come into Cabinet discussions without the excessive intrusion of departmentalism and that such a Cabinet would be a highly effective instrument composed of a limited number of wise men.

Mr. L. S. Amery, a Conservative ex-Minister of considerable experience, has given attention to the matter in his *Thoughts on the Constitution*, and is probably the extreme exponent of the small Cabinet of supervising non-departmental Ministers. Mr. Amery seeks to combine the recommendations of the Haldane

Committee (which, by the way, did not recommend a small peace-time Cabinet of supervising Ministers only) with the features found most useful in the Cabinet organization of the last thirty years. His aim appears to be to devise machinery which will distinguish without 'creating a divorce between planning and administration'. 'At the apex of the whole structure, and as the necessary link between policy and administration', he 'would have a Cabinet of about half a dozen, all entirely free from ordinary departmental duties. This Cabinet would deal with current administrative questions, as did the War Cabinets of the last two wars, by bringing into its discussions the departmental Ministers directly affected. But it should also have regular meetings definitely set aside for the discussion of future policy.'

For these duties, Mr. Amery urges, the Cabinet would be assisted by two groups of committees:

(*a*) standing and *ad hoc* committees under non-departmental chairmen to be concerned with 'co-ordinating and adjusting the current work of departments'; and

(*b*) standing 'Policy Committees', whose official chairman should be the Prime Minister. He should appoint a Cabinet Minister 'as standing deputy chairman of each committee and acting head of its staff'.

'The Cabinet Minister so appointed would be much more than a mere "co-ordinator". . . . He would be the recognized Policy Minister for his group of departments, with the knowledge and authority derived from his regular handling of his subject-matter both on current affairs committees and on his Standing Policy Committee, and he would have his own staff behind him.'

This second group of committees would correspond to the Defence Committee and would study 'policy in the main fields of External Affairs, Economics, and Social Welfare, each with its own adequate research and planning staff. These staffs should not be self-contained bodies, but, like the Joint Intelligence and Planning Staffs developed in the last war, should be manned by members of the intelligence and planning staffs of their several offices at . . . "the official level".' Among the advantages for the kind of organization he advocates Mr. Amery states that 'the Cabinet Ministers charged with co-ordinating duties would do so primarily from the policy point of view'. This would, he thinks, meet 'the conclusive objection to the small Cabinet of super-Ministers, each directly responsible for the administration, as well as the policy, of a group of departments, which has often been advocated. For, in the absence of a clear distinction between the functions of policy and administration these would tend to be even more over-burdened, in Cabinet and in Parliament, with administrative responsibilities, and even less capable of thinking ahead than the members of the present type of Cabinet'. He also urges that 'it should be possible . . . to secure a real co-ordination of the work of departments in the light of coherent policies thought out beforehand in place of the weak compromises, postponements, and fluctuations which have so often resulted from the attempt to reconcile conflicting departmental policies as and when a problem has obtruded itself upon the attention of an overworked Cabinet'; e.g. Palestine, which he describes as a field of conflict between the traditional view of the Foreign Office and the constructive view of the Colonial Office.

The principal objections to Mr. Amery's scheme have already been touched upon. The Cabinet is not just a group of backroom boys brooding over future policy. As Mr. Amery knows from experience, the Cabinet has to give political leadership to the party in power, to the House of Commons and to the country as a whole. Its members have to be closely in touch with opinion, both inside the House and out, and have to carry with them the loyalty and active support of all the different strands of opinion within their party. It is difficult to see how six men, however chosen, could do this. Whilst in any party there are two or three Ministers who carry particularly great weight, there are always ten or more who carry some weight and who have the confidence of a particular section. To leave these out would not make for party unity and indeed to leave out the energetic and up-and-coming Minister might be asking for serious trouble. A Cabinet without departmental Ministers would be deficient in that day-to-day administrative experience which makes a real contribution to collective decisions.

It seems to me that in his enthusiasm Mr. Amery has carried his idea much too far. It is possible to avoid the very large Cabinet and to use non-departmental Ministers to secure a measure of co-ordination and policy planning without restricting the Cabinet to six super-Ministers.

Mr. Attlee's Views and Practice

Mr. Attlee, in his well-known book *The Labour Party in Perspective*, published in 1937, gave considerable thought to the organization of the Cabinet. He criticized the 1937 Cabinet of twenty-two Ministers, most of whom had heavy departmental duties, on the ground that 'The Cabinet, as now constituted, sins against the first principle of good administration, in that it does not distinguish between the function of planning broad strategy and making decisions as to the detailed execution of plans'. He stated that 'It is . . . essential to make a distinction of function between Ministers who are responsible for detailed administration and those to whom is entrusted the work of dealing with the broader issues'. He urged that the non-departmental Ministers' posts should be 'filled by Ministers who have the faculty of directing broad issues of policy. They should be in charge of functions not departments. Each should . . . be . . . the representative of the Prime Minister in relation to a particular group of services, and should preside over a committee of the Ministers charged with administration.' On the relations of the co-ordinating Ministers with the Prime Minister, Mr. Attlee said: 'The Prime Minister is necessarily the responsible head of the Ministry, but he needs to be assisted by a small group of members of the Cabinet whose specific function is co-ordinating policy and giving general direction.' He also declared that 'the Ministers who are charged with co-ordination will be in constant and close contact with the Ministers in their respective groups, who will, through them, be able to make their views felt more effectively'.

To a considerable extent, though not in every detail, Mr. Attlee lived up to these principles in the constitution and work of the Labour Governments of 1945–51. He manifested considerable ability in the delicate business of delegation, thus improving the organization of government and relieving himself as Prime Minister of impossible burdens. He delegated to me, as Lord President and Deputy Prime Minister, a considerable amount of co-ordinating work including the Chairmanship of a number of Cabinet Committees, and there fell to me, as

Leader of the House of Commons, not only the management of Parliament and the handling of our relationships with the Parliamentary Labour Party in association with our excellent Chief Whip (Mr. William Whiteley) but, subject to the Future Legislation Committee and the Cabinet, the shaping and the organization of the legislative programme.

Mr. Ernest Bevin, the Foreign Secretary, had very heavy duties to discharge at the Foreign Office, but he was also broadly regarded as co-ordinating Minister for overseas affairs generally. His services were utilized at times on domestic affairs related to his special industrial experience and he was Chairman of Cabinet Committees from time to time.

Sir Stafford Cripps and, later, Mr. Hugh Gaitskell, after my functions relating to economic co-ordination had passed to the Chancellor of the Exchequer, were charged by the Prime Minister with extensive duties of co-ordination over the wide field of economic policy. The Minister of Defence, Mr. A. V. Alexander and, later, Mr. Shinwell, relieved the Prime Minister of part of his co-ordinating functions in relation to defence.

Taken together this delegation covered an enormous field of work. If either the Prime Minister personally or the Cabinet collectively had tried to do this work directly, the men and the machine might have broken down within six months, and the country would have suffered.

In presiding over the Cabinet, Mr. Attlee was essentially the good Chairman, giving guidance, maintaining the relevance of discussion and leading it to a generally acceptable conclusion. He was not dictatorial. The Cabinet Committee system itself helped to build up a spirit of co-operation and common outlook over the various fields of policy. So the Cabinet had a considerable sense of working as a team. The Cabinet Committees relieved the Cabinet of much labour and reduced the size of the agenda, thus leaving time for the superior body to deal more adequately with subjects which were properly of Cabinet concern, without weakening the status and authority of the Cabinet itself.

Non-departmental Ministers

The Labour Governments of 1945–51 made full use of three or four Ministers of considerable political standing to act as

Chairmen of Cabinet Committees and to co-ordinate policy and administration in various fields for the Cabinet. It is, therefore, well to say something of the place and contribution of the non-departmental Minister.

Every Government contains a certain number of non-departmental Ministers with little or even no direct administrative responsibilities. There is much work to do of a special non-departmental or inter-departmental character. In the previous chapter we saw that sometimes a departmental Minister may serve as Chairman of a Committee. But often that is inappropriate. It may be difficult for him to be considered impartial. And in any case the burden of departmental work can be considerable, particularly if membership of the Cabinet and of Cabinet Committees is added to it. In so far, therefore, as departmental Ministers are used it is generally in connexion with subjects of an *ad hoc* or limited character. There are exceptions when the Minister is departmentally responsible for a field of co-ordination, as, for example, the Chancellor of the Exchequer for economic affairs, or the Home Secretary for Civil Defence. Let us look at the, in the main, ancient non-departmental offices whose holders are available for more permanent inter-departmental duties.

Prime Minister

The first and most important non-departmental Minister is the Prime Minister himself. He has many duties and plenty of work to do, but he has no departmental functions, although he is responsible for a number of specific things including proposals to the Sovereign for the appointment or transfer of Ministers, recommendations for honours and ecclesiastical patronage. As the head of the Government he is *primus inter pares*. He is the leader of his party.

Until recent years he usually acted as Leader of the House of Commons, but, as his duties have become heavier, it is now usual for him to arrange for another Minister to take over these responsibilities. No fixed rule has been made. It is open to any future Prime Minister to make such arrangements as will seem wise to him. Much depends on his own work, his personality, the men available, and even the composition of the House. He usually takes a special interest in defence and overseas affairs and during a war it is highly probable that the Prime Minister will also be Minister of Defence. But here again much will depend upon his personality and the circumstances of the time.

The Prime Minister has to keep abreast of a wide range of matters. He cannot know everything that is going on over the whole field of government and it would be foolish of him to try, but he must know enough to be ready to intervene if he apprehends that something is going wrong. All these things were done by Mr. Attlee, and he was readily available when his colleagues sought counsel or advice. He maintained steady contact on parliamentary matters with the Leaders of the Houses of Parliament and the Chief Whip, and was frequently in consultation with the Foreign Secretary.

The Prime Minister presides over some Cabinet Committees. He is, of course, eminently a co-ordinating Minister and, up to a point and only up to a point, a supervising Minister, though even he will be wise not to overdo it. He is not the master of the Cabinet. Perhaps the habit of referring to Prime Minister's directives across the Floor of the House of Commons or asking the Prime Minister to direct one or more of his colleagues to do this or that has been overdone. It is right, and indeed in most cases inevitable, that the Prime Minister should have a special authority; if for no other reason it is bound to emerge because of the fact that he recommends to the Sovereign the appointment of Ministers and can ask for resignations. He is the leader of the Government, but (except on occasions of emergency) he ought not to, and usually does not, presume to give directions or decisions which are proper to the Cabinet or one of its Committees, even though his position is rightly one of special authority and Parliament and the country quite properly look to him for leadership and inspiration.

In talking in my younger days to a high civil servant who had formerly worked under me I was vigorously—perhaps in the circumstances too vigorously—denouncing the policy of his new master, my successor in office. At a moment when it became clear to me that I was somewhat embarrassing him, he said, 'Well, Mr. Morrison, I can only say that different Ministers have different ways', which illustrated the meritorious loyalty which the Civil Service quite properly owes and practises towards Ministers. Well, Prime Ministers have their different ways too. One has only to consider the long list of men who have held this great office to realize that it has been held by varied personalities with varied techniques. Mr. Ramsay MacDonald, for example, did not pretend to have clear views on the legislative programme, and was greatly amused by the competition of Ministers for places in the King's Speech, so I suppose the places went to the obstinate and the persistent or the skilled and persuasive. And then consider Mr. Balfour, who, during the two years or so when his Cabinet was sharply divided on tariff reform, brilliantly kept the Government together by evasion, by formulas which meant little, and by public declarations which annoyed a good many of his party on both sides of the controversy and pleased very few. It was brilliant, but the price was in part paid at the General Election of 1906. Mr. Neville Chamberlain was cold and shy, but a capable administrator. He assumed a special authority in foreign affairs at the time of Munich. There could be no greater contrast in Cabinet Chairmanship than between Mr. Attlee and Mr. Churchill.

Lord President

Next there is the Lord President of the Council. The direct duties of his office are limited. They include responsibility for the work of the Privy Council Office and he presents the business to the Queen and the Council at the formal and not very frequent meetings of Her Majesty's Most Honourable Privy Council. He is answerable for the work of the Department of Scientific and Industrial Research, the Medical Research Council, the Agricultural Research Council, and the Nature Conservancy, for these are technically Committees of the Privy Council. He is charged with a general oversight of scientific activities on the civil side, the Minister of Defence having similar duties on the military side. That about completes the official duties attributable to the Privy Council Office. Though the scientific part of the Lord President's work is important, the Research Councils do much of it, and clearly he is available for other duties. Before the Second World War he was frequently a Peer, sometimes Leader of the House of Lords, and indeed that became the case again when Lord Addison was appointed Lord President in March 1951.[1] In the MacDonald–Baldwin Government of 1931 to 1935, Mr. Baldwin was at the beginning Lord President under Mr. Ramsay MacDonald and later on Mr. MacDonald became Lord President under Mr. Baldwin. What duties they had outside those of the Privy Council Office I do not know. It was, I think, in Mr. Churchill's War Government that the Lord President first emerged as a powerful senior Minister. This is indicated by the fact that leading colleagues were selected for this office. Mr. Neville Chamberlain, after ceasing to be Prime Minister, became Lord President. On his death he was succeeded in this office by Sir John Anderson who was in turn succeeded by Mr. Attlee, already holding the title of Deputy Prime Minister. All these Lord Presidents had an extensive amount of ministerial co-ordinating work to do as Chairmen of Cabinet Committees. When I held the office of Lord President in the Labour Government the Prime Minister delegated many duties to me. The Lord President of the Council can be used in a variety of ways. The duties of the man rather than the office are for determination by the Prime Minister of the day and will vary not only according to the person appointed but also to the general set-up of the Government, and the availability and suitability of other Ministers for co-ordinating work.

Lord Privy Seal

We pass to the next non-departmental Minister, the Lord Privy Seal. He has absolutely no duties pertaining to his office whatever, except perhaps the safe keeping of the Privy Seal. The position is none the less useful, for the holder can be assigned special duties by the Prime Minister. For example, Sir Stafford Cripps was Lord Privy Seal when he was Leader of the House of Commons for a short time in 1942. Mr. Attlee combined the office of Lord Privy Seal with the Chairmanship of two major Cabinet Committees and other work from May 1940 to February 1942. Mr. Arthur Greenwood was appointed Lord Privy Seal in August 1945 and later combined this office with that of Paymaster-General. Lord Addison combined the office of Lord

[1] In November 1952 Lord Salisbury, who was already Leader of the House of Lords, was appointed Lord President.

Privy Seal and the Chairmanship of certain Committees with the Leadership of the House of Lords from October 1947 to March 1951, as did Lord Salisbury in the Conservative Government of 1924 to 1929. Mr. J. H. Thomas was Lord Privy Seal from June 1929 to June 1930 when Mr. Ramsay MacDonald allocated to him duties in connexion with unemployment.

Chancellor of the Duchy of Lancaster

A fourth non-departmental Minister is the Chancellor of the Duchy of Lancaster whose direct duties relate to certain Crown estates which involve, I gather, about half an hour's work a week; so this office also is available for a Minister with other duties. Between 1945 and 1948 it was held by Mr. John Hynd and Lord Pakenham when, successively, they were the Ministers concerned with the administration of the British Zone in Western Germany, work which kept them fully occupied. Subsequently responsibility for that work was transferred to the Foreign Office and Mr. Hugh Dalton, on rejoining the Government, became Chancellor of the Duchy and available for special duties. He was succeeded in due course by Viscount Alexander of Hillsborough. Lord Swinton became Chancellor of the Duchy in the Conservative Government in 1951, was put in charge of raw materials and had certain responsibilities for public relations; he also functioned as Deputy Leader of the House of Lords.

Paymaster-General

A fifth Minister with negligible departmental duties is the Paymaster-General. For the first year of the Labour Government this office was not filled, and then Mr. Arthur Greenwood held it in addition to the office of Lord Privy Seal. In March 1947 he was succeeded as Paymaster-General by Mr. H. A. Marquand until in July 1948 the appointment was again combined with that of Lord Privy Seal under Lord Addison. Following him, Lord Macdonald of Gwaenysgor became Paymaster-General and was available for special duties. In Mr. Churchill's Government, formed after the General Election of October 1951, Lord Cherwell, who held the office in the War Government outside the Cabinet, became Paymaster-General with the exceptional status of Cabinet membership. He was put in charge of atomic energy development and discharged special duties for the Prime Minister, having under his control the Prime Minister's Statistical Section. The fact that the position of Paymaster-General can range between a full Cabinet Minister and a minor office illustrates how usefully adaptable the ministerial structure can be.

Minister without Portfolio

There can be a sixth non-departmental Minister, a Minister carrying the hardly inspiring title of Minister without Portfolio; indeed, subject to certain conditions there can be more than one such Minister. Mr. Arthur Greenwood held the office during his membership of the War Cabinet and also for a short while in 1947 and at the same time presided over certain Cabinet Committees. But it is not usual for such a Minister to be created.

Minister of Defence

The Minister of Defence is partly an executive and partly a co-ordinating Minister. His title and functions give him rather more authority than the ordinary co-ordinating non-departmental Minister. He has the duty of direct consultation with the Chiefs of Staff and at times the making of recommendations in association with them on problems of strategy. He may be personally concerned with matters which are common to the three Service Departments. But he does not run the Admiralty over the head of the First Lord, and if I know their Lordships of the Board of Admiralty, he will have his work cut out to try. He does not run the War Office over the head of the Secretary of State and the Army Council, or the Air Ministry over the head of the Secretary of State and the Air Council.

Their use: their Staffs

In practice, three or four non-departmental Ministers in addition to the Prime Minister are quite adequate; indeed with four it is not always easy to provide them with full employment. Recently their duties have varied between single full-time functions (administration of the British Zone in Germany) and the varied duties of the Lord President and Deputy Prime Minister from 1945 to 1951.

The non-departmental Ministers (including the Prime Minister), not being immersed in day-to-day departmental duties, are in a position to give time and careful study to the shape of things to come. Their minds should be free of those biases which may, quite understandably, influence the mind of the departmental Minister. They can, therefore, make a contribution to Cabinet thinking which fills a gap that otherwise might exist. Provided the Prime Minister chooses these Ministers with an eye to their suitability for this work and for the function of co-ordination, the presence of a suitable number of non-departmental Ministers in the Cabinet is a real advantage. But the Cabinet should also include departmental Ministers, for between them they will bring to bear on the Papers and proposals of their non-departmental colleagues the experience, mind, and outlook of the day-to-day administrator, which are indispensable if the divorce between policy and administration is to be avoided.

If long-term thinking and planning is to be done it is also desirable that the Government, as a whole, should have at its disposal suitable non-departmental official machinery as well as inter-departmental working parties. The Cabinet Secretariat, the Economic Section, the Central Statistical Office, and the Government scientific organizations are valuable official organizations for examining broader problems or seeing that they are examined.

The staffing of the non-departmental Minister's office will depend upon the nature of his work. If his work is limited and deals with relatively simple and straightforward affairs, he may not need more than a private secretary and possibly a personal assistant. But if he is involved in extensive co-ordination, looking out for difficulties that are likely to arise in the future, and engaging in the longer-term thinking and planning, he will need a staff, not large, but of suitable quality and tact. To leave such a Minister with a private secretary and a personal assistant only is to make it impossible for him properly to discharge his functions. He has to live at peace with the Departments; it is right that he should draw on departmental knowledge and co-operation; but it is no less right that he should also have on his own staff persons who are looking at things free from departmental loyalties and boundaries. It is clearly of importance that these officers should know their way about Whitehall and should maintain good personal relations with the departmental civil servants. The non-departmental Minister's small staff will, in great measure, be drawn from the Departments, and in some, though not all, cases it may be well if the officers have had experience of Departments with which the co-ordinating Minister is concerned. For example, if he co-ordinates work relating to the socialization of industry, it would be well if he has somebody on his staff with experience of one or other of the Departments dealing with publicly owned industries or services. And if, as was so in my case, he is also Leader of the House of Commons, he may need a person (who would do other work also) experienced in parliamentary affairs or capable of learning about them, and having a real respect for the House of Commons. However, the Leader of the House receives extensive help from the Whips' Office.

The practice of Prime Ministers in the staffing of No. 10 varies and, of course, there is a great difference in conditions between war and peace. Mr. Lloyd George in the First World War built up a considerable personal staff, including what was known as the 'garden suburb' in the grounds of No. 10. It is said that this substantial and busy staff led to friction with the Departments and their Ministers, particularly the Foreign Office. Mr. Churchill did not, I think, have such an extensive staff in the Second World War but he had at his disposal some personal assistants, including Lord Cherwell who, with the staff of the Prime Minister's Statistical Section, did special work for him and briefed him on many matters. Mr. Churchill was also Minister of Defence. He had at his disposal the Chiefs of Staff Committee and its Secretariat under General Sir Hastings Ismay. Apart from his Public Relations Adviser (Mr. Francis Williams and, later, Mr. Philip Jordan), Mr. Attlee had an economic adviser for a time but relied mainly upon his private secretaries and their assistants. He drew freely on the common service organizations and the Departments for any advice or help he needed; and it must be remembered that he was wise enough to delegate extensively to co-ordinating Ministers.

Co-ordinator or Overlord?

The precise status, authority, and responsibility of certain senior Ministers became prominent in Sir Winston Churchill's not very happy experiment in the first two years of his present Cabinet. The principle of the supervising Minister was apparently applied, or perhaps I should say attempted to be applied. The Lord President of the Council (Lord Woolton) was put in a supervisory position over the Ministers of Agriculture and Food, and made responsible for concerting—as *The Times* put it—the policy of those two Departments. A new Minister, the Secretary of State for the Co-ordination of Transport, Fuel and Power (Lord Leathers), was apparently given similar responsibilities in relation to the Ministry of Transport, the Ministry of Civil Aviation (associated with Transport), and the Ministry of Fuel and Power. These Ministers promptly became known as the Overlords. How far Lord Swinton and Lord Cherwell could be placed in a similar category is uncertain. Controversy about their appointments and status arose in both Houses of Parliament. The case for the appointments was stated in a number of ministerial pronouncements and Press comments.

The brief official announcements of the appointments were to some extent amplified by the Parliamentary Correspondent of *The Times* on 31 October 1951. He remarked:

> Some of the further Cabinet appointments announced yesterday show that Mr. Churchill has to some extent moulded a functional Cabinet in which many of the key men are to be coordinators of the policies of groups of departments.
>
> The Prime Minister himself is also Minister of Defence, to whom the three Service Ministers will be answerable; Lord Woolton, as Lord President of the Council, is to supervise and coordinate the policies of the Ministers of Food and Agriculture; Lord Leathers is to be a coordinator on an even bigger scale; and Lord Cherwell, the Paymaster-General, is to be responsible for the coordination of scientific research and development. An eighth Secretaryship of State has been created and Lord Leathers is to hold this as Secretary of State for the Coordination of Transport, Fuel and Power.

Speaking on 6 November in the debate on the Address in reply to the King's Speech, Mr. Attlee criticized the arrangements on three main grounds: the strain imposed on the Prime Minister;

the position of the supervising Ministers; and the obscurity of responsibility for economic affairs. Mr. Churchill, he said,

has taken on the positions of Prime Minister and Minister of Defence. I think that is quite right in war-time, but I believe it is generally agreed that in peace-time rather different considerations apply. . . . The work of the Prime Minister in these days is very, very heavy. So is the work of a Minister of Defence. There is a danger, on the one hand, that defence may cease to be effectively done with a Ministry of Defence which is not a Department but with a Defence Minister co-ordinating the activities of the head Ministers of the Fighting Services, because of the Prime Minister's necessary absorption with other business; or, on the other hand, that the Prime Minister's interest in defence may lead him to find that he has not time for the rest of his work. . . .

He then went on to ask about the position of the supervising Ministers.

Here it seems that the power of decision is left with Ministers in another place, and we here are to be faced only with Departmental Ministers responsible merely for administration. I want to know this: when questions of major policy arise concerning food and agriculture and transport and fuel and power, who will answer in this House? Will some Cabinet Minister answer?

I am not quite sure who is the Minister who will co-ordinate economic activity. It may be the Chancellor of the Exchequer. If so, the Chancellor of the Exchequer has a very heavy job. Further, I am not sure about the relationship of the Chancellor of the Exchequer to these supervising Ministers. I do not believe very much in the system of supervising Ministers. I think that duty is better done by co-ordination within a Government rather than by professed co-ordinating Ministers, because one is apt to take away responsibility from the Departmental Minister. I should like to know just how the machinery is to work. (493 *H.C. Deb.* 66–67.)

In his reply Mr. Churchill asserted that Mr. Attlee should be familiar with 'the exact relationship between supervising Ministers and the Ministers responsible to this House', 'because it was a process which continually operated during all the years of the Great War and was found very beneficial in many ways'. Mr. Churchill continued:

But the rights and responsibilities of the Members of Parliament are in no way affected by the fact that these problems are studied in the larger bracket from a position of some detachment from the Departments which are grouped together. I believe very much in the policy of grouping Departments where it is possible, and that really is the designing principle upon which the Government was constructed.

The right hon. Gentleman asked me whether I was not burdening myself too much by taking the Ministry of Defence as well as the office of Prime Minister. I am well aware of the burden of both these offices, but I did feel that I must, at any rate at the outset, master the situation in the sphere of defence and leave the future to be decided later on. That is what I propose to do. I do not feel that I shall have difficulty in discharging these two functions, at any rate until I am fully possessed of the actual situation in which we stand at the present time. (493 *H.C. Deb.* 74–75.)

(In March 1952 Field-Marshal Lord Alexander of Tunis was appointed Minister of Defence.)

I put my own criticisms when moving an amendment to the Address:

I come to this serious constitutional point about Lord Leathers and Lord Woolton and any other Ministers in a similar position. It has been publicly announced that they are specifically responsible for certain things, either co-ordination or the over-all policy of the Departments with which they are connected. The Prime Minister says there is nothing new about this; it was done in the war. With great respect, I do not agree with him, and I think my right hon. Friend the Leader of the Opposition, who had a hand in all that, will bear me out.

There were Cabinet Committees and there were chairmen of Cabinet Committees, as there were in the late Labour Government. That is domestic to a Government, and Sir John Anderson always took the view that it is desirable that they should be secret and not announced. I respectfully agree with that. But this is a domestic matter within the Government. There is no need for there to be answerability for Chairmen of Cabinet Committees, in other than exceptional cases where the chairman of a Cabinet Committee is announced or his function is announced, as mine was in relation to the Information Services.

These have been announced. These Ministers have specific responsibilities which will move the responsibilities away from departmental Ministers. . . . Therefore, I want to know who is to answer for those two noble Lords in the House of Commons. This is an important matter. If it is said that the departmental Ministers will answer, that is an impossible situation, because the departmental Ministers have no longer responsibility for this sphere of activity.

Where more than one Minister is responsible, there is the Prime Minister in reserve. Should policy questions on transport, civil aviation, fuel and power, food, and agriculture and fisheries all be put to the Prime Minister? I hope we can be told, because obviously someone must answer for these two Ministers with specifically stated public functions who sit in another place. (493 *H.C. Deb.* 834–5.)

Naturally we pressed the Prime Minister on various occasions to clarify the responsibility of these Ministers, and how they were to be made answerable to the House. At the end of Question Time on 20 November 1951 Mr. Churchill made a statement about arrangements for securing answers to Parliamentary Questions:

Questions about the Department of Scientific and Industrial Research and the scientific research councils, for which the Lord President of the Council is responsible, should be put down to the Parliamentary Secretary, Ministry of Works, as representing the Lord President, and will be placed after Questions to the Minister of Works on Tuesdays.

Questions on the more important matters of policy, which are the concern of the Secretary of State for the Co-ordination of Transport, Fuel and Power, the Paymaster-General, or the Lord President, except the Questions I have just mentioned relating to his scientific responsibilities, and which cannot be dealt with by a Departmental Minister, should be put down to me.

Questions relating to the Ministry of Materials for which the Chancellor of the Duchy of Lancaster is responsible should be put down to the Secretary for Overseas Trade, as representing the Chancellor of the Duchy, and will be placed after Questions to the President of the Board of Trade on Thursdays.

I have arranged that Questions addressed to me as Minister of Defence should be placed after other Questions addressed to me on Wednesdays. (494 *H.C. Deb.* 229.)

There was a further governmental defence of the arrangements in a Supply debate on 21 November. On 30 April 1952 Lord Woolton made a statement in the House of Lords which inevitably aroused much criticism and reinforced doubts about the constitutional position of the Overlords. Lord Woolton then said:

I must explain what I conceive to be the clear issue of responsibility, and it is this. Ministers of the Crown are responsible to Parliament for the Departments to which they are charged. The Minister of Agriculture is responsible to Parliament for what he does. In this House, when your Lordships raise issues, then either his Parliamentary Secretary or I reply for him. The Minister of Food is responsible in the House of Commons. Of course, there is no Parliamentary Secretary here, and I reply for him just as I reply for the Minister of Health in this House. My own Parliamentary responsibilities as Lord President of the Council are quite clearly defined. I am responsible for the work of the Privy Council and I am responsible for civil science in this country. In my view, the work of the co-ordinators is not a responsibility to Parliament; it is a responsibility to the Cabinet. It is true that in Mr. Churchill's present Government we have not, as we had in his previous Government and as I gather noble Lords opposite had in the last Government, a Committee for food and agriculture. Instead, Ministers are good enough to confer with me, bringing their departmental staff with them. (176 *H.L. Deb.* 475–6.)

Next day in the Lords, Lord Shepherd on behalf of the Opposition asked Her Majesty's Government whether they agreed with Lord Woolton's view that 'the work of the co-ordinators is not a responsibility to Parliament; it is a responsibility to the Cabinet'. Lord Salisbury replied:

My Lords, what my noble friend had in mind was that the co-ordination of the work of Departments is a function within the Government, an allocation of duties by the Prime Minister for purposes of administrative convenience. It does not affect the direct responsibility to Parliament of Departmental Ministers, which, as before, remains with these Ministers once the Government have taken their decisions; nor, equally, does it affect the long-established ministerial responsibility to Crown and Parliament.

When pressed for further explanations of the precise powers of the Overlords, Lord Salisbury was no clearer. For example, in reply to a point made by Lord Stansgate, the Conservative Leader in the Lords said:

. . . what the Secretary of State is responsible for is co-ordinating transport, fuel and power. That does not mean that he has power to give orders to the Minister of Fuel and Power or the Minister of Transport. (176 *H.L. Deb.* 523–7.)

The position was not made any clearer by a statement said to have been made by Lord Leathers to the *Evening Standard*

(1 May) and quoted by Lord Stansgate on 2 May in the House of Lords. The quotation was:

'I suppose we approach it differently', Lord Leathers tells me of himself and the Ministers with whom he works. 'I do, anyway. It is a heavy task. Lord Woolton may have a reason for putting it the way he does. He may be shaping his course differently. He is wanting to preserve the standing of the Ministers, no doubt. I do not want to take any limelight from the Ministers. But I could not agree that the job is a minor one.' (176 *H.L. Deb.* 599–600.)

We felt we had a right to know just what was the responsibility of these super-Ministers and whether they reduced the full accountability of the departmental Minister to the House of Commons. Had these 'Overlords' been in the Commons we could, of course, have more quickly settled the issue, for they would have had to accept or deny responsibility when all kinds of Questions were put to them. Their presence in the Lords obscured the issue and up to a point made it easier for them to get away with it. But if they were to have important policy functions their place was obviously in the House of Commons.

On 6 May 1952 Mr. Churchill made another attempt to explain, this time by claiming that the Overlords were a natural development of the system of Chairmen of Cabinet Committees as operated during the war and during Mr. Attlee's Administrations. He then said:

During the war the Lord President of the Council, in particular, discharged extensive co-ordinating responsibilities on this basis; and it is well-known that similar arrangements were in force during the period of office of the late Government. The responsibilities assigned under the present Government to Lord Woolton and Lord Leathers carry this development a stage further in one respect, and in one respect only, namely, that the specific area of co-ordination assigned to each of them was publicly announced on his appointment.

Indeed, so far as concerns my noble Friend, Lord Leathers, it was made explicit in his title. Coal, gas, electricity, oil and transport represent a homogeneous group of subjects which call for co-ordination. Moreover, it includes the basic services which have passed under public ownership under Socialist schemes of nationalisation; and there is clear scope for co-ordination . . . of the Government's relations with the public corporations administering those services. Lord Leathers' co-ordinating functions do not differ, in the constitutional sense, from those of my noble Friend, Lord Woolton.

The co-ordinating Ministers have no statutory powers. They have, in particular, no power to give orders or directions to a Departmental Minister. A Departmental Minister who is invited by a co-ordinating Minister to adjust a Departmental policy to accord with the wider interests of the Government as a whole always has access to the Cabinet; and, if he then finds that he cannot win the support of his Ministerial colleagues, he should accept their decision. No Departmental Minister can, of course, be expected to remain in a Government and carry out policies with which he disagrees.

Thus, the existence and activities of these co-ordinating Ministers do not impair or diminish the responsibility to Parliament of the Departmental Ministers whose policies they co-ordinate. Those Ministers are fully accountable to Parliament for any act of policy or administration within their Departmental jurisdiction. It does not follow that the co-ordinating Ministers are 'non-responsible'. Having no statutory powers as co-ordinating Ministers, they perform in that capacity no formal acts. But they share in the collective responsibility of the Government as a whole, and, as Ministers of the Crown, they are accountable to Parliament.

In conclusion, I should perhaps make it clear that the Minister of Defence is not in the same sense a co-ordinating Minister. His appointment was authorised by a Statute—the Ministry of Defence Act, 1946—which defines his powers and duties in general terms. Broadly speaking, his responsibility is to apportion between the three Services the resources—in men, materials and money—which are made available for them all. And, on this apportionment and on all the questions which arise from it, he is directly accountable to Parliament in the same way as any Departmental Minister is responsible for matters within his jurisdiction. But it is the Service Ministers, and not the Minister of Defence, who are responsible to Parliament for the use which each of them makes of his share of those resources and for the administration of the Service under his charge. (500 *H.C. Deb.* 188–96.)

In commenting on this statement Mr. Attlee put his finger on one of the main issues. Stressing that the Minister of Defence had statutory responsibilities for which he was answerable to Parliament in the same way as any departmental Minister, he pointed out that Lord Leathers and Lord Woolton had no such clearly defined or limited responsibility. It was therefore not possible to say who, for example, should be questioned about transport policy—the Minister of Transport or the Secretary of State for the Co-ordination of Transport, Fuel and

Power. Either the previous policy of not disclosing the purely internal responsibilities of senior Ministers or Committee Chairmen should have been followed or, if a named Minister was given public responsibility for a particular field of work the extent of his accountability to Parliament should have been clearly laid down.

Whether as a result of these criticisms, or of the difficulty of operating such a system, or for other reasons, it later became clear that the arrangements were in the process of modification. It was not until 4 September 1953, however, that with the resignation of Lord Leathers the system came to an end. Its termination was publicly announced.

Comment on the Supervising Minister

I regard the idea of the supervising Minister as not being in accordance with the spirit of our system of parliamentary government and as likely to develop irresponsibility and friction. A departmental Minister is appointed to administer the affairs of a Department of State, and I think it is wrong and anomalous that he should not be fully responsible to Parliament for the work of his Department. If he is not responsible for the policy of his Department and another Minister is, there is first of all the difficulty of finding where policy ends and day-to-day administration begins. If in answering Parliamentary Questions and debates he has to protect himself by showing that another Minister and not he is responsible for the policy of the Department, confusion is likely to arise and Parliament to be annoyed. If, on the other hand, he accepts parliamentary responsibility where he is not responsible, that is unfair and frustrating. Moreover, the civil servants in his Department would tend to have a dual responsibility to him and to the supervising Minister: he would not be fully master of his own Department. The authoritative intervention of the supervising Minister by way of verbal or written instructions or otherwise may well be resented by the departmental Minister; the civil servants may be confused, if not resentful, because they are uncertain to whom they are responsible.

The supervising Minister himself will either experience a steady fight to assert his authority or, in the interests of a quiet life, he will give up the attempt to discharge his supervisory functions. And supposing, as may well happen, there is disagreement between the supervising and departmental Minister or Ministers, what then? Quite awkward situations may arise requiring the attention of the Prime Minister or even the Cabinet, almost inevitably involving a loss of that goodwill and *camaraderie* which is necessary to successful Cabinet government. Is the supervising Minister to answer directly in Cabinet, at any rate on policy, for the Departments he supervises, or are the departmental Ministers also to be present to argue the case out with him in front of his colleagues in case of disagreement? If the former, and the supervising Minister puts the case in a way which is not agreeable to the departmental Ministers, there will be misunderstanding and trouble; if the latter, Cabinet meetings could become awkward and unhappy affairs. If I were asked to prophesy who would win in the end my guess would be the Departments which have strong Ministers. For the Departments of State are powerful organizations, and even though victory would partly depend on the personality of the departmental Minister, it must be remembered that the supervising Minister would tend to be somewhat isolated, and in the case of a difference of opinion would be battling not only with the departmental Minister but in all probability with the Department behind that Minister. If the supervising Minister is to be in a powerful position, whose word in respect of the Departments concerned is ultimately supreme, subject only to the Cabinet, I think it would be a task of doubtful attraction. He would, I think, live a lonely life in his little office, faced with the dilemma of doing little or nothing on the one hand, or fighting his way through resistance and friction on the other.

I am not unconscious of the difficulties which arise from the growth in the number of Departments of State, but believe the co-ordinating—rather than the supervising—Minister is the solution. In my view the supervising Minister idea imperils an essential of our Constitution, namely the responsibility of Ministers to Parliament for their Departments. There is a real distinction between a supervising and a co-ordinating Minister. If the former means anything it means that he has the power of decision and direction. The co-ordinating Minister usually works as Chairman of a Cabinet Committee and as such can consult, urge and seek to persuade, but he is normally subject to the decision of the Committee as is the departmental Minister. He is a helpful colleague and not a master.

'But', I can almost hear somebody saying, 'you have got it all wrong. A supervising Minister is not intended to be a man who gives directions or orders. It is not desired to upset the responsibility of a Minister for his Department. The supervising Minister is a co-ordinator, a helpful colleague, a reconciler in the field of inter-departmental troubles.' The Press announcements at the time of the formation of the 1951 Government, however, gave a different picture of the work of the Overlords. Not all the advocates of the supervising Minister would take this mild view of his responsibility. There is no doubt that some of the advocates, faced with the considerations set out above, would fall back on this explanation, but it really will not do. The *Concise Oxford Dictionary* says that the word 'supervise' means 'direct or watch with authority the work or proceedings or progress of, oversee'. If the milder view of the apologist be accepted, the idea of the super-Minister—as the idea is commonly described—falls down. If those who take the milder view intend that he should be a co-ordinating Minister only, that is quite a different and indeed sensible idea. Let us, therefore, now consider co-ordinating Ministers and how they should set about their work.

How Co-ordinating Ministers Work

First of all the Chairman of a Cabinet Committee will be wise not to think of himself as, or assume himself to be, a supervising Minister. He should be a sympathetic and understanding friend of the departmental Ministers with whom he is dealing. They have to take the blows in Parliament and elsewhere when trouble or criticism is abroad, and similarly a co-ordinating Minister should never seek to rob them of the credit of their successes whether they or he are responsible. He must be content to be behind the scenes. His functions may be guessed at by intelligent Members of Parliament, but they must not normally, at any rate at the time, be publicly proclaimed. This was once done when it was disclosed by the Press and later confirmed in the House that Sir Samuel Hoare (now Lord Temple-wood) was responsible for the co-ordination of agricultural policy. Before he knew where he was the back-benchers and the Opposition demanded his participation in a debate on agriculture. Sir Samuel Hoare was certainly not below the average of ministerial ability in that Government, but this did not prevent him from having a very difficult passage, for attempts were made to extract answers from him on matters of detailed administration which could hardly have come within his duties as a co-ordinating Minister.

The wise departmental Minister will not be too proud to take his headaches to his co-ordinating colleague for consultation and friendly advice. It should help him to arrive at the right conclusions and may be of assistance to him in Cabinet or Cabinet Committee later. The greatest compliment that the co-ordinating Minister can enjoy is that his colleagues develop the habit of voluntarily and freely coming to him in this way.

Conclusions

I have sought to summarize the case for the small Cabinet with as much fairness as I can, as well as quoting supporting arguments for the idea. I must say that, as the result of experience in four Governments over an aggregate period in office of nearly fourteen years, I am not convinced of its suitability for peace-time conditions. In war the case for the small Cabinet is really strong, though even in that case I agree with Mr. Churchill's decision not to make the War Cabinet of 1940–5 one of non-departmental Ministers alone. For whilst there should be in all Governments a proportion of non-departmental Ministers, there are, even in conditions of war, some departmental Ministers of such significance in relation to the prosecution of the war and the economics of war that it would be unreal to leave them out. Moreover, personalities and their public standing cannot be ignored in the constitution of Cabinets.

From May 1940 to October 1940 I was Minister of Supply and from October 1940 to November 1942 I was Home Secretary and Minister of Home Security outside the War Cabinet, but I was in frequent and, in the second capacity, almost regular attendance. I entered the War Cabinet (retaining the offices of Home Secretary and Minister of Home Security) on

22 November 1942 and remained a member until the break-up of the War Government in May 1945. One of the things I noticed was that the number of occasions on which War Cabinet Ministers alone were present was very limited. To most of the meetings a substantial number of departmental Ministers from outside the War Cabinet were invited, including a few 'constant attenders'. In practice, therefore, it is difficult and, as I think, undesirable to keep the departmental Ministers out of discussions in which they are directly or indirectly concerned. This indeed is conceded by many advocates of the small non-departmental Cabinet, though the more extreme might argue that the departmental points of view can be represented by the supervising Cabinet Ministers. That, however, involves such a degree of indignity to the departmental Minister and weakening of his authority that it would not be tolerated by him. The fact is that a peace-time Cabinet of Ministers without Portfolio would be a body of somewhat lonely men, rather cut off from pulsating departmental and parliamentary life, and the public. They would not bring to the Cabinet that intimate experience of day-to-day affairs and work which is part of the valuable experience behind the contribution the departmental Minister makes to Cabinet discussions. Even the clash of departmental opinion—which is often much exaggerated—is not wholly to be deplored. Out of the clash of argument truth sufficiently frequently emerges to make the argument worth while.

Therefore, in my own view, a Cabinet of a moderate size, say sixteen to eighteen, which includes a limited number of non-departmental Ministers and the rest departmental Ministers, is probably best. Even so, other Ministers in charge of Departments will be called in from time to time on business in which they are interested, and the Prime Minister will be wise to give special consideration to their inclusion among the members of appropriate Cabinet Committees so that they also may be able to make their contribution to collective discussions and decisions.

CHAPTER IV

Ministers and Parliamentary Secretaries

THIS chapter deals with the status and problems of those Ministers who are not members of the Cabinet. They can be divided into three broad categories: Ministers in charge of Departments, Ministers of State, and Parliamentary Secretaries.

Departmental Ministers

Ministers in charge of Departments, but not members of the Cabinet, are often known as Ministers of Cabinet rank, a term that is disputed, though I personally see no great harm in this description. However, the last official pronouncement of which I heard declared that Ministers of Cabinet rank was a wrong term and that they were Ministers not in the Cabinet, which certainly cannot be disputed on grounds of literal accuracy.

The Ministers in charge of Departments but not in the Cabinet will vary from Government to Government; it is a matter for the Prime Minister's discretion. They are no less in charge of their Departments than Ministers who are in the Cabinet. They have the same discretion about what they will take to the Cabinet or Cabinet Committees and what they will not. They conduct their Parliamentary Business and are answerable to Parliament in the same way as Cabinet Ministers. They are at liberty to circulate papers to the Cabinet or its Committees on their departmental business and, on exceptional occasions with the consent of the Prime Minister or the Chairman of the Committee concerned, they can even bring forward memoranda on subjects outside their departmental sphere. They can make suggestions and representations to the Prime Minister or other Ministers. As has already been recorded, they discharge important duties within the field of collective discussion and decision at Cabinet Committees; as members of such Committees they have the same rights as Cabinet Ministers. They attend the Cabinet or Committees of which they are not members on matters with which they are departmentally concerned and possibly on subjects of which they have special knowledge. They receive Cabinet Agenda Papers and Conclusions together with a number of other documents. Indeed, to put the matter shortly, Ministers in charge of Departments but not members of the Cabinet have substantially the same rights and responsibilities as Cabinet Ministers apart from the fact that they are outside the Cabinet.

Ministers of State

The Minister of State usually has a status intermediate between that of a full Minister and of a Parliamentary Secretary.

The first Minister of State was Lord Beaverbrook who held that office for a time from 1 May 1941. Lord Beaverbrook, however, was a full Minister and a member of the War Cabinet. During the war Ministers with unusual titles were created. Mr. O. Lyttelton was Minister of State, Resident Middle East from July 1941 to February 1942 and was succeeded in that office by Mr. R. G. Casey of Australia. Both these Ministers were members of the War Cabinet. There were also for a time Ministers Resident at Washington, in West Africa, and at Allied Headquarters in North-West Africa, but they were not included in the War Cabinet. None of these war-time Ministers, however, conformed in status to the post-war practice.

The first Minister of State at the Foreign Office (Mr. Richard Law) was appointed during Mr. Churchill's War Government. That post continued in the Labour Governments during which similar positions were instituted at the Treasury and the Colonial Office. These three posts were filled when Mr. Churchill's Conservative Government was formed in 1951, though after a time he, like Mr. Attlee, dropped the office at the Treasury. Mr. Churchill nominated a Peer as Minister of State for Scottish Affairs in 1951, who would normally be resident in Scotland. A fourth Minister of State was created in September 1953 when the Secretary for Overseas Trade was replaced by a Minister of State at the Board of Trade whose duties were to 'give special attention to the promotion of exports and to the problems of oversea trade generally'. A fifth was created when Lord Reading was promoted Minister of State at the Foreign Office in November 1953.

In practice the general idea of the Minister of State is to create a Minister of higher status than that of a Parliamentary Secretary who could relieve heavily-burdened departmental Ministers of material parts of their work to an extent which might not be considered appropriate in the case of Parliamentary Secretaries.

I have been to some trouble to ascertain whether a Minister of State is a Minister of the Crown. Such Ministers, like a Minister without Portfolio, are apparently appointed by virtue of the Re-election of Ministers Act, 1919, Section 2 of which provides:

> 2. Where, before or after the passing of this Act, a member of His Majesty's Privy Council has been or is appointed to be a Minister of the Crown at a salary, without any other office being assigned to him, he shall not by reason thereof be deemed to have been or to be incapable of being elected to or of sitting or voting in the Commons House of Parliament, and the office of such Minister shall be deemed to be an office included in the above-mentioned schedules:
>
> Provided that not more than three Ministers to whom this section applies shall sit as members of that House at the same time.

It would appear from this that, provided a Minister without Portfolio or a Minister of State is a Privy Councillor, he is a Minister of the Crown. However, any action taken by a Minister of State who is subordinate to the Minister in charge of a Department would be on behalf of the Minister under delegated powers; the Minister in charge would still be answerable to Parliament.

Parliamentary Secretaries

Each departmental Minister usually has a Parliamentary Secretary to assist him, but in some of the larger Departments there may be two. Mostly they are Members of the House of Commons, or if not then of the House of Lords. They must not, of course, be confused with the Permanent Secretary who is the senior civil servant in the Department. Nowadays they are selected by the Prime Minister in consultation with the Minister concerned.

According to authoritative advice Parliamentary Secretaries are not Ministers *of the Crown*, for they are not appointed by the

Sovereign (though the Sovereign is informed of such proposed appointments). Constitutionally they have no 'powers'.

Collective Responsibility

Even though not members of the Cabinet, the above Ministers, like other members of the Administration, are bound by Cabinet decisions. Parliamentary Secretaries are rarely summoned to the Cabinet and then usually only in the absence of their ministerial chiefs. The deputy Chief Whip may attend in the absence of the Chief Whip. Nevertheless, the doctrine of collective responsibility extends to all of them, and if any were publicly to proclaim his disagreement with the Government his resignation would almost certainly be required. Indeed, this happened with Mr. Stanley Evans, who was required to resign the office of Parliamentary Secretary to the Ministry of Food after making a public statement on agriculture which conflicted with Government policy. All Ministers therefore, whether members of the Cabinet or not, share a collective responsibility, including that for Cabinet or Cabinet Committee decisions in the reaching of which they have taken no part whatever. This may sound rather rough; indeed, from time to time it is. But the Government must stand together as a whole and Ministers must not contradict each other, otherwise cracks will appear in the governmental fabric. That is liable to be embarrassing or possibly fatal, and indeed injurious to good government. All this is part of the contract of service. It has to be endured as a condition of acceptance of office.

The growth in the number of Ministers and Parliamentary Secretaries needs to be watched; even the number of Parliamentary Private Secretaries should be limited. If their numbers become excessive the free functioning of Parliament is endangered. All of them are inevitably tied to the Government by speech and vote, though not officially quite so tightly in the case of Parliamentary Private Secretaries. It is undesirable that the proportion of Members of Parliament so placed should be needlessly high.

Help for Hard-worked Ministers

I now propose to deal with the relations between the ministerial head of a Department and his Parliamentary Secretary.

As the latter exists to assist the former, I cannot do better than start by giving a picture of the heavy burdens now borne by a departmental Minister.

How is the ministerial day spent? There are considerable variations according to the nature of the office. In the Labour Governments I imagine that the Ministers working the longest hours were the Prime Minister, the Lord President, when I held that office, the Foreign Secretary, and the Chancellor of the Exchequer. We had to hold or attend many meetings and consultations, to do much paper work, and, as in the case of other Ministers, to see a good many people; in addition we all had to discharge our parliamentary duties.

The average Minister will reach his office at about 9.30 or 10.0 a.m.; the Private Secretary will probably seek his directions about urgent correspondence or messages received; the Permanent Secretary and other higher civil servants will wish to see him for the discussion and decision of problems which have arisen or to receive instructions on the preparation of a Cabinet Paper. There may be one or more office consultations attended by the Parliamentary Secretary and quite a number of civil servants. There will be minutes and papers to read. At any time of the day appointments may have been made for deputations or individual people to be received. Time has to be reserved for meetings of the Cabinet or of Cabinet Committees.

On most days, according to the nature of the Business, or if it is his Question day, the Minister will have to attend the House of Commons. Indeed, when Government majorities are small, as in the case of the Parliaments resulting from the elections of 1950 and 1951, there will be many days on which most Ministers will be unable to leave the House of Commons while it is sitting. This adds to the strain, not only because of the additional hours but also because the House is a somewhat distracting place and it is more difficult to do consistent work in the Minister's room there than in the Department.

If the parliamentary situation and duties permit, or during the recess, many Ministers will pay visits to various parts of the United Kingdom to visit local offices, if the Department has them, to meet local authorities, or to inspect work being done by the Department or by local or other authorities in which the Department is interested. These are pleasant breaks from office routine and the Minister is all the better for getting out of Whitehall and seeing people and things as well as reading about them.

In a number of cases the Minister may have a Bill or Bills to pilot through Parliament. If it is a big Bill this involves a considerable amount of preparation and the almost endless task of settling Government amendments and deciding the attitude to be adopted to amendments promoted by Members of the House of Commons or of the House of Lords. If the Committee stage is taken in Standing Committee upstairs there will be morning meetings of the Committee starting at 10.30. If it is a large Bill or controversial such meetings may also take place in the afternoon or even the evenings. In these circumstances some of the Minister's work which would ordinarily be done at the office has to be done at the House.

The Minister will also have dinners and other functions to attend, either under Government auspices, or given by Associations having a relationship to the work of his Department, by Commonwealth High Commissioners, or by Ambassadors representing foreign countries. The Minister will be wise to try not to overdo attendance at functions, for they can be tiring and may well involve resuming paper work after they are over. In any case the more heavily burdened Ministers will have to work late into the night.

I have only been able to give a very broad and general picture of ministerial life, for it varies from day to day and from Department to Department. Much of the time of the Foreign Secretary, for example, is taken up in office consultations and receiving visits from Ambassadors as well as attending United Nations and other international gatherings and visiting foreign countries.

My short experience as Secretary of State for Foreign Affairs made it abundantly clear that under present-day conditions the burden of the Foreign Secretary is excessively heavy. At the Ministry of Supply I got to bed about 1 or 2 a.m. and up again at 8 a.m. In the height of the war at the Home Office the work on civil defence was very heavy; reading was extensive, requiring great care and attention in connexion with death sentences, detentions under Regulation 18B, and internments of aliens. The review of any death sentence required the most conscientious and meticulous consideration. I was naturally most anxious not to keep anybody in detention or internment beyond a point that was reasonably necessary for the security of the State. All this, together with Mr. Churchill's little custom of calling late ministerial meetings, involved a bedtime of about 3 or 4 a.m. and sometimes later, and up at 8 a.m. At both the Ministry of Supply and the Home Office I was liable to be wakened by anti-aircraft fire and find the buildings and my bed shaking severely as a result of the explosion of nearby bombs. However, this was war, and the vital importance of victory for our country and our people helped to keep one going. But at the Foreign Office one was working in days of peace, even though it was a disturbed and troublesome peace. I had inherited many problems which had accumulated during the illness of my distinguished predecessor (Mr. Ernest Bevin), and a series of new difficulties and grave problems descended upon my desk during the seven months I was Foreign Secretary. Indeed, my successor, Mr. Eden, told me that when he returned to the Foreign Office towards the end of 1951 he found the work had about doubled as compared with what it was when he left the Foreign Office in 1945. Sometimes it was 2 a.m. and sometimes much later when I got to bed, the average being about 3 a.m., and I would be up again at 8 a.m. or thereabouts.

I slept at 11 Downing Street, and in the summer months the glory of the dawn would have appeared over St. James's Park by the time I went to bed. The birds were fresh and lively, full of song. More than once I said to myself, 'Ah, little birds, you went to bed early last evening; you have had a good night's sleep; now you have wakened fresh and full of song. I almost wish I were a little bird.' Fortunately I sleep well, and when I could I had half-an-hour's 'snooze' in the afternoon, though that was by no means regular.

Relations between departmental Ministers and Parliamentary Secretaries

The powers of a Department are the powers of the Minister. To the extent that they are exercised by others, those others are acting on his behalf by virtue of a delegation of his authority. In this respect there is no difference between a Parliamentary

Secretary and a permanent officer: both are exercising the Minister's powers.

It is thus a matter for the Minister in his discretion to determine what decisions or classes of decision may be taken, without reference to him, by a Parliamentary Secretary or a permanent officer. The Minister in any event remains fully responsible.

What happens when the Minister is absent from the Department, on holiday or by reason of illness? Day-to-day decisions can be taken by others on his behalf in accordance with policy which he has previously approved. But particular care must be taken about new decisions of policy or other matters of political importance. The guiding principle should be that permanent officials should not settle questions of policy which would normally be referred to the Minister without obtaining political guidance. On some occasions it will be appropriate that the Permanent Secretary should obtain this guidance from the Parliamentary Secretary, with whom he should consult freely. But on matters of major political importance he should also be required to refer to some other Minister, preferably a member of the Cabinet, authorized to act on behalf of the absent Minister. Indeed, if a Minister is going to be away for a substantial period, it is customary and desirable for another Minister to be nominated to act on his behalf.

Special care must also be taken in any formal exercise of a Minister's statutory powers during his absence. With some exceptions, the powers of a Secretary of State can be exercised by another Secretary of State. But there are limits to the extent to which one Minister may act for another in the formal exercise of statutory powers.

The 'Zinoviev Letter'

It is not quite analogous, but an interesting and unfortunate situation arose in connexion with civil servants acting on behalf of a Minister in 1924. This was the famous 'Zinoviev letter' case. It arose during the General Election of 1924—an awkward circumstance—when Mr. Ramsay MacDonald was both Prime Minister and Foreign Secretary. Information reached the Foreign Office alleging that Mr. Zinoviev of the Third (Communist) International had addressed a letter to the Communist Party of Great Britain instructing them to engage in revolutionary activity of a serious character. When the matter became public its authenticity was denied both by the Soviet Government and the British Communist Party; that was to be expected, but to this day one cannot be absolutely sure about it, even though its wording was not out of harmony with Communist language and principles.

As the Soviet Government had undertaken not to interfere in our internal affairs, Mr. MacDonald took a very serious view about the letter and gave instructions that a draft protest to the Soviet Ambassador should be prepared for consideration. This was done, but Mr. MacDonald was engaged in a heavy electioneering tour of the country. He dealt with the draft in Wales, making corrections in his own handwriting. He returned it to the Foreign Office, but—most unwisely—appended no specific minute of instruction as to action—just the amended draft. When it reached the Foreign Office it came to their knowledge that the *Daily Mail* had a copy of the 'Zinoviev letter' and was about to publish it. Mr. MacDonald could not be got hold of on the telephone. Polling would take place in a few days.

Did the Prime Minister and Foreign Secretary mean publication or did he not? Was it a 'revise' intended for further consideration? If the Office did not publish he might be cross if he were accused by opponents of not taking action. If they did publish there would be a greater assumption of the letter's authenticity. Either way, it could be embarrassing to the Prime Minister electorally. A nasty dilemma. They decided that publication by the *Daily Mail* as a 'scoop' without any announcement of Government action would be the greater evil and to assume that Mr. MacDonald's amended draft meant that he intended delivery and publication. So the Office published both the 'Zinoviev letter' and the Foreign Secretary's note of protest to the Soviet Ambassador. The whole thing at once became a first-class electoral issue. The Labour Party's troubles were added to by the fact that Mr. MacDonald gave little or no clear leadership on the issue in his speeches. Candidates took various lines about it. We lost the election, many Labour Members of the dissolved Parliament (including myself) losing our seats. The 1924 contest has since been known as the 'Red Letter' Election.

I was very conscious of this unhappy episode when I was Foreign Secretary during the 1951 election and kept a tight hold on things, even sacrificing one provincial tour. A nerve-racked Foreign Secretary is an electoral menace.

Of course, Mr. MacDonald was at fault in not sending a specific minute of instructions to the Foreign Office and in not giving the Party a clear lead. It could also be argued that the Foreign Office, in the absence of a minute of instruction, should not have acted. But I must say that the Prime Minister and the *Daily Mail* between them had put the Foreign Office into a very difficult situation.

Life of a Parliamentary Secretary

The life of the Parliamentary Secretary can be interesting and fairly full, or, on the other hand, uninteresting and rather empty according to the attitude of the Minister and, to some extent, the higher civil servants. If, departmentally, he is left out in the cold or given little or nothing to do it is, I think, cruel, foolish, and unfair. It is cruel because it will develop unhappiness and bitterness in the heart of the Parliamentary Secretary; it is foolish because the Parliamentary Secretary of today is a possible Minister of the future and it is desirable for him to learn all he can, including the taking of responsibility; it is unfair because, apart from creating a feeling of frustration, it makes a fool of the Parliamentary Secretary when he hears through other channels of things he ought already to have known about, and is driven to tell inquiring M.P.s that he is sorry but he knows nothing about it. Nor should it be forgotten that he has important duties to discharge with and for the Minister from the Treasury Bench. Moreover, there is the important consideration that the proper employment of the Parliamentary Secretary can lighten the burden of the Minister. These things I say although I have never myself been a Parliamentary Secretary.

In the case of the Minister being a Peer, it is of course absolutely essential for the Parliamentary Secretary in the Commons to be in 'on the ground floor' of departmental discussions, for he is the departmental spokesman in the House of Commons. A similar need arises where the Minister is in the Commons and the Parliamentary Secretary is in the Lords.

There are some matters of exceptional secrecy which even Parliamentary Secretaries cannot be told about, but generally speaking the more they know about the work of the Department and the more they can take a positive or consultative part in the appropriate fields of administration the better. I have listened to many sad confidential complaints from Parliamentary Secretaries about all this, and have always done what I could discreetly to help them.

One of the difficulties may be the unwillingness not only of the Minister but of the higher civil servants to bring the Parliamentary Secretary in, but this is by no means universally the case. I can understand the apprehension of the Permanent Secretary and the higher civil servants that if the Parliamentary Secretary minutes against their views they will have to argue a matter twice over which would add to their labours. But I think the fear of this can be exaggerated; in any case it should be accepted for the sake of the general good and happiness.

A Parliamentary Secretaries' Charter

I will now record what I did about this problem at the Home Office when I was Home Secretary and Minister of Home Security in 1940–5, controlling two Departments, each with its Permanent Secretary. I had a special problem at Home Security, so did the Permanent Secretary, for there were two Parliamentary Secretaries, Mr. William Mabane and Miss Ellen Wilkinson, both of whom served me well. In addition I was served at the Home Office by Mr. Osbert Peake and, later, Lord Munster as Parliamentary Under-Secretary.[1] The Home Office side was fairly easy, but with two Parliamentary Secretaries at Home Security it was not so easy because it was my wish as well as my duty to allocate duties between the two Parliamentary Secretaries in such a way as not to cause any feeling of unfairness. As a whole I think I can say that we succeeded.

I called for a memorandum giving me a picture of the functions of the branches in the two Departments. This supplied, the task then was to allocate duties between myself, as Secretary of State and as Minister of Home Security, the Parliamentary

[1] When the Minister is a Secretary of State, the 'Parliamentary Secretary' is known as the Parliamentary Under-Secretary of State and the 'Permanent Secretary' as the Permanent Under-Secretary of State.

Under-Secretary at the Home Office, and the two Parliamentary Secretaries of Home Security. First I determined upon a limited number of matters of special secrecy or delicacy which were to come to me direct for decision. Among them were top-secret Home Security matters; in the Home Office, death sentences, detentions under Defence Regulation 18B, subversive activities, matters relating to security services, &c. On most matters, however, the files and memoranda were to come to me through the appropriate Parliamentary Secretary, it being his duty in such cases to read the papers and minute his comments and suggestions. Finally, I delegated quite a number of the less important matters to the Parliamentary Secretaries for decision, subject to the understanding that they would be referred to me either if the Parliamentary Secretary considered that they were of special importance or might lead to trouble or if there was a disagreement between the Parliamentary Secretary and our civil service advisers.

At the Foreign Office I was fighting hard to do the same kind of thing and to distribute delegated functions between the Minister of State and the two Parliamentary Under-Secretaries. I got some way with this and would have got farther in time, but it was hard going. There were warnings of practical difficulties, of possible mistakes, or of things being done with which I would not agree; and that Parliament would (quite properly) hold me personally responsible. I would have persisted, however. Whether it would have been right to tell Parliament frankly about it and publicly state the responsibility to Parliament of the subordinate Ministers for certain matters is disputable. His excessively heavy work at the Foreign Office killed Ernest Bevin; and Mr. Eden experienced grave illness during 1953. If there is not to be a heavy sickness and mortality rate among our Foreign Secretaries, something like what I have suggested will have to be done. The alternative seems to be to carve up the Foreign Office, which would be a pity. Another expedient may be worth thinking about, namely, an additional Minister of State at the Foreign Office[1] who should not go to overseas gatherings on other than exceptional occasions. Thus one of the Ministers of State would be in continuous contact with the

[1] Lord Reading was appointed an additional Minister of State in November 1953.

work of the Foreign Office. However, there is always the hope that the world may become rational and that foreign affairs may quieten down.

There is another possible injustice to Parliamentary Secretaries, namely, leaving them out of office consultations and conferences. Obviously it is not always right or convenient to have them present, but systematically to leave them out means that they do not know the background of policy decisions. Moreover, even listening to their chief handling such meetings is an experience and an education which may help them if and when they come to shoulder bigger responsibilities. It was my general rule, therefore, to give instructions that the appropriate Parliamentary Secretary or Secretaries should be present at such gatherings, and I would see to it that they had an opportunity of contributing their views, even though they were by no means always accepted. This not only assisted our deliberations and brought them into the inside of things, but helped them to learn the delicate art of the ministerial handling of civil servants. In the end I would give a decision, but, even though it was a decision that some did not want, everybody would go away happier for having had a share in the deliberations.

Ellen Wilkinson, a brave soul in the blitz, whose early death in 1947 was a great loss to the country and the Labour Party, told me that she had thought of a dirge for unhappy Parliamentary Secretaries: it was 'Less than the dust' from the *Indian Love Lyrics*. Let us hope that the foregoing may constitute something in the nature of a charter for all Parliamentary Secretaries.

were of the present Office, however, their answer is the one that the work may become tedious and that having [illegible] they [illegible] down.

There are more [illegible] images of Parliamentary secre- [illegible] moments, a [illegible] part of the Office's business and con- [illegible] it [illegible] convenient, to have [illegible], but [illegible] to [illegible] them out [illegible] not [illegible] background of the [illegible]. Moreover, even listening to all that familiar succession of ex- [illegible] may [illegible] them, and when [illegible] to another [illegible] it was my general [illegible] they [illegible] appear. Parlia- mentary [illegible] should be [illegible] with [illegible] had no [illegible] though they were [illegible] means [illegible] I [illegible] and brought them [illegible] but helped them to [illegible] without [illegible]. In the end I would give a [illegible] though it was a decision that some did not want; everybody would [illegible] have [illegible] for having had a [illegible] in the field [illegible].

[illegible] the [illegible] all to the [illegible] told me that she had [illegible] mentary [illegible] them [illegible] [illegible]

PARLIAMENT

CHAPTER V

The Monarchy as Part of Our Parliamentary Democracy

PERHAPS the best statement of the relationship between the Monarchy and Parliament is given in the recital of every Act of Parliament: 'Be it enacted by the Queen's most Excellent Majesty, by and with the advice and consent of the Lords Spiritual and Temporal, and Commons, in this present Parliament assembled, and by the authority of the same, as follows:—' It will be observed that whilst the enactment is by the Queen, it is made effective not only by and with the advice of both Houses of Parliament, but by and with their consent. Moreover, the authority for the statute is clearly stated to be that of Parliament. The assertion of parliamentary responsibility could not be more clear, yet it is put in the best possible way from the point of view of the dignity of the Sovereign by the commencing words: 'Be it enacted by the Queen's most Excellent Majesty'. Moreover, before a Bill can become an Act it requires the Royal Assent, which is generally signified to Parliament not in person but before Lords Commissioners, on behalf of Her Majesty, by the Clerk of the Parliaments, at an impressive ceremony which takes place in the House of Lords with the Commons present.

The Queen and Parliament

There are other associations between the Queen and Parliament. The Sovereign approves the appointment of the Speaker of the House of Commons. The Houses, and indeed individual Members of the Lords, have the right of access to the Monarch, though it is not often exercised.[1] On appropriate occasions

[1] Erskine May (15th ed., 1950), pp. 86 and 87, says: 'The privilege of access is enjoyed by the House at large, with their Speaker. . . . Far different is the privilege enjoyed by the House of Peers. Not only is that House, as a body, entitled to free access to the throne, but each peer, as one of the hereditary counsellors of the Crown, is individually privileged to have an audience of the king.'

messages are sent by the Sovereign to Parliament and from Parliament to her. I shall describe the ceremonial in connexion with such messages in Chapter VI.

The House of Commons discharges the delicate responsibility of settling the public income of the Sovereign to provide for the maintenance of the Queen and the Royal Family and to cover expenses connected with the discharge of the various Royal functions. This is called the Civil List. In order that it may be considered in detail, and evidence taken from those competent to advise, the House appoints a Select Committee under the Chairmanship of the Chancellor of the Exchequer. Leading Members of the House and back-benchers are included among its members. Its report, with recommendations, is submitted to the House and is usually debated and often challenged in certain respects. A Bill follows, which is of course debatable, and amendments may be, and often are, moved. During part of the reign of Queen Victoria, when there was a noticeable republican movement, and when the Monarchy was being actively criticized, debates on the Royal finances were liable to be exciting and even stormy. The fact that Parliament sustains the Monarchy by grants of public money is in itself an indication of the power and authority of Parliament, and particularly of the House of Commons, which alone can grant supplies even though the Bill leading up to the Civil List Act has to pass the House of Lords. Such public grants were, however, in their origin an exchange for some of the hereditary land revenues of the Crown surrendered by George III on his accession.

The outstanding occasion which demonstrates the happy association of the Queen with Lords and Commons is at the beginning of each Session when she opens Parliament. This is the occasion of the Queen's Speech, usually delivered by the Sovereign in person from the Throne in the House of Lords with the Commons present. It is a great occasion. There is a Royal procession from Buckingham Palace. Her Majesty is received at the House of Lords by the Earl Marshal and the Lord Great Chamberlain. A procession is formed, and the Queen, accompanied by the Duke of Edinburgh, and preceded by the Great Officers of State (the Lord Chancellor, the Lord President of the Council, and the Lord Privy Seal) and by the Earl Marshal, the Lord Great Chamberlain, the Heralds, and others, makes her progress towards the House, and is eagerly watched by wives of M.P.s and other members of the public who have been able to obtain tickets. In the House of Lords itself are assembled the Lords, including the Judges, the Archbishops, and the Bishops in their respective robes; Peeresses are in the Gallery, with wives of Ministers and of leading members of the Opposition—some Peeresses being accommodated on the benches below—whilst a large number of Members of the House of Commons are crowded behind the Bar, headed by their Speaker. At the beginning the Lords are standing, but the proceedings begin by the Queen saying, 'My Lords, pray be seated'. The Speech is handed to Her Majesty by the Lord Chancellor, kneeling, and upon his resuming his place is read by the Queen from the Throne. If the Sovereign is ill, or for some other sufficient reason is unable to be present, the Speech is read by the Lord Chancellor or another member of the Commission of Peers, but this has been exceptional throughout the present century. When the Speech has been delivered the Queen hands it back to the Lord Chancellor, the procession re-forms, and the Queen with the Duke and her attendants departs and returns to the Palace. The Session has begun.

The Speech itself has been composed by the Government, for it is a public declaration of Government policy and intentions for the coming Session. The basis of its language is what 'My Ministers' think and propose to do. The Cabinet considers and settles the draft, which goes to the Palace for the consideration of Her Majesty. Of course, she cannot upset the policy, for that would be unconstitutional, though she can raise questions about it; certainly the Sovereign can and often does make suggestions for revision of wording, either because it is thought to be better for delivery or to make a sentence more appropriate or attractive. All such suggestions from the Palace are given that respectful and sympathetic consideration which is their due, but the last word is with the Cabinet, and as regards policy the first word as well.

The new Session opens with debates in both Houses on the Address in reply to the Gracious Speech. The Address is usually moved and seconded by two back-benchers on the Government side who, without undue provocation, welcome the proposals in the Speech. The proposals are debated and amendments to the Address are moved, on the basis, of course, that the Cabinet is entirely responsible for the Speech.

Choice of Prime Minister

So much for the actual personal relationships between the Queen and Parliament. Let us now consider the relationship between the Queen and her Ministers. The most important political act of the Sovereign is appointing the Prime Minister and commissioning him to form a Government. Nowadays, the choice is usually obvious. The essential point is that the new Prime Minister should be able to command a majority in the House of Commons, and not merely be able to form a Government, for the Government cannot live without a parliamentary majority. In most cases there is little or no doubt who should be sent for; there was no doubt that it was the Leader of the Labour Party after the substantial Labour electoral victory of 1945. The General Election of 1950 gave Labour an overall majority in the House of Commons of only six, but it was still right that Mr. Attlee should again be Prime Minister. And when the election of 1951 resulted in a small Conservative overall majority —though somewhat larger than the 1950 Labour majority—it was equally right that the Leader of the Conservative Party, Mr. Churchill, should be sent for.

Even if a Prime Minister dies in office the choice of his successor can be reasonably obvious, though careful consideration would no doubt always be given to the likelihood of the person appointed being acceptable to a majority in the House of Commons. Including and since Mr. Churchill's War Government, the position of Deputy Prime Minister has been publicly announced, though not constitutionally recognized. The position has been held in conjunction with the office of Lord President or Foreign Secretary. So far the holder has not been (though he could be) the Chancellor of the Exchequer.[1] The Deputy Prime Minister might be specially considered by the Sovereign, though there would be no obligation to do

[1] Mr. R. A. Butler, Chancellor of the Exchequer, was acting Prime Minister during a period in the summer of 1953 when both Sir Winston Churchill and Mr. Anthony Eden were absent through illness.

so, especially as I gather that the Sovereign does not recognize such an office.

There are circumstances, however, in which the choice of Prime Minister is not easy. Such conditions may arise when a Coalition Government is being formed, or (subject to the observations above) when a Prime Minister dies in office or retires, or when a political party has, at the crucial moment, no recognized leader. The Sovereign's choice in these conditions has much constitutional significance. The choice may be a very delicate one and involve embarrassing complications. The Sovereign would, of course, take all relevant considerations into account, and be at great pains not only to be constitutionally correct, but make every effort to see that the correctness is likely to be generally recognized. The Sovereign is free to seek or not to seek the advice of the out-going Prime Minister, and can also receive counsel and advice from such Privy Councillors as she may wish to consult.

The Crisis of 1931

An exceptional problem in this respect faced King George V in connexion with the financial crisis of 1931, which precipitated division within and ultimately the fall of the Labour Government. Here I think it desirable to set out my personal views, though I recognize that the passages that follow may be controversial. The Cabinet (of which I was a member) decided to invite the Prime Minister (he assenting) to tender to the King the resignation of the Government. Mr. MacDonald went to the Palace and submitted the resignation of the Government. But the King, on the advice of Mr. MacDonald, brought into consultation Mr. Baldwin, Leader of the Conservative Party, and Sir Herbert Samuel, who was acting Leader of the Liberal Party in the absence of Mr. Lloyd George, who was ill and who disagreed with the line taken by his Liberal colleague. In Sir Harold Nicolson's *King George V, His Life and Reign*, a valuable account is given of these events which I believe to be substantially correct, though I do not find myself able to agree that the King's action was wise.

Sir Herbert Samuel made the suggestion that Mr. MacDonald should be invited to continue in office as Prime Minister at the head of a Government of personalities or a Coalition.

Sir Herbert was a Privy Councillor and had the right to give such advice once the King had brought him into consultation; and the King had a right to receive and consider it. Mr. Baldwin acquiesced in this advice, at any rate to the extent of indicating that he would be willing to co-operate. Mr. MacDonald is said at first to have resisted, but ultimately to have agreed (without, however, consulting the Labour Cabinet), and this can fairly be construed as giving the King personal advice as Prime Minister (though a resigning one) to that effect. The King invited Mr. MacDonald to continue as Prime Minister at the head of a Coalition or a Government of personalities, and to the surprise of the Cabinet Mr. MacDonald came back to Downing Street and told us what had happened.[1] Most of us regarded this action of Mr. MacDonald as a blunder at the best and a betrayal at the worst, and indicated our unwillingness to help in a venture which we regarded as bad in itself and about which we had not been consulted. Only a handful of Labour M.P.s gave him support in the new Government. He had ceased to possess representative parliamentary value. The case for the step taken by the King was that he had advice to that end from the three party leaders, including that of the Prime Minister, and that he was convinced that the step was essential to the well-being of the nation at a grave and critical time; a view with which I cannot agree because I consider that a Conservative–Liberal Coalition could have done all that the so-called National Government did. Mr. MacDonald and his few supporters brought no real strength to the new Government, though their action much increased the bitterness in Parliament and the country.

It may well be that the King had the impression that Mr.

[1] See the evidence of Philip Snowden, one of the few former Labour Ministers who entered the National Government under Mr. MacDonald. 'Mr. MacDonald at the Palace meeting on the Monday morning agreed to the formation of a National Government, with himself as Prime Minister, without a word of previous consultation with any of his Labour colleagues. He knew he would have the great majority of the Labour Cabinet against him, and practically the whole of the Parliamentary Labour Party. He had, in fact, at that time, no assurance that he could take any of his late colleagues with him. Mr. Baldwin and Sir Herbert Samuel were in a different position. They could count confidently on carrying their Parties with them. Mr. MacDonald at the best could not hope to have the support of more than a mere handful of Labour members.' *An Autobiography*, Philip, Viscount Snowden, vol. ii, p. 952 (1934).

MacDonald would carry a majority, or at any rate a substantial proportion, of the Parliamentary Labour Party with him, and had that been true it would have strengthened the case for his action. But this did not prove to be so. He would have been wise to have ascertained what was likely to happen by inquiry of one or more Labour Privy Councillors likely to know. He might have asked the Prime Minister to ascertain the view of the Labour Cabinet; but no action was taken to ascertain the general Labour view. King George V was, I feel sure, actuated by sincere motives. And certainly the financial and economic situation of the country was serious. Nevertheless, I think his judgement was at fault. He was himself, I apprehend, over-favourable to a very speculative course of action. The very formation of what was styled the National Government was a highly controversial step; it led to bitter parliamentary debates, for Mr. MacDonald did not carry the Labour Party with him. While the defections from the Labour Party were so small that they could not be described as a split, the consequence of Mr. MacDonald, Mr. Snowden, and Mr. J. H. Thomas associating themselves with the Conservatives at the subsequent election led to a dramatic Labour Party defeat so far as seats were concerned (the fall being from 288 to 52[1]), although Labour polled nearly 6,650,000[1] votes as compared with about 8,390,000 in 1929. According to Mr. D. E. Butler, in his valuable study *The Electoral System in Britain, 1918–51* (p. 175), the average percentage vote per Labour candidate (calculated as a percentage of the average vote cast in each constituency at each election) fell from 39·3 per cent. in 1929 to 33·0 per cent. in 1931, whereas Labour seats in the House of Commons fell from 46·8 per cent. (288 seats) in 1929 to 8·5 per cent. (52 seats) in 1931. This curious and abnormal election created an unhealthy parliamentary situation because of the unnatural smallness of the Opposition. We would have been defeated anyway, but the association of distinguished former Labour Ministers with the Coalition made things much more serious.

As I see it, the King had unwittingly become involved in what he no doubt regarded as action essential to meet a national crisis but what millions of his subjects regarded as an unneces-

[1] These figures for 1931 include the votes for I.L.P. candidates (five of whom were elected) who had not been endorsed by the Labour Party Executive.

sary and unpleasant political manœuvre by Mr. MacDonald and his new allies, calculated to inflict grave injury on the Labour Party and to benefit the Conservatives—as it did. Moreover, the national necessity really did not, as I see it, require the formation of what was called the National Government. Although it was clear that the minority Labour Government could not survive, it seemed to me that the natural and appropriate parliamentary solution, if the Labour Government was defeated in the House or resigned (as it did) of its own volition, was that the Conservatives should take office, probably with Liberal support. Mr. Baldwin, as Prime Minister, would no doubt have been granted a dissolution if he had asked for it. On a balance of considerations, therefore, my own view is that in this instance King George V received bad advice and that he himself made a mistake in accepting it, though I would not go so far as to assert that his action was unconstitutional. He may have taken the view (from which I would respectfully differ) that the crisis required a National Government, and that it would be helpful if Mr. MacDonald (for whom he had a warm regard) continued as Prime Minister. I have set out my own view though I recognize that many authorities may not agree with it.

King George V had a full share of constitutional problems to face. There was, for example, the conflict between the Commons and Lords in 1910 over the Parliament Bill which followed the Lords' rejection of the 1909 Budget, when the Liberal Government asked His Majesty to create a large number of Peers so that the Conservative majority in the Lords might be out-voted. He had inherited this problem from King Edward VII, who had just died. Ultimately King George V agreed in principle to the Liberal Government's demands, subject to certain conditions. When this became known the Conservatives made a great attack on the Liberal Government, alleging that it had given the King wrong and unconstitutional advice.

The Queen and Her Ministers

It is an axiom of our system of Constitutional Monarchy and parliamentary democracy that whilst many State actions take the form of decisions by the Monarch, they are and should be in fact decisions of Ministers responsible to Parliament. In form, the Queen makes many Orders in Council; it is, for example, the Queen in Council who appoints the Governors of the British Broadcasting Corporation. She appoints Ambassadors to represent her abroad, and approves the appointment of Ministers of the Crown. She exercises the Royal Prerogative of Mercy (the Prerogative of relieving an offender of all or some of the consequences of a conviction or of a sentence or penalty imposed by the Criminal Courts) by granting free pardons, conditional pardons, or remissions; and murderers may be reprieved on condition that the sentence of death is commuted to one of life imprisonment. She is the Head of each of the three Armed Forces, and she appoints and promotes their officers. Many other examples could be given of the Sovereign's varied actions. Nevertheless, they are all taken on the advice of Ministers, and if, as may well be the case, controversy ensues, it is the Ministers who are responsible to Parliament and the public, whether the action has been taken on the advice of individual Ministers or of the Cabinet.

Nevertheless, it is perfectly legitimate for the Sovereign to discuss any matter with the Minister or Ministers concerned, and naturally this is particularly so where the Royal Prerogative is involved, as, for example, in the mitigation of sentences of the Law Courts. George VI twice discussed particular death sentences with me when I was Home Secretary. He expressed his views ably and reasonably and, naturally, I gave them every consideration. However, I did not feel able to accept His Majesty's view in either case, and when I respectfully told him so he accepted my decision with every good grace. Such specific discussions are the exception rather than the rule, though general discussions on public affairs, including foreign policy, are common, and it is quite competent for Ministers to modify their proposals in the light of the discussions or not. Most of the issues involved are not party-political, but occasionally the Sovereign may have to concern himself with a matter which is causing very great bitterness between the parties. King George V, for example, sought to have the Irish question discussed in a reasonable atmosphere by the party leaders; they did not reach agreement, but he did bring them together.

While on a visit to South Wales King Edward VIII made public declarations about unemployment which could be construed as criticism of his Government. It was a Conservative Government and the words in themselves were acceptable to the Labour Party. But I did not think well of it, for it was a case of the Sovereign publicly expressing views on matters which were the subject of political controversy. However, he would appear also to have political views adverse to the Labour Party. That became clear in the course of an article by him in a Sunday newspaper of 24 May 1953 when he condemned the passing of aristocratic luxury and privilege and was severely critical of those who had brought this about. By this time, of course, the former King Edward VIII had become H.R.H. the Duke of Windsor. Such an expression of opinion critical of any political party on the part of a former Monarch is, I think, unfortunate. It confirms my personal view that ex-Monarchs are wise to be silent and not to live in a country or countries over which they formerly ruled.

Walter Bagehot in his *English Constitution*[1] put the case for free discussion between Sovereign and Ministers in the following words:

> To state the matter shortly, the sovereign has, under a constitutional monarchy such as ours, three rights—the right to be consulted, the right to encourage, the right to warn. And a king of great sense and sagacity would want no others. He would find that his having no others would enable him to use these with singular effect. He would say to his minister: 'The responsibility of these measures is upon you. Whatever you think best must be done. Whatever you think best shall have my full and effectual support. *But* you will observe that for this reason and that reason what you propose to do is bad; for this reason and that reason what you do not propose is better. I do not oppose, it is my duty not to oppose; but observe that I *warn*.' Supposing the king to be right, and to have what kings often have, the gift of effectual expression, he could not help moving his minister. He might not always turn his course, but he would always trouble his mind.
>
> In the course of a long reign a sagacious king would acquire an experience with which few ministers could contend. The king could say: 'Have you referred to the transactions which happened during such and such an administration, I think about fourteen years ago?

[1] World's Classics edition, Oxford University Press, pp. 67–68.

They afford an instructive example of the bad results which are sure to attend the policy which you propose. You did not at that time take so prominent a part in public life as you now do, and it is possible you do not fully remember all the events. I should recommend you to recur to them, and to discuss them with your older colleagues who took part in them. It is unwise to recommence a policy which so lately worked so ill.' The king would indeed have the advantage which a permanent under-secretary has over his superior the parliamentary secretary—that of having shared in the proceedings of the previous parliamentary secretaries.

I rather think that Bagehot put the Sovereign's language in somewhat stronger terms than would now be used and stronger than I personally have experienced; but it must be remembered that *The English Constitution* was first published in 1867 in the days of Queen Victoria, who had fairly strong views on her powers and authority.

King George V when Duke of York received the services of Mr. J. R. Tanner, of St. John's College, Cambridge, who was engaged in March 1894 to instruct the Duke in the law and practice of the Constitution. The story of the King's studies and the resultant summary he wrote is recorded in Sir Harold Nicolson's excellent volume *King George V, His Life and Reign* at pages 61–63.

. . . It must be admitted that the visits of Mr. Tanner to York House are recorded with less frequency than those of Mr. Tilleard, the philatelist. Mr. Tanner none the less did succeed in inducing the Duke to read and analyse some at least of the sparkling pages of Walter Bagehot's *English Constitution.* There exists at Windsor a school note-book, in the opening pages of which the Duke summarised in his own careful handwriting the precepts which Mr. Bagehot, in his confident way, had laid down for the instruction and guidance of our English kings. In these few notes the Duke crystallised those very conceptions of the functions and duties of a constitutional monarch which, when he came to the throne, he applied with consistent faithfulness. His summary deserves, therefore, to be quoted in its entirety:

Monarchy

'(1) The value of the Crown in its *dignified* capacity.
  (*a*) It makes Government *intelligible* to the masses.
  (*b*) It makes Government *interesting* to the masses.

(*c*) It *strengthens* Government with the *religious* tradition connected with the Crown.

After the accession of George III the Hanoverian line inherited the traditional reverence of Stuart times.

(*d*) The *social* value of the Crown.

If the high social rank was to be scrambled for in the House of Commons, the number of social adventurers there would be incalculably more numerous & indefinitely more eager.

(*e*) The *moral* value of the Crown.

Great for good or evil.

Compare the Courts of Charles II and George III in their influence on the nation.

(*f*) The existence of the Crown serves to *disguise* change & therefore to deprive it of the evil consequences of revolution, e.g. The Reform Bill of 1832.

'(2) The value of the Crown in its *business* capacity. The Crown is no longer an "Estate of the Realm" or itself the executive, but the Queen nevertheless retains an immense unexhausted *influence* which goes some way to compensate for the formal *powers* which have been lost; this influence can be exercised in various ways:

(*a*) In the *formation* of Ministries; especially in choosing between the Statesmen who have a claim to lead party.

(*b*) During the *continuance* of Ministries. The Crown possesses *first* the right to be consulted, *second* the right to encourage & *third* the right to warn. And these rights may lead to a very important influence on the course of politics, especially as under a system of party government, the Monarch alone possesses a *continuous political experience.*

(*c*) At the *break up* of a Ministry (but this can be treated best in connection with the House of Lords).

'Thus, though it would be possible to construct a system of political machinery in which there was no monarchy, yet in a State where a monarchy of the English type already exists, it is still a great political force & offers a splendid career to an able monarch; he is independent of parties & therefore impartial, his position ensures that his advice would be received with respect; & he is the only statesman in the country whose political experience is continuous.'

Sir Harold Nicolson comments:

The Duke of York possessed neither an eager imagination nor wild thoughts. His faith in the principle of Monarchy was simple, devout even; but selfless. All that he aspired to do was to serve that principle with rectitude; to represent all that was most straightforward in the national character; to give to the world an example of personal probity; to advise, to encourage and to warn.

To few men has it been granted to fulfil their aspirations with such completeness.

The essential point is that such discussions are legitimate, provided they are conducted on the basis (which in my own experience they always are) that in the end it is the view of the Minister or Ministers that prevails. For consider the consequences of the alternative. If the Sovereign actually exercised a power to overrule ministerial advice or decision, what would happen, especially if the matter were controversial? Questions might arise in Parliament or elsewhere asking why such-and-such a thing had been done. If the Minister were truthful (and he would have a right to be) he would say, 'This was not my action; it was that of the Sovereign; and I personally did not agree with it.' Then the controversy would descend upon the Sovereign as well as upon the Minister, because the critics would say the Sovereign was wrong on the merits of the decision and because general opinion would say he or she was wrong in overruling ministerial decision or advice. The Minister himself would be criticized on the ground that he had permitted the Sovereign to overrule him. I would say that the strength of the British Monarchy, particularly in the present century during which respect for it has grown and its popularity has increased, rests upon the general acceptance of its impartiality. The saying that the Queen can do no wrong—precisely because she cannot make decisions of a political or controversial character—protects the Sovereign from controversy. Therefore the responsibility of Ministers to Parliament for what are nominally actions of the Sovereign is right, not only from the point of view of parliamentary democracy, but from the standpoint of the well-being and the popularity of the Monarchy itself.

There are some actions, lying outside the field of executive government, in which the Queen will not only take a personal interest but may indeed reach her own decision. For example, although most honours are conferred on advice, the Queen herself decides in the case of the Order of Merit, the Garter, and the Thistle, as well as the Royal Victorian Order.

The Sovereign's Heavy Duties

Because the responsibility for action rests with Ministers, it should not be thought that the Sovereign's work is light or nominal. The duties are in fact heavy. Cabinet Minutes and Papers, Foreign Office, Commonwealth Relations Office and Colonial Office telegrams, and other official papers are sent to the Palace day by day. To my own knowledge King George V and King George VI engaged in extensive reading of such official material covering a wide field of public administration and overseas policy. Indeed, in my own personal conversations with King George VI he took a delight in catching me out by demonstrating that he knew something that I did not (though I must add, in self-defence, that no single Minister can be expected to know everything). I feel sure that Queen Elizabeth II is keeping herself well informed by reading these numerous official papers. Moreover, the Queen receives a large number of documents to sign and these and the attendant papers and minutes also involve her in much reading. There are, for example, appointments in the Services and remissions or modifications in sentences or fines imposed by Courts of Law, right down to very small matters. When I was at the Home Office I was worried about the number of this last class of documents which King George VI was called upon to sign. Having regard to his heavy labours, I took the opportunity of discreetly sounding him as to whether he might wish to delegate the smaller of these signing operations to the Home Secretary, especially as that Minister has to countersign them anyway. But the very conscientious view he took of his duties caused him to decline the proposal.

It must be remembered also that the Queen of the United Kingdom is also Queen of Canada, Australia, New Zealand, South Africa and Ceylon, and of the Colonies, and in India[1] she is recognized as Head of the Commonwealth. Therefore she has responsibilities in relation to Commonwealth countries overseas, even though, in most of them, they are delegated to Governors General, who, however, no doubt keep her informed.

As Queen of the independent self-governing countries of the Commonwealth, Her Majesty has relations with them separate

[1] At the time of writing the position in Pakistan is the subject of consideration and debate in that country.

and distinct from her relations with the United Kingdom. The fact that our Queen is also the Queen of other independent countries in no way implies British interference with those countries, for all the self-governing nations of the Commonwealth are equal in status and their Governments have the exclusive right to advise Her Majesty on their own affairs. There is a real danger of the Sovereign being overworked, but if her labours in the United Kingdom could be appropriately adjusted it would be a fine thing if a systematic plan could be worked out whereby she could from time to time open Parliamentary Sessions in other Commonwealth countries with a Speech from the Throne as she does at Westminster.

As the ceremonial Head of the State, the Queen is, so to speak, the incarnation of the State, the esteemed non-party representative of the nation as a whole. She has to carry through many ceremonial duties, including visits to various institutions and parts of the country, and to perform opening ceremonies. When the Heads of other States or distinguished representatives of Commonwealth and other countries visit our country she receives and entertains them. There is the conferring of honours and receiving the homage of Bishops. There are also the garden-parties and other functions held at the Palace and attended by people of all walks of life.

All of these activities, as I can testify from my personal observation, involve heavy physical labour as well as mental strain. The fact that the Monarchy has become a popular institution is a fine thing, but it has added to the labours of the Sovereign. It is therefore necessary that her duties and engagements should be carefully examined with a view to easing the load. I agree with Miss Jennie Lee that the time has come when parties for the presentation of débutantes could be abandoned. I have never been to one but I gather that they are functions rather more suitable to an earlier and more aristocratic age. In any case it is clearly desirable that the personal contacts of the Sovereign should not be confined to the aristocratic and better-off sections of society; and with the onward march of democracy there have been improvements in this respect. The Queen has a heavy task and she must discharge her duties; but there is a responsibility on everybody concerned not to overload her.

Hereditary Sovereign or President?

It must be remembered that our present parliamentary democracy is the result partly of acute struggle but in the main of peaceful development and evolution over several centuries. The basis of the growth of parliamentary power as against that of the Monarch was Parliament's power of the purse, exercised through the voting of supply. Our Parliament is supreme. No Republic has a Parliament of greater authority.

Nowadays there are not many republicans in our country. Some of the reasons for this situation will be apparent from what I have already written. However, let us consider whether we should be better served by an elected President and a Republic rather than by our system of Constitutional Monarchy and parliamentary democracy.

The President of the French Republic discharges functions which are somewhat similar to those of the British Monarch and are similarly limited, for France has a Prime Minister and a Cabinet. The President of France is normally, if not always, a man who has had long and active experience in party politics. It is true that he is expected, upon becoming President, to divorce himself from party politics and, in general, I think it can be said that he does so. Nevertheless, I doubt whether we should take kindly to the idea of the Head of the State having been an active party politician until he took presidential office. Also a former politician in the office would cause it to lose much of that glamour and colour to which the British Monarchy has accustomed us and which I think helps the wheels of democracy to move smoothly round. The French President is elected by the Members of both Houses of Parliament for a period of seven years.

In our case also the election of a President with limited powers would presumably be by Parliament; maybe by the two Houses sitting in joint Session, although it is probable that Labour would urge that the election should be by the House of Commons alone. Popular election would give the President too much authority at the expense of the Government and Parliament. In any case there would be every possibility of friction and party bargaining of a kind seen in the election of the French President in 1953. There would be the risk that the person elected President would not command that universal assent and support of the people enjoyed by the Sovereign. Moreover, the limited period of office of a President has disadvantages as compared with the continuing reign of an hereditary monarch. The British Sovereign, whilst divorced from party politics, acquires over the years as a result of intimate contact with the Governments of varying parties and, indeed, with leading personalities in all parties, a rich experience of public affairs which in itself is advantageous. When a Prime Minister has to be selected and a Government formed, or at times of crisis, the British Monarch can function as the Head of the State and in a sense as the incarnation of the State in a way that no President drawn from among the politicians could do. The Crown provides a link between the countries of the Commonwealth which could not be as well, if at all, provided by an elected President.

I have referred to the action of King George V in bringing the party leaders together at the Palace so that they might confer among themselves about the serious situation which had arisen from the Liberal Government's Bill granting Home Rule to Ireland and the bitter opposition to the Bill shortly before the First World War. On carefully chosen occasions such as this (and they must be chosen with great care and discretion) the Sovereign can render useful public service more easily than a President probably could.

It has been said that Ministers come and Ministers go but that the Permanent Secretaries go on for ever. This is better than a system whereby Permanent Secretaries change with each change of Government, for Ministers would be denied that long departmental experience which Permanent Secretaries have acquired. Similarly in the case of the Sovereign the experience gained, the memory of difficulties and problems of the past is of value. Governments come and Governments go but the Sovereign goes on. The Sovereign in our country is, so to speak, an hereditary President. It is, of course, most important that the Monarch should be conscious of being an impartial public servant and should have no wish to exercise the executive rights and powers of government. That is absolutely vital. It is not only vital that it should be so: it is equally vital that it should appear to be so to Parliament and the public. If ever this ceased to be so the Monarchy and the nation would be in trouble.

I have not compared the British Monarchy with the Presidency of the United States. For—although they are not always sufficiently recognized—there are fundamental differences between the Constitution of the United Kingdom and that of the United States. The President of the United States is a party politician and elected as such; he is not and does not pretend to be politically impartial. He is not a President on the French model, for he is the Government. During his first term of office I asked President Franklin D. Roosevelt whether he would be standing for a second term, a question to which I do not think he wished to give a categorical answer. What he did say was: 'Morrison, being President of the United States is a terrible job. I am, so to speak, King, Prime Minister, and party leader, in a very big country. It is a hard—a very hard—life. Who would want a second term?' Nevertheless, he had a second term and indeed a third, and began a fourth before his much deplored death in 1945. He was right about the strain, for the job killed this great man. But the significance of his observation was that the President of the United States is King, Prime Minister, party leader—all rolled into one. The greatest political compliment one can pay the people of the United States is that they make their Constitution, which has worked out far differently from the way its founders ever contemplated, function as a whole successfully. But it is not a Constitution that would be acceptable to the British people. We should not wish to confer upon one man the enormous powers that are possessed by the President of the United States, even though he could be pulled up and put into great difficulties by Parliament and the Courts as the American President can be. Our people much prefer the British Monarchy to the Presidency of the United States or even to the Presidency of France, a country whose Constitution is more like ours, though owing to the relative weakness of the Executive in Parliament it works very differently.

There is another argument sometimes adduced by our few advocates of a republican régime, namely, that a President would be cheaper to maintain than the Royal Family. I do not know what the overall costs of the French and American Presidencies are, and in any case the circumstances are not analogous. But, assuming that there would be a noticeable saving in public expenditure,[1] it would be very small in relation to our total national budget, and, after all, the amount is determined by the House of Commons after examination in fair detail by a Select Committee of the House. The money argument is a small affair compared with the undoubted advantages of the British Monarchy as it is now working. If it continues to be strictly impartial, to be animated by a high sense of public duty, it will continue to achieve its almost universal popularity. It is not for me to pronounce upon the merits of the republican régimes in France, in the United States, or elsewhere: that is the business of the nations concerned. But for our country Constitutional Monarchy is a success and deserves the support and respect which it undoubtedly receives from the people.

Popularity of the Monarchy

It is true that in the course of this development of the power of Parliament as against the Crown one king lost his head and another had to flee the country. We do not talk too much about these things, for we do not like violence in our internal political affairs, and the violence of monarchs at the expense of their subjects is now far back in our history. The thing of which we are proud, and of which we are entitled to be proud, is the predominantly non-violent evolutionary process towards the final supremacy of a great electorate, embracing both sexes on the basis of adult suffrage, and the steady growth towards some degree of perfection in our system of parliamentary democracy. Notwithstanding the fact that the Crown has lost its original great powers it can be said, certainly of the present century, that as those powers passed and the Monarchy became strictly constitutional, the Monarch has become increasingly popular in the hearts and minds of the British people. No Monarchy in the world is more secure or more respected by the people than ours. The steady increase in the esteem of the nation for King George V and King George VI was something of which we are all aware. The welcome to the young Queen Elizabeth II was real and sincere, and her Coronation in 1953 became a great national festival. Wherever she goes she is

[1] And the matter of the former hereditary land revenues of the Crown (see p. 74) should be kept in mind.

assured of a great and genuine welcome. When the people cheer the Queen and sing her praises, they are also cheering our free democracy.

On great occasions, such as jubilees and coronations, the people are in it in their own way as much as the notables and elected representatives. The home-made decorations, the tea-parties, and other assemblies in the working-class back streets of London, in the great cities, and in the countryside, are a demonstration that the Monarchy is regarded by the masses of the people as their own as much as it is of those who sit in the seats of power. Perhaps this feeling of the ordinary people was most dramatically expressed on a great Royal occasion at a street-party in an East London slum, when a banner was strung between the upper windows of the houses across the street carrying the humorous slogan, 'Lousy but loyal'.

The security and popularity of the British Monarchy today are largely the result of the fact that it does not govern and that government is the task of Ministers responsible to a House of Commons elected by the people. The Monarchy as it exists now facilitates the processes of parliamentary democracy and functions as an upholder of freedom and representative government.

CHAPTER VI

How Government and Parliament Live Together—or Die

No Government can be successfully formed or survive unless it is sustained by the House of Commons. That means that the Government must have a majority in the House. Usually the party supporting the Government has a majority over all other parties but there have been exceptions. For example, the two minority Labour Governments of 1924 and 1929–31 were usually dependent on Liberal support and as they had difficulties from time to time among their back-benchers these Governments had insecure and uncertain lives. Similarly, the Liberal Governments which emerged from the General Elections of 1910, not having a clear majority of their own party, needed the support of the Irish Nationalists to survive. But their situation was easier than that of the two Labour Governments, for as long as they seriously sought to promote Home Rule for Ireland they could, in general, rely on Irish Nationalist support; moreover, they usually had the support of the Labour M.P.s. However the House of Commons' majority may be composed, the Government must have one or it will fall. That is the basis of our parliamentary democracy.

The Parliamentary Balance of Power

In our country, unlike France, there is a delicate balance of power between the Cabinet and the House of Commons. The Government, for the sake of itself and its party, cannot be indifferent to defeat in the House. It must do everything it can to avoid defeat. In France defeat is most unlikely to lead to the dissolution of Parliament and a General Election, or even necessarily to a change of policy: what happens is that one Government of mixed elements goes out and another Government (sometimes after serious delay) of the same or differently mixed elements comes in. But in the United Kingdom the defeat of the Government on other than trivial matters is serious. It will most probably involve the resignation of the Government, and unless it is possible to form another Government with a parliamentary majority, dissolution and a General Election will follow. I think that this is to the good and that it is to be preferred to the working of the French system of parliamentary government.

Some people think that the British practice puts too much power into the hands of the Government and its Whips. However, whilst it can be and sometimes is abused, generally speaking that is not so—particularly if we assume, as I think we should, that a Government of democratic strength is to be preferred to a minority or peace-time Coalition Government of wobble and weakness. Some price has to be paid to avoid confusion. If the House of Commons sets aside the policy or wishes of the Government, the Prime Minister can seek a dissolution from the Sovereign, and this is a deterrent to parliamentary revolt. But equally the Government must seek to retain the support of a parliamentary majority by persuasion, goodwill, mutual understanding, and, upon occasion, must make concessions, because the consequences to itself and to its electoral support are likely to be damaging if it goes to the country with its ranks divided. And it is essential that Governments should take parliamentary and public opinion into account. A Cabinet that proceeded to ride rough-shod over the feelings and wishes of its supporters, relying on the Whips to enforce its will, would be asking for trouble; and it would not be long before it got it. It must be ready to take a firm line on essential matters of public interest, but a Government cannot hold its majority together unless it takes trouble to do so. Therefore, if Governments are often saved from parliamentary defeat by the back-benchers' fear of a dissolution, it is no less true that Governments must treat their supporters with respect and understanding, because this is in accordance with the spirit of our parliamentary democracy and it is essential to the success and survival of the Government and its political party.

Indeed, we should go further than this. On many matters of policy the Government will resist the Opposition and the Opposition will fight the Government. This is natural and right. It breathes life and zest into our parliamentary proceedings and, let us hope, educates the nation. The duly elected majority must rule; but the Opposition has its rights and duties. The Opposition has been elected by its supporters to put their point of view in Parliament. And it is in accordance with the spirit of our parliamentary democracy that the Government should be prepared to listen to and to consider Opposition arguments and representations, for our belief in government by majority certainly does not mean that that majority should act in an arbitrary spirit. It is silly as well as intolerable if the Government, without considering the merits, assumes that every Opposition amendment to a Bill or opinion on policy is wrong and, therefore, to be rejected out of hand. Oppositions can be right and Governments can be wrong. Therefore, Ministers should fairly consider arguments seriously advanced from both sides of the House. It is also the duty of the Opposition fairly to consider arguments seriously advanced by the Government. It may be that these desiderata are somewhat idealistic, having regard to the hurly-burly of parliamentary life, and I know that there are and will be many occasions when they are not observed. I would, however, assure the reader that they are observed more often than many people think, and that there are many Acts of Parliament in which can be found words and ideas that have been suggested from both sides of the House. Administration is also affected—and rightly affected—by criticisms and suggestions from various quarters in the House.

Just as the Government has not, and ought not to have, absolute power, neither have nor ought the back-benchers to have absolute power. If back-benchers could freely do just as they liked according to their individual wishes or prejudices, or even according to the moods they were in on some particular day—and, believe me, there are moods of the day as well as Orders of the Day—we should have parliamentary chaos, and the orderliness and authority of government would be seriously impaired. It is not in the interest of good government, of Parliament, or of our democratic institutions generally, that there should be no sense of coherence or collective responsibility on the back-benches. In France Governments are sometimes made and unmade every few weeks, largely because the power of the National Assembly is excessive as against the authority of the Government. The means of enforcing a real sense of responsibility are absent. So just as the British Government must be careful to win the respect and support of the House of Commons, it is also necessary that the Members of Parliament should be actuated by a proper sense of responsibility in casting or even not casting their votes in the House. Intelligence, a fair weighing up of the pros and cons, proper consideration of public opinion, a sense of loyalty and comradeship to one's political associates, consideration of the overall or longer-term interests of the country, as well as the merits of the immediate issue involved—all these are factors which are, or should be, in the mind of the back-bencher.

In a debate on the Conservative Government's proposal for commercially sponsored television, a Conservative back-bencher (Mr. Beverley Baxter) said that he hated the Government's proposal, but that he hated the possibility of a Socialist Government still more; that on the balance of considerations he would vote with the Government. This is by way of illustration; I do not say that I agreed with him, for in any case I considered that the Government Whips should have been taken off.

Parliamentary Obstruction

Obstruction in the House of Commons has a long history. Its greatest practitioners were the Irish Nationalist Members. Their sole mission in life being the achievement of Home Rule for Ireland, they were not called upon to expound any settled political philosophy. They could vote in the House with either Liberals or Conservatives according to what was, in their view, expedient for the moment for Home Rule or the achievement of changes such as Irish land reform. It was a matter of indifference to them whether the British parliamentary system worked or not; indeed, their bias was in favour of stopping it from working, for the greater the nuisance they could make of themselves the sooner might come the day when the British would be glad to be rid of them by conceding Home Rule.

The Conservatives and Liberals and the Labour Party have practised obstruction, the art of using up parliamentary time with the object of preventing the Government from getting its controversial measures through, or of upsetting the Government's parliamentary time-table. I think there has been a change for the better in the feeling of most M.P.s about obstruction, except perhaps when great measures of an acutely controversial character are before the House. In earlier years obstruction—even though often annoying and boring—was accepted as a more or less legitimate form of parliamentary activity or amusement. There was, and still is, in some quarters an impression that to accuse a party or a Member of obstruction is unparliamentary, but this is not so, for it has been ruled that it is a legitimate parliamentary allegation.

There was, of course, obstruction by Conservatives in the Parliaments of 1924 and 1929–31 against the minority Labour Governments. At that time there was no time-limit on the discussion of supplementary estimates. Consequently, even if the amounts were negligible, it was easy for the Conservative Opposition to keep debate going for quite a long time, seeking further information and charging the Government with having failed to estimate properly. On legislation there were many time-wasting speeches. We who were members of the Labour Party and supporters of the Government naturally found all this not only boring but irritating, though allowance must be made for our not unnatural bias. I personally felt, in addition, that what I described in my own mind as 'this playing the fool' was humiliating to the parliamentary institution itself and not calculated to bring credit to the House of Commons as a whole.

I think that things are materially better now and that this has been brought about not only by changes in parliamentary procedure, but also because there is a general feeling in the House that the obstruction of business which is not really disputed, and the spinning out of needless and rather boring speeches (even if at times they are clever) is not conducive to that public respect for the House of Commons which we all desire. In the Parliament of 1945–50, which had a large Labour majority, there was not much silly obstruction, though the Guillotine had to be used on three Bills. In the 1950–1 Parliament, with a Labour majority of only six, obstruction was practised by putting down Prayers against Orders[1] to keep Ministers and their supporters up late but with no real intention of opposing the Order or dividing in favour of its annulment. This experiment of the Opposition did not go well. It was really

[1] See Chapter VIII, p. 152.

unpopular inside and outside the House, and when the Government was driven to retaliate by adjourning the House before Prayers were reached the protest was nominal rather than real and agreement was soon reached whereby abuse was avoided. There has been some obstruction in the Parliament elected in 1951, but not as heavy or persistent as in earlier years. I, personally, am very pleased at the tendency for purposeless and needless obstruction to be dropped. Hard fighting against measures which arouse really genuine and strong feeling is another matter. But obstruction, even brilliant obstruction which is merely playing the fool, is not a good thing.

Of course, if a Government with a very small majority brings in highly controversial legislation which is not urgent in the public interest, it is asking for trouble. The logical deduction from a close election result is that the electorate has 'put the brakes on' for the time being and that there is little or no mandate for exciting things. And if the Opposition is genuinely convinced that the Government has no mandate for controversial measures and that they are not urgent, it has a moral justification for sustained opposition.

Even if a Government has a working majority there is a duty upon it to avoid highly controversial legislation or administrative policies for which it has no proper mandate from the people, unless circumstances have arisen which make action necessary in the public interest. If the Opposition is to be given no moral case for obstruction, the Government must 'play the game' and respect the principles of parliamentary democracy, otherwise representative government will be endangered. However, the public interest comes first, and if action is necessary to protect it, action must be taken.

Contacts between the Government, its Friends, and the Opposition

Now let us look behind these general ideas and try to see how the Government lives day by day with its supporters and the Opposition, and how the back-benchers influence the Government by public and private criticism. Later, in Chapter VIII, I will examine the widespread belief that the back-bench M.P. is merely a cog in the machine without an individual life of his own and without any real power to influence the course of legislation or administration.

I propose to describe the methods by which Ministers keep in close touch with the views of their supporters in the House and the machinery for settling business between the Government and the Opposition.

Before dealing with the formal machinery I would like to stress the very great deal of informal intercourse between Ministers and M.P.s of their party and of the Opposition, and indeed between all M.P.s. Ministers spend a considerable amount of time at the House (not necessarily in the Chamber), though not as much as formerly when their departmental duties were less onerous. In the long hours Members spend in the House—in the Lobbies, the Library, the Smoking- and Dining-rooms—there are plenty of opportunities for M.P.s, whether Ministers or not, to get to know each other and to exchange views. Most Ministers and M.P.s have grown up in their party and in the House. They have helped each other at elections, met at the annual party conference and on many other party occasions. Some back-benchers will be new to the House and perhaps not yet well known, but many others will be men and women of long experience and on friendly terms with members of the Government. A Government and its supporters are not a collection of strangers brought together for a particular purpose but a group, most of whom have lived together in the House and their party for many years and who share the same broad aims. Formal machinery is necessary for certain purposes, but the informal relations that exist are perhaps even more important.

The formal machinery can most conveniently be described under two broad headings. On the one hand, there are the Whips, Parliamentary Secretaries and Parliamentary Private Secretaries, and the Leader of the House, who are obviously part of the machinery of government. On the other hand, there is the general organization of the party in the House and the relations which obtain between its leaders and its members, which is discussed in the next chapter. Until recent years there was perhaps an inadequate appreciation of what an important part was played by party organization in the working of the British Constitution. The back-bencher's chances of getting his views considered have, I think, improved as the organization of the parliamentary parties has developed and become more comprehensive.

The Whip

This British term 'Whip' is very confusing to foreigners and is probably imperfectly understood even by the bulk of the British people. Its origin, so far as I can ascertain, is the hunting-field, where the whipper-in drove the hounds with the whip back into the pack so as to prevent them from straying. The phrase 'whipping them in' is quoted by the *Oxford English Dictionary* as one which found favour with Burke in 1769 when he was describing the Ministry's sending for their friends from the north and from Paris. In 1792 a political dictionary defined a whipper-in as 'a fellow that sends for Members to carry a question when the Minister is hard run'. In the nineteenth century the abbreviated form of the name came into use and the term Whip is now applied both to a member of a particular party in Parliament whose duty it is to secure the attendance of members of that party for divisions and on all other necessary occasions, and to the written appeal or circular notice by which he summons members of his party and informs them of the programme of Parliamentary Business. The word sounds aggressive, tyrannical, and even physically painful. Doubtless this adds to the widespread feeling that the Whips are more terrible people than they are.

The Party Whips

Each of the main parties in the House has its Chief Whip, Deputy Chief Whip, and a varying number of junior Whips. All are M.P.s. Most of the Government Whips are paid out of public funds. The Opposition Whips receive no special pay, i.e. they receive only the remuneration of ordinary M.P.s.

The junior Government Whips carry varying offices and designations. For example, in November 1953, three of the political Officers of Her Majesty's Household were at the same time Whips, namely the Treasurer, the Comptroller, and the Vice-Chamberlain. Five other junior Whips held the office of Lords Commissioners of the Treasury; and there were five described as 'Assistant Whips (unpaid)'. The Whips who are Officers of the Household appear at the Palace on certain occasions. One of them, namely the Vice-Chamberlain, sends a daily summary of and commentary on parliamentary proceedings to the Sovereign. He also takes Commons Addresses to the Queen and brings back her replies. Equipped with a white stave, he stands at the Bar of the House to deliver 'A Message from the Queen, Sir, in reply to a loyal and dutiful address from this House', and then proceeds up the Floor to read the message in front of the Table and finally delivers it to the Clerk.[1] So far as I know, Lords Commissioners of the Treasury have no Treasury duties other than the signing of formal documents from time to time.

The Government Chief Whip has an office at 12 Downing Street, where there is also accommodation for the junior Whips. This Downing Street accommodation emphasizes the nearness of the Chief Whip to his party leader (the Prime Minister). The Chief Whip is also often referred to as the Patronage Secretary, but his official title is Parliamentary Secretary to the Treasury, even though he has little if anything to do with the departmental business of the Treasury. The term Patronage Secretary comes from the days when the Chief Whip exercised a material influence on numerous Government appointments.

When I went to the Home Office in 1940 I found (though I cannot say whether this was the case under the minority Labour Governments) that the opinions and recommendations of the Whips were received and, presumably, considered on judicial appointments of recorders and stipendiary magistrates. Such a channel of recommendation to judicial appointments was liable to be politically biased and I gave instructions at once that the opinion of the Whips should not be considered. I instituted a practice whereby, although having, as Home Secretary, the last word, I consulted the Lord Chancellor, the Attorney-General, and the Solicitor-General, between whom one should be able to get impartial and objective advice even though they did not always agree with each other, nor were they bound to do so.

In earlier times when honours were bought and sold for the benefit of the party funds under Tory and Whig and Conservative and Liberal Governments, it was said that the Chief Whip

[1] More important messages from the Crown are delivered by the Prime Minister, the Lord Privy Seal, or the Home Secretary, who stands at the Bar of the House and on being called by the Speaker says: 'A Message from the Queen, Sir, signed by her own hand'. He then proceeds up the Floor and hands it to the Speaker who reads it to the House.

had a considerable voice in determining recommendations for honours. Even since these earlier crude practices were abolished it is probable (and not unreasonably so) that the recommendations of the Chief Whip are considered; indeed, he may be consulted about a number of recommendations by the Prime Minister.

In forming a Government or replacing Ministers who have died or resigned, most Prime Ministers consult the Chief Whip as well as senior colleagues, though they are not obliged to do so. It has been said that some Prime Ministers have paid excessive attention to the opinion of the Chief Whip. Sometimes, when a ministerial appointment has been made which nobody can understand, the Chief Whip, rightly or wrongly, has been blamed for it, especially if the Prime Minister of the day rather rejoices in not knowing the bulk of his own supporters.

The main work of the ministerial Chief Whip, however, is the organization, under the Prime Minister and the Leader of the House, of Government Business, the organization of the party in the House, ensuring the maximum practicable attendance of members of the party, promoting support for Government policies, and seeing to it that Ministers are aware of the opinions and apprehensions of back-benchers. The Government Chief Whip has a very small civil service staff headed by the Private Secretary who is not infrequently consulted by the Leader of the House of Commons. The Opposition Chief Whip discharges equally responsible duties for his own side. He has no special salary and no ministerial status or duties.

The 'Usual Channels'

The two Chief Whips constitute what are known as the 'usual channels'. Frequently, when the Opposition asks the Leader of the House for facilities for a debate the answer will be, 'I am not sure if this can be arranged, but perhaps it might be discussed through the usual channels.' That suggestion means that the two Chief Whips should talk and see what, if anything, can be done. It may be that facilities can be agreed upon outright; but the Government Chief Whip may require from the Opposition Chief Whip an undertaking that the Opposition will facilitate the completion of other business in order that the necessary time may be found without an excessive overall loss of Government time; or it may be that they cannot agree and that the Government Chief Whip will take the view that the Opposition should use some of the time at their disposal for the Business of Supply.[1] The Opposition Chief Whip receives advance notice of the Business the Government proposes to submit to the House in the following week, and it is not finally settled until after conversations between him and the Government Chief Whip to try to reach agreement.

The two Chief Whips are responsible to their respective sides and are loyal to them, but normally their personal relations are good, and in the interests of the smooth running of the House of Commons it is desirable that this should be so. Otherwise the efficient organization of Parliamentary Business would be so impaired that not only the Government but also the Opposition would be inconvenienced. There is so much attacking and counter-attacking between the two sides of the House that this perhaps is the reason why Chief Whips do not normally take part in debate, for it is desirable that at all times some people representing Government and Opposition should be on speaking terms, though it is remarkable how even the most extreme members of either side engage in furious attacks in the Chamber and maintain friendly relations outside. This British characteristic is in contrast to the practice in the old German Reichstag in the days of the Kaiser, the days of very rigid separation of the German parties even to the provision of separate dining-rooms. (Something of this—though not so much, I suspect—survives today in Bonn.) The Whips' Office and the 'usual channels' are a necessary element in parliamentary machinery. Their work is conducive not only to the smooth running of the House of Commons, but also to the mobilization of the party forces on great parliamentary occasions, when the most vigorous attacks and counter-attacks take place, culminating in a division to which Members have been summoned by a three-line Whip.

Both Chief Whips have a busy time. They must attend a certain number of meetings. They respectively have to be available to their other Whips, to Ministers on the Government side, and to party leaders on the Opposition side. Many M.P.s will want to see them during the day. They spend a good deal of time in

[1] See p. 106.

the Chamber itself (at all times not less than one Whip of each side must be on the Front Bench), and the Chief Whips must be ready to come into the Chamber at any time if difficulties requiring their advice or attention should arise. It is the Government Chief Whip who nowadays (formerly, I am told, it was the Minister in charge) customarily moves the closure (namely 'That the Question be now put'), thereby frequently incurring vocal denunciation and sometimes real hostility from the Opposition benches accompanied by cries of 'Gag! Gag!' He must put up with this, together with a good deal of misapprehension in the popular mind about his duties: all this is in part what he is paid for. The Opposition Chief Whip has duties which are not markedly less heavy than those of his opposite number on the Government side.

The Deputy Chief Whip has general duties. The junior Whips are not only generally at the service of the Chief Whip and their Front Bench, but also have the duty of keeping contact with and being available to M.P.s from Scotland, Wales, Northern Ireland, and what may be called the political regions of England. The systematic contact with individual Members is therefore a duty of the junior Whips rather than the Chief Whip, though he must be available to individual Members and be familiar with them. The junior Whips who have this close contact with their respective groups of Members have a duty to convey to the Chief Whip warnings of possible trouble on the back-benches, or criticisms of Ministers or party leaders, and it is then that the Chief Whip has to decide what to do. The Whips of each side meet daily to consider the Business of the House and other matters.

A Two-way Traffic

It is a widespread belief that the Whips have no other duty than to bully and coerce Members against their will into voting in the party lobby and speaking in accordance with the 'party line'. This is an inaccurate and incomplete picture of the functions of the Whips. It is persuasion rather than bullying that is the rule; it is reasoning with a recalcitrant Member rather than coercion that is the general practice. The good Whip seeks to avoid a situation in which the troubled or troublesome Member is driven to choose between forced, humiliating conformity, and flagrant revolt which may raise all the difficult problems of official disciplinary action. There are extreme cases from time to time which may justify and, indeed, necessitate straight speaking, but peaceful persuasion, friendly reasoning, and argument based on the need for keeping the party together, are far more normal and effective.

Moreover, the Whips' Office conducts a two-way traffic. During the nearly six years that I was Leader of the House of Commons I impressed upon the Labour M.P.s and the Whips that the Whips had just as much a duty to convey to me and to other Ministers the anxieties, worries, and unhappiness of back-benchers as they had to convey to the back-benchers the wishes of the Government. I would myself see troubled—or troublesome—M.P.s if necessary. Such interviews were normally pleasant and helpful. This part of the Whips' functions was fully discharged. They were the ears and eyes not only of the Government but of the back-benchers. Indeed, they would be incompetent Whips who did not warn Ministers when in power, or the Front Bench when in Opposition, of potential trouble, though they should not be frightened too easily. Frequently, the Chief Whip is asked by Government or party leaders, 'What is the feeling in the party about this?', or, 'Is there likely to be trouble about that?' Clearly, it would be impossible for the Chief Whip to give an intelligent answer unless he and his colleagues not only took steps to be in touch with the back-benchers, but had such a good relationship with them that the back-benchers did not hesitate to pour out their anxieties and troubles.

The Whips and Procedure

The Government Whips, in particular the Chief Whip, have the responsibility of seeing that Government Business is not impeded by procedural failure on the Treasury Bench. They are supplied with notes on the Business of the day and indications when this or that must be moved and by whom. For example, if on a Supply day it is agreed that a debate should take place on the Adjournment, the House has to go through a metamorphosis before this business can properly proceed. The Speaker having called 'The Clerk will now proceed to read the Orders of the Day', the Clerk announces 'Supply; Committee'.

The Speaker then leaves the Chair and sits on an obscure part of the Treasury Bench. At this point the Serjeant-at-Arms or his assistant gravely walks up the Floor of the House from the Bar, lifts the Mace from the Table and rests it under the Table as an indication that the Speaker is no longer in the Chair. He then returns to his seat behind the Bar. The Chair at the Clerk's Table is taken by the Chairman of Ways and Means who reads out the proposed Motion for the granting of Supply. It is at this point that the Government Chief Whip must be prepared to move that the Chairman do report progress and ask leave to sit again, even though there has been no progress. This being agreed to, the Chairman then leaves the Chair, to make his report to Mr. Speaker. The Serjeant-at-Arms again makes his ceremonial progress up the Floor, replaces the Mace on top of the Table and, after the Chairman has made his report, the Government Chief Whip (Mr. Speaker now being in the Chair) then stands in his place and says, 'I beg to move that this House do now adjourn'. And when that Question is proposed from the Chair but not, of course, determined at that point, debate is opened on the stipulated subject either by a Minister or by a member of the Opposition Front Bench. No wonder that my old friend Ernest Bevin, when Foreign Secretary, who was perfectly frank about his relative lack of knowledge of parliamentary procedure, would say either to myself or to the Chief Whip, 'I can't understand all this, so tell me when I've got to get up', and at the right point we would dig him in the ribs and say 'Up you go, Ernie', and up he went.

Well, there is parliamentary meaning behind all this. Under Standing Orders a number of days are allotted for the consideration of the estimates in Committee of Supply. The subjects for debate are chosen by the Opposition, but changes in legislation cannot be discussed. If for some reason they prefer to use one of these days for a debate on the Adjournment or some other Motion, which would enable legislation to be discussed, the House must first go into Committee of Supply so as to get rid of the allotted day. The Committee of Supply is a Committee of the Whole House with the Chairman of Ways and Means (or his deputy) in the Chair and not the Speaker, whereas a debate on the Adjournment of the House must find the Speaker or Deputy Speaker in the Chair. If the Chief Whip or other Whip acting for him should fail to move the right Motion at the right time, or to see that the Minister concerned does so, serious confusion would result and the Speaker or Chairman of Ways and Means would be put into an embarrassing position.

Let me illustrate. One night shortly after midnight we had the rare experience of a junior Whip of the Labour Government nearly making an understandable but serious slip, which was rectified in time, otherwise the Business of the House for the next sitting could not have proceeded. The Business before the House was to be continued at the next sitting. The Speaker called from the Chair, 'Debate to be resumed?' Now it being after midnight the right answer was 'This Day', but unfortunately the junior Whip nearly replied 'Tomorrow', but just checked himself in time.

An incident of another character occurred in the House in the early hours of 26 November 1952. This was at the end of the first day of the two days' debate on the Second Reading of the Conservatives' Iron and Steel Bill. About half an hour before the debate was due to be adjourned to the second day it came to the knowledge of some Labour Members that the attendance of Government supporters was very thin. Colonel George Wigg, Labour M.P. for Dudley, made a quick check and thought it likely that there were not forty Conservative Members available to form a quorum, although there were plenty of Labour Members in the building. The other Labour Members were advised to keep out of the Chamber and Colonel Wigg, from his place, rose to call attention to the fact that a quorum was not present in the Chamber. The bells were ordered to be rung but the necessary number of Conservative M.P.s did not appear. As it was known that no division would take place they had apparently been allowed by the Whips to go home, or at any rate had gone. So the House stood adjourned without Question put.

This incident caused considerable parliamentary excitement and trouble. The Leader of the House and the Government Chief Whip, both of whom would be accountable to the Prime Minister in the matter, were of the opinion that Colonel Wigg had pursued unfair tactics and claimed that their side had never done such a thing when the Labour Government was in office.

The Labour answer was that as Government Business was being taken it was clearly the responsibility of the Government Whips to see that they had at least the necessary quorum present; that it was for them to 'keep a House'; and that far from getting cross with the Opposition they should really have got cross with themselves for having failed in their duty. The Labour Members concerned hoped that the progress of the Iron and Steel Bill would be set back. The upshot was that after the raising of lengthy and, as I thought, substantial points of order with Mr. Speaker, the Government gave way for the moment, but in the end got its revenge by compressing two days' Business into a single sitting which resulted in the House deliberating till 9 o'clock in the morning and then having to recommence at 11 a.m. This in turn led to a Labour Motion of Censure on the Government for failing to conduct the Business of the House of Commons properly, which was moved but not carried in the following week. So the Government first saved its day and then lost it.

Pairing

Members are not expected to leave the House without consulting the appropriate Whip. Indeed, there are times when the Whips stand at the doors leading to the outer regions to question Members who appear to be leaving. This work of keeping the maximum possible number of Members present was particularly heavy for the Whips in the Parliament of 1950–1 under the Labour Government and the next one under the Conservative Government. Of course there are days when the Business is of a character which enables a more tolerant view to be taken about absences. But in these two Parliaments we were all more or less prisoners. The sense of lack of reasonable freedom leads to a feeling of frustration and irritability which will be understandable to any humane person, and is certainly understandable to those who are, so to speak, prisoners in the parliamentary cage. This is an inevitable characteristic of Parliaments in which there is a small majority, unless very extensive pairing were allowed, and then the public would soon become critical about low numbers in divisions and allege that M.P.s were neglecting their duties. However, what is known as pairing does take place.

Pairing means that two M.P.s—one on each side—will agree to be absent from a given day's Business or a given division or divisions. Alternatively, a Member may ask his Whip to fix up a pair with the Whips' Office on the other side. The result is that the majority is unaffected although the total votes on each side are diminished to the extent that pairing has taken place. Members are expected to get the approval of their Whips' Office and register the pair with them, though to the annoyance of the Whips this does not always happen. As the strain on the Government supporters in Parliament with a narrow majority tends to be greatest it may be that the Government Whips have, except on special occasions, been more willing to give pairs than the Opposition. Some degree of misunderstanding or friction is always liable to occur about pairing, and sometimes individual Members are accused by their Whips or their colleagues of engaging in excessive 'private enterprise' in the matter. When Business is subject to a three-line Whip pairing is only grudgingly arranged, for each side naturally wants to keep its numbers up, apart from the wish of the Government to keep its majority as high as possible and that of the Opposition to bring it down.

My own view is that pairing—if not abused—is a legitimate parliamentary amenity. It is not a good thing that Members should be perpetually tied to the Palace of Westminster, otherwise they would find it difficult ever to be in their constituencies on parliamentary days or to engage to a desirable extent in political education and propaganda in the country. Moreover, Members must sometimes, quite properly, be abroad on public business, and it would be wrong to refuse them pairs. And reasonable relaxation is not a bad thing for M.P.s. If a Member is ill the decent thing is to provide him with a pair if one is available. Nevertheless, the Whips are right to insist on the pairing being transacted through their Offices and in stipulating that Members should exercise a necessary degree of restraint.

The Documentary Whip

'The Whip' is a document normally posted by the respective Chief Whips to their Members on Friday, though special Whips can be circulated in the week as required. The Whip recites the

On Monday, 27th October, 1947, the House will meet at 2-30 p.m.

Continuation of the General debate on the Address.
Discussion on Germany until 8-30 p.m., then
Opposition Amendment on Imperial Security. (Mr. J.P.L. Thomas).

Your attendance at 3-30 p.m. and throughout the Sitting is requested. A division will take place at 11 p.m.

On Tuesday, 28th October, the House will meet at 2-30 p.m.

Debate on the Address.
Opposition Amendment.

Your attendance at 3-30 p.m. and throughout the Sitting is requested.

On Wednesday, 29th October, the House will meet at 2-30 p.m.

Conclusion of the debate on the Address.
Opposition Amendment.

Your attendance at 3-30 p.m. and throughout the Sitting is particularly requested. A most important division or divisions

On Thursday, 30th October, the House will meet at 2-30 p.m.

Consideration of the Reports from the Committee of Privileges relating to the cases of the Hon.Members for Gravesend (Mr.Garry Allighan)and Doncaster(Mr.Evelyn Walkden).

Your attendance at 3-30 p.m. and throughout the Sitting is requested. **There will be a free Vote of the House.**

On Friday, 31st October, the House will meet at 11 a.m.

Expiring Laws Bill; Committee & remaining stages.
Jersey and Guernsey(Financial Provisions)Bill; 2nd Reading.
Motions to approve the Fish Sales(Charges)Order and the 4 Purchase Tax Orders on the Paper.

Your attendance at 11 a.m. and throughout the Sitting is requested.

WILLIAM WHITELEY.

Note.

During the week it is hoped to consider the Motion relating to the Parliamentary Electors(War-Time Registration)Act,1944.

A Prayer has been tabled for consideration on Tuesday.

On MONDAY, 1st November, 1948, the House will meet at 2.30 p.m.

Continuation of the Debate on the Address.

Debates on the Economic Situation and then on Food.

Your attendance is particularly requested.

On TUESDAY, 2nd November, the House will meet at 2.30 p.m.

Debate on the Address.

Debate on the Official Opposition Amendment.

Your attendance is particularly requested.

On WEDNESDAY, 3rd November, the House will meet at 2.30 p.m.

Conclusion of the Debate on the Official Opposition Amendment to the Address.

A most important Division will take place and your

attendance by 9.30 p.m. is particularly requested.

On THURSDAY, 4th November, the House will meet at 2.30 p.m.

Wages Councils Bill; 2nd Reading.

Recall of Army and Air Force Pensioners Bill; 2nd Reading.

Your attendance is requested.

On FRIDAY, 5th November, the House will meet at 11 a.m.

Expiring Laws Continuance Bill; Committee and 3rd Reading.

Colonial Stock Bill; 2nd Reading, and Committee stage of the Money Resolution.

Debts Clearing Offices Bill; 2nd Reading, " "

Savings Banks Bill; 2nd Reading, " "

Your attendance is requested.

PATRICK BUCHAN-HEPBURN.

Business to be taken in the following week and may indicate who the Front Bench speakers will be. Each item is underlined. If the underlining is one line it is a fair indication that no division is expected. If two lines, the Business is fairly important and a division may take place. A three-line underlining indicates that a division is almost certain to take place, that it will be of first-class importance, and that every Member is expected to be present unless unavoidably absent through illness. The wording will vary according to these underlinings. It may be that 'Your attendance is requested by . . . p.m.' In a three-line Whip it is likely to be that 'A most important division will take place and your attendance by . . . p.m. is particularly requested' (or 'is essential'). The wording has to be carefully studied by the Whips for, if he can, the Member who fails to put in an appearance will be quick to point out in his defence that the wording was not clear. For the information of the reader two sample Whips have been reproduced (by courtesy of the Labour and Conservative Chief Whips) on pages 110–113. One is the Labour Government Whip for the week ending 31 October 1947, and the other is the Conservative Opposition Whip for the week ending 5 November 1948.

The receipt of the weekly Whip by an M.P. is a recognition that he is a member of the party which has issued the Whip, so if the Whip (namely, this document) is withdrawn and no longer sent to him then he is in effect excommunicated or expelled. In most cases it follows, unless he should be readmitted, that the Member will not be adopted as a candidate for the next election, or at any rate will not be endorsed by party headquarters. Both parties have had occasion to withdraw the Whip. I cannot be sure what follows in the Conservative Party but, although quiet, it is very likely none the less effective. If the Whip is withdrawn by the Parliamentary Labour Party, the National Executive is informed so that it can consider consequential action either in a Member's constituency or otherwise. As the Executive is the endorsing authority for candidates there obviously must be some appropriate contact.

In the later stages of the 1945–50 Parliament the National Executive itself initiated action against certain Labour M.P.s by expelling them from the party on policy grounds. So, as they were no longer members of the Labour Party, it was necessary to withdraw the parliamentary Whip from them. They all stood independently at the General Election of 1950, but they were all defeated by official Labour candidates who had been chosen in their stead by the constituency parties concerned with the approval of the National Executive. Another expulsion at about the same time was that of Mr. Alfred Edwards, then Labour M.P. for Middlesbrough, on the ground that he had been excessively critical of party policy, notably in respect of the nationalization of the iron and steel industry. He has since joined the Conservatives, as did Mr. Ivor Thomas (now Mr. Ivor Bulmer-Thomas, and not to be confused with Mr. Ivor Owen Thomas, Labour M.P. for The Wrekin), who stood unsuccessfully as Conservative candidate at Newport at the 1950 Election following his resignation from the Labour Party on somewhat Conservative grounds. Mr. Edwards was also defeated at Middlesbrough in 1950.

The Parliamentary Secretary and the Parliamentary Private Secretary

All departmental Ministers have a Parliamentary Secretary or Secretaries who are members of the Government. As I have explained in Chapter IV, Parliamentary Secretaries are available to assist their Ministers in the Office and on the Front Bench, but among their important duties is to be accessible to Members who seek information or wish to make representations or complaints so that their Ministers may be made aware of parliamentary apprehensions and opinions. Many of these matters can be dealt with by the Parliamentary Secretary on his own responsibility. But he should always have in mind the possible desirability of taking things to his Minister or warning him about trouble ahead.

There is also the Parliamentary Private Secretary. He is an M.P.; he receives no pay for his duties, which can be considerable; but he is not a Minister and must be careful not to speak or to conduct himself as if he were a member of the Government. He performs many duties for the Minister calculated to lighten the ministerial load. He usually has modest accommodation in the Department and knows such things as are proper about what is going on. The relationship between Ministers and their Parliamentary Private Secretaries will vary according to the personal factors involved, but ideally it should be cordial, frank, and confidential, for it is of help to the Parliamentary Private Secretary to know the Minister's mind as it is helpful to the Minister to have the advice and counsel of the Parliamentary Private Secretary about rumblings in the House or the state of parliamentary opinion. The good Parliamentary Private Secretary will know 'what is cooking' in the House, as the saying is. Upon occasion he must not hesitate to warn the Minister that he is heading for trouble, or even to criticize him to his face, but he has to be careful not to overdo it in case he demoralizes him. However, their relationship should be sufficiently frank for them to be able to have a plain and friendly talk, for the Parliamentary Private Secretary is a valuable channel of information and contact with the back-benchers, additional to the Whips and the Parliamentary Secretary. I was successfully, faithfully, and very frankly served in 1929–31 by G. R. Strauss; in the War Government by John Jaggar and Fred Watkins; and during 1945–51 in turn by Christopher Mayhew, Patrick Gordon-Walker, Stephen Taylor, and Edward Shackleton. They were good colleagues whose hard work, loyalty, but no less frankness and independent judgement, I valued very highly. Like the Whips, the Parliamentary Private Secretary conducts a two-way business of conveying the Minister's views and wishes to the back-benchers and the troubled thoughts or even anger of the back-benchers to the Minister. In cases that warrant it he will arrange interviews between a back-bencher (or back-benchers) from either side of the House and the Minister to try to clear up misapprehensions or misunderstandings.

I have written about various indirect means whereby back-benchers can make their views known to Ministers. It should not be assumed, however, that Ministers themselves are not available to M.P.s. They are and should be. But the great bulk of M.P.s are considerate people; and realizing how heavily pressed Ministers are, they are happy in most cases to put their case to the Whips, the Parliamentary Secretary, or the Parliamentary Private Secretary.

The Leader of the House of Commons

Until 1942 the Prime Minister (unless a Peer) was also usually Leader of the House of Commons. But Mr. Churchill did not so act after February 1942, nor did Mr. Attlee during the period 1945–51. In Churchill's present Administration the Lord Privy Seal and former Minister of Health (Mr. Harry Crookshank) has acted as Leader of the House. This development reflects in large part the very heavy pressure on the Prime Minister's time, though it may also reflect the growth of party discipline which makes it less necessary for the Prime Minister always to be present to give a lead. It is, however, for any future Prime Minister to decide whether or not he will lead the House of Commons.

The Leader of the House of Commons (whether the Prime Minister or another Minister) has, subject to the Cabinet, an overriding responsibility for the Business of the House and the Government's programme. In my case he was—and in my view should be—Chairman of the Cabinet Committee on Legislation and of the Committee dealing with the future legislative programme. He makes the weekly Business statement to the House and answers supplementary Questions about it.

He has a particular responsibility to the House as a whole in leading and guiding it on procedural difficulties, on privilege matters, on domestic affairs, and on ceremonial occasions if the Prime Minister does not himself act. He has a general responsibility to safeguard what one may term the decencies and to ensure that Business arrangements have regard to what is right and proper in the interests of the House as a whole.

Under the Leader of the House, the Chief Whip manages the Government's programme of Business and makes the day-to-day arrangements apart from his responsibilities for securing majorities for the Government and the other duties already mentioned.

How much time does the Leader of the House require for his duties? There is no fixed answer. It depends on the man, the habits and temperament of the Prime Minister, the parliamentary majority, and the Government programme. I do not accept the view that it is a full-time task. In my own case (though it is difficult to be precise) I should say that it varied between a quarter and a third of my working day. But it is fair to add that my working day ranged between fifteen and eighteen hours.

It is most desirable that the Leader of the House of Commons should be conscious of five responsibilities: to the Government, to the Government's own supporters on the back-benches, to the Opposition, to the House as a whole, and to the individual Minister in charge. He should, within reason, be accessible to both sides of the House. His relations with the Government Whips should be close, cordial, and co-operative, and he must be ready to listen to them even though he is not always bound to agree with their view. When Leader of the House I owed much to the Whips and in particular to William Whiteley, a good friend and an able Chief Whip, and to R. J. Taylor, his deputy. The Leader of the House should meet all the Whips from time to time to hear their views, to counsel them, to encourage them, and to thank them for their work. He can criticize them privately, but he should not let them down in public.

After the Government was formed and from time to time later I met Ministers or Parliamentary Secretaries who were new to the Treasury Bench to advise them about Parliamentary Business and relations with the House when answering Questions and when in charge of Government Business.

The Leader of the House should possess an intuitive instinct about what is going on in the minds of Members on both sides, and if some trouble blows up he should be able to estimate in a flash what the nature and extent of the commotion is. He stands at that Box alone and may have to give a decision on the spot; he will either get away with it or he will be in trouble. Though never lightly setting aside the public interest, he must be ready to bend to strong parliamentary pressure, especially when it comes from both sides, for he is eminently the servant of the House as a whole. On the other hand, he should not be afraid of mere numbers if they have been somewhat artificially manufactured.

In my day an independent Member circularized all M.P.s (enclosing a reply post-card) asking them to put down their names to a Motion. Now many M.P.s, like the late President Hindenburg of Germany, have a weakness for signing things. So, week by week the number of favourable answers to the honourable Member's 'plebiscite' grew; and week by week the honourable Member put the question to me: 'Would I give facilities for the discussion of his Motion?' and week by week the answer was in the negative. The time came when he asked me whether I was aware that the number of signatories had reached something near a majority of the House and what I would say next week if he had got a majority. I had to think quickly and carefully. I concluded that it was my duty to continue to take a firm line. I held the view very strongly that the freedom and responsibility of the proceedings of the House of Commons would be imperilled if Members signed on the dotted line on particular issues before debate and voting took place, and that collecting signatures on the Order Paper with a view to coercing the Government to give time, merely because it was intimidated by the number of canvassed signatures, would weaken the responsibility of Government to Parliament as an institution; and would in time weaken public respect for M.P.s. So I declared that even if the honourable Gentleman achieved such a success in his 'plebiscite' or 'referendum' I would still say no, as I considered that this was not a responsible, proper, or dignified way in which to conduct Parliamentary Business. The House did not throw me over—indeed, I suspect it rather liked my spirit. Nevertheless, I might have had a very rough time.

On the other hand, the Leader of the House should quite properly keep in mind the duty of the Government to promote all reasonable facilities for the House to debate matters about which it is genuinely concerned. He should not, either in the House or in the party meeting, be a protector of Ministers who are unwilling to face the music. Parliament and the party meeting have the right to argue things out and all reasonable facilities should be available. The Leader of the House is the guardian of the legitimate rights of the Opposition as well as those of the Government. He should be among the foremost champions of the rights of Parliament as a whole and resist ministerial pressures from any quarter to deny the House its rightful opportunities. I will give one example: Supply days are Opposition time, and the Opposition decides what is to be discussed on those days. It can be somewhat hard on ministerial supporters when they are asking for subjects to be debated which would be appropriate for Supply days. I was more than once asked that the Government or its supporters should have a voice in the selection of subjects on such occasions. I advised my friends to see what they could do to persuade the

Opposition, but adhered to the view that Opposition time was sacred to the Opposition and that I was unwilling to interfere with their rights. Thus the Leader of the House must regard himself, not only as a member of the Government, but as one of the principal guardians of the rights of the House of Commons as a whole.

CHAPTER VII

Party Organization in Parliament

It will be of assistance in understanding this somewhat subtle matter of the relationship between the Government and its back-benchers if I describe how things went in the Parliaments of 1945–51 as compared with those of 1924 and 1929–31. Later, I will describe any differences in the organization of the Parliamentary Labour Party now that it is in opposition. I will also do my best to describe the working of Conservative Party organization in Parliament, though on that I cannot pretend to be expert.

Difficulties under Minority Labour Governments

Under the two minority Labour Governments of 1924 and 1929–31 the relationship between the Government and the back-benchers was rather imperfect. My own view was that, although there were elements among the back-benchers who were fractious, difficult, and needlessly troublesome, the fault rested as much if not more with the Government. There was a tendency on the part of some Ministers to sidestep the party meeting by not being present when they ought to have been. This naturally irritated the back-benchers, and the fact that the Minister or Ministers concerned might then have been asked to attend a later party meeting sometimes annoyed Ministers. One felt that some of the Ministers regarded party meetings and the back-benchers as nuisances, whilst many of the back-benchers felt that some leading Ministers (the late Arthur Henderson being an outstanding exception) were deliberately avoiding party meetings, and that there was a lack of good fellowship and healthy social contact between Ministers and back-benchers. There is, of course, this to be said for the Ministers in the minority Labour Governments: they had an awful life; every day brought its crisis, and as a consequence—apart from heavy departmental work—ministerial meetings of one sort or another were so frequent that the time they could spare for contact with the back-benchers was limited. However, the gulf between Ministers and a substantial proportion of the back-benchers was there and the psychological consequences were unfortunate. Relations degenerated into a state of almost settled and accepted non-co-operation. As so often happens, the bad feeling radiated from Parliament to the constituencies, and made its contribution to the defeats we experienced in the elections of October 1924 and October 1931.

A Consultative Committee of a dozen or so members was elected by the Parliamentary Party in 1924 and in 1929–31 with its own back-bench Chairman, but on which one or two Ministers sat to provide liaison with the Government. One of the principal duties of the Committee was to maintain a happy link between the back-benchers and the Government, but I fear that this aim was not achieved. When trouble was afoot the appropriate Ministers were asked to meet the Consultative Committee and possibly unhappy back-benchers. Sometimes the result was satisfactory. Sometimes the consultations were ineffective or did not result in agreement, or some back-benchers would resist the advice of both the Government and the Consultative Committee. Perhaps the Committee itself was not always a happy team. Whatever the cause, I was convinced that there had been a marked failure under those two minority Labour Governments to build up good relations between the Government and its supporters. Of course, the minority situation added to the difficulties. The Government could not fully answer for its conduct in Parliament because on any day it was liable to be coerced or pushed about by the other two parties who, between them, constituted a majority. The Government often did not know whether or not the Conservatives and Liberals would combine against it.

In the inter-war years, when Labour was in opposition, we had fewer difficulties, but there were some, despite the existence of party standing orders which were supposed to keep things right.

During the War Coalition Government of 1940–5 a similar Committee was elected by the Parliamentary Labour Party, but called the Administrative Committee. It consisted of the Leader of the party, the Chief Whip, an elected Chairman and Vice-Chairman, and sixteen members elected by the party as a whole, of whom not more than three were to be Ministers. Apart from a few inevitable minor crises, the Committee worked well. It was, however, large, and proceedings were at times a little protracted.

Changes in 1945–51

As Leader of the House of Commons in 1945 it fell to me, in consultation with the Prime Minister and the Chief Whip, to try to get a happier start and to keep things sweet. We decided to recommend the appointment, not of twenty members as in the earlier Administrative Committee, but of a small Liaison Committee which would not attempt to lead the party. Its principal duty would be to arrange for Ministers to attend the party meeting itself so that, subject to the limitations stated later on pages 135–7, they could explain their policies or Bills or deal with any criticism or dissatisfaction. It was to aim at anticipating possible misunderstanding or trouble and not to wait for it to emerge in the House itself. Whenever possible, it was to see that the party had its opportunity in good time for discussion, suggestion, and criticism with the appropriate Minister present. But Governments have to govern and they are responsible to the House of Commons as a whole. So, as a general rule, it is not possible to inform or consult the party meeting in advance of decisions, as some of the back-benchers urged, particularly in the early days.

Our forthcoming attitude towards the party meeting was appreciated by the back-benchers and did much good. They knew at all times that, if they desired the presence of a Minister, from the Prime Minister downwards, at a party meeting, the Liaison Committee, in consultation with the Minister, would make the necessary arrangements. In general, it was the responsibility not of the Liaison Committee but of Ministers to give leadership and advice to the party meeting and to defend themselves.

We gave careful consideration to the composition of the Liaison Committee. We recommended, and it was agreed, that it should consist of a back-bench Chairman and Vice-Chairman (elected by the Parliamentary Party), the Leader of the House of Commons, the Chief Whip, and, in order to give it a non-ministerial majority, a Labour Peer who was not a Minister. It was later decided that the party meeting should elect an additional Vice-Chairman, which gave the Committee a clear House of Commons non-ministerial majority. The smallness of the Committee was conducive to smooth working. I think I can say that, as distinct from the Consultative Committee of 1924 and 1929–31, our meetings were uniformly happy. Our first Chairman and Vice-Chairman were Mr. Neil Maclean and Mr. Maurice Webb. Later Mr. Webb became the Chairman and Mr. Frank Bowles the Vice-Chairman. When the latter became Deputy Chairman of Ways and Means, he was succeeded in the office of Vice-Chairman by Mr. George Daggar. Following the General Election of 1950 it was decided to appoint an additional Vice-Chairman, and Mr. Anthony Greenwood was elected. When Mr. Webb became Minister of Food in 1950 he was succeeded as Chairman by Mr. W. Glenvil Hall, and after the death of Mr. Daggar Mr. C. W. Gibson became Vice-Chairman.

Parliamentary Party Groups

Whether in opposition or in power the Parliamentary Labour Party has since 1944 officially established Subject and Area Groups with their own chairmen and vice-chairmen and with secretarial service from the staff of the Parliamentary Party, at the head of which was its Secretary, Mr. Carol Johnson. Labour Peers as well as Commoners are among the members of the Subject Groups. Before 1944 there were a few Subject Groups, but they were not systematic and part of the ground was covered by Advisory Committees of the National Executive on which some M.P.s served. The Subject Groups meet to discuss matters within their terms of reference, and the Area Groups questions affecting their regions. Under a Labour Government they can make representations to Ministers and the Liaison Committee; and Ministers concerned will attend meetings by mutual arrangement. In opposition they make representations or recommendations to the Parliamentary Committee (the elected Opposition Front Bench) and, from time to time, to the party meeting.

The Area and Subject Groups of the Parliamentary Labour

Party for the Session of 1952–3 were as follows (they may be taken as roughly indicative of the groups which existed in the days of the Labour Government):

Area Groups

Scottish Labour Group
Welsh Labour Group
Northern Group
Lancashire and Cheshire Group
Yorkshire Group
West Midlands Group
East Midlands Group
Eastern Group
London and Middlesex Group
South and South-Western Group.

These areas are related to the Labour M.P.s on the lists of the junior Whips and to the organizing regions of the Labour Party outside. So a junior Whip attends each of the Area Groups and each Area Group appoints an M.P. to serve on the corresponding Regional Council of the Labour Party.

Subject Groups

Agriculture, Fisheries, and Food
Arts and Amenities
Commonwealth and Colonies
Defence and Services
Education
Finance and Economic
Foreign Affairs
Health and Social Insurance
Legal and Judicial
Local Government
Nationalized Industries
Public Information
Statutory Instruments (for examination of delegated legislation)
Trade Union.

It is common for Groups to set up standing committees. For example, the Agriculture Group had a Fisheries Committee; Defence and Services had three, i.e. Navy, Army, and R.A.F.

Committees; the Finance and Economic Group had four: Finance, Labour, Trade and Industry, and Textiles Committees; Health and Social Insurance had its Health Services and National Insurance Committees; Local Government its Blitzed Areas, Civil Defence, Housing, and Town and Country Planning Committees; and Nationalized Industries its Civil Aviation, Fuel and Power, Inland Transport, and Steel Committees.

There were other *ad hoc* committees set up by the Groups and their committees (e.g. on the Finance Bill and on Films). Working parties were appointed for the Conservative Government's Transport and Iron and Steel (de-nationalization) Bills of 1952–3. They examined the Bills in detail and organized the work of the Opposition.

According to their nature and the Business coming before the House, the Subject Groups meet with varying frequency. Some of the Groups or committees may be dealing largely with limited matters of current concern not requiring lengthy or continuous study, but quite a number of the Groups, for example, Foreign Affairs, Defence, Finance and Economic, will be dealing with matters requiring continuous attention, owing to the magnitude of the subjects or to developing or changing circumstances or to the frequency with which the matters concerned are likely to arise in Parliament. Notices, and often agenda papers, are circulated and at times informative or argumentative memoranda. Outside experts are sometimes brought in, and party leaders will take part in the proceedings as circumstances require. The recognized Subject Groups are valuable in clarifying the minds of the Members taking an interest in their work. It does not follow that either the Parliamentary Committee or the party meeting will accept the view of a Group. As a whole I regard the work of the Subject Groups and, although of a different nature, that of the Area Groups, as of value in our parliamentary life.

Labour in Opposition

When, as a result of the 1951 General Election, the Labour Party went into opposition it was obviously necessary to make changes in the organization of the Parliamentary Party. These changes were settled by the party meeting and I will now describe the arrangements obtaining in 1953.

Three officers are elected by the Parliamentary Party at the beginning of each Parliamentary Session: the Chairman and Leader of the party; the Vice-Chairman and Deputy Leader; and the Chief Whip. Even though more than one nomination for each of the three offices is infrequent, every member of the Parliamentary Party has a right to nominate any other member with his consent. If there is more than one nomination a ballot is held.

The Chairman and Leader of the party is recognized as the Leader of the Labour Party not only in Parliament but also in the country; he is *ex officio* a member of the National Executive Committee of the Labour Party and he is free to attend any of the sub-committees of the Executive as an *ex officio* member if and when he wishes to do so. He is the leading spokesman of the Opposition in Parliament. Each week he (or, in his absence, the Deputy Leader of the Opposition) asks the Leader of the House to state the Business to be taken in the following week. His position is not only officially recognized in parliamentary practice, but it is also now recognized by statute, for under the Ministers of the Crown Act, 1937, passed by a Conservative Government, a salary of £2,000 a year is payable to the Leader of the Opposition. He presides at Parliamentary Party meetings and meetings of the Parliamentary Committee. The Vice-Chairman and Deputy Leader presides when he is absent, assists the Leader of the Opposition generally, undertakes special tasks from time to time, and acts on his behalf in his absence. As a result of an amendment to the party constitution made at the 1953 Margate Conference the Deputy Leader is now also *ex officio* a member of the National Executive. He also has power to serve on any sub-committee of the Executive. The duties of the Chief Whip have already been described in Chapter VI.

At the beginning of each Parliamentary Session the Parliamentary Party in the Commons elects twelve members who, with the three officers just mentioned, the Leader (or Deputy Leader) and the Chief Whip of the Labour Peers and one other elected Peer, constitute the Parliamentary Committee. The nominations for the Committee members are usually numerous and a ballot is necessary. Members of the Parliamentary Committee sit on the Opposition Front Bench whether ex-Ministers or not. Permission for Members who are not ex-Ministers to sit on the Front Bench was given by an earlier Speaker after careful consideration by him and after argument had taken place in the House, some Conservative Members having been critical of the innovation. However, this privilege of the members of the Parliamentary Committee in no way prejudices the right of ex-Ministers belonging to the official Opposition to sit on the Front Bench and if called upon in debate to speak at the Dispatch Box. Indeed, the Opposition Front Bench, like the Treasury Bench, can be very crowded at times.

In most weeks the Parliamentary Labour Party in opposition has two party meetings, the members of the Parliamentary Committee sitting on the platform with the Chairman and Leader in the Chair. Labour Peers are members of the Parliamentary Party and are free to attend its meetings, though they do not vote on matters of special concern to the Commons. One meeting is held in the morning, though it is dispensed with from time to time by decision of the party meeting or of the Parliamentary Committee. This morning meeting may settle the general policy on matters pending in the House or which it is desired to initiate in Parliament or questions of Parliamentary party organization. Subjects for discussion can be initiated not only by the Parliamentary Committee but also by individual Members if notice has been given and sometimes on reports by the appropriate party Group. Important matters arranged for discussion are usually notified on the notice summoning the meeting.

If any of the recommendations of the Parliamentary Committee are regarded as unimportant or uncontroversial they will be dealt with informally from the Chair. If important or controversial the recommendations will be introduced and defended by the member of the Committee (possibly the Chairman) who has been chosen for the purpose, and it may be that he, or another member of the Committee, will wind up the debate. If an item is down in the name of a Subject Group the case for the Group will be stated by its Chairman or other authorized member, and probably a member of the Parliamentary Committee will intervene. Debate is free, and a vote is taken if agreement is not reached.

The second party meeting is on Thursday evenings to receive

and consider the recommendations of the Parliamentary Committee about speakers and the general line to be taken on the Business of the House for the following week.

Labour Party Standing Orders

For many years before the war the Parliamentary Labour Party had its standing orders giving guidance on the conduct of its members to encourage co-operation between them and cohesion in action by the party as a whole. It cannot be said that they were always effective. If any member or members cause serious offence to the party as a whole by acting out of harmony with party policy or the decisions of the party meeting they will be seen and talked to usually more in sorrow than in anger by the Chief Whip or, in exceptional cases, by the Deputy Leader of the party or even the Leader of the party himself. If the conduct is serious and persistent there is only one real sanction, namely, the withdrawal of the Whip or a clear warning that this will happen unless there is improvement. But back-benchers and Front Benchers alike are reluctant to take such serious action unless there is a very strong case. On rare occasions the Whip has been withdrawn. The Conservative Party also sometimes acts in this way and indeed the technique of the two great parties in handling disciplinary problems is much the same, though the Labour Party is more formally democratic, and publicity is more likely, for the recommendation would have to go to the party meeting and the member or members would have a right to be heard both by the Parliamentary Committee and the party meeting.

Soon after the Labour Government was returned in 1945 I came to the conclusion as Leader of the House of Commons that it would be a worth-while experiment to suspend the Labour Party's standing orders. We discussed the matter on the Liaison Committee and, with the agreement of my colleagues and the Prime Minister, I proposed that the standing orders should be suspended for a period and the situation then reviewed. We made it clear that the party would expect its members to practise good comradeship and to work as a team, it being understood that the power to withdraw the Whip in extreme cases still existed. This action was appreciated by the great majority of the party though it was looked upon with some misgiving by a minority. I believe, however, that it contributed to a happy spirit in the party and helped rather than weakened that good fellowship and co-operation without which a parliamentary party whether or not in power cannot succeed. There were some troubles from time to time which produced a demand for the reimposition of the standing orders. My own feeling was that it would not help to do so and in fact we suspended the standing orders from January 1946 to March 1952. Even in the early days of opposition we maintained the suspension, but when fifty-seven Labour M.P.s abstained from voting on a party motion relating to national defence there was very serious concern in the party. Indeed the Parliamentary Committee recommended that those of the fifty-seven who would not give an undertaking for better conduct in the future should have the Whip withdrawn from them. This, however, proved not to be acceptable to the majority of the Parliamentary Party and one of the factors in the compromise reached was that the standing orders should be revised and reintroduced. This was done. The standing orders of the Parliamentary Party, revised in March 1952, read as follows:

1. The privilege of membership of the Parliamentary Labour Party involves the acceptance of the decisions of the Party Meeting. The Party recognises the right of individual Members to abstain from voting on matters of deeply held personal conscientious conviction.

2. The Parliamentary Party have the right to withdraw the Whip on account of things said or done by Members of the Party in the House. The Member or Members concerned shall have the right to be heard at the Party Meeting before the Whip is withdrawn.

3. The National Executive Committee shall be informed of any decision to withdraw the Whip.

4. It is the duty of the Parliamentary Committee to bring before the Party Meeting cases of serious or persistent breaches of Party discipline, and in appropriate cases to recommend to the Party Meeting that the Member or Members concerned shall be reported to the National Executive Committee. The Member or Members concerned shall have the right to be heard by the Parliamentary Committee and the Parliamentary Party.

5. For the purpose of securing concerted action in the House, Members shall consult the Officers of the Parliamentary Party before

tabling any motion, amendment or prayer, or other proposal which may involve Party policies or decisions.

These Standing Orders may be amended, rescinded, altered, added to, suspended or reinstated for such period and under such conditions as may be determined, after due notice, by a duly constituted meeting of the Parliamentary Labour Party.

Conservative Party Organization

Naturally I am not as well informed about the organization of the Conservative Parliamentary Party, but I got some impressions of its working while I was a member of Mr. Churchill's War Cabinet and worked officially with Conservative as well as Labour Whips. The Conservative Party is not and would not claim to be as democratic in its internal organization as is the Labour Party, although I suspect that there is more democracy in practice than meets the eye, more particularly in its parliamentary organization. It values traditions and precedents. The Conservative Party has a much longer history than the Labour Party. It is probable that many of its customs have been handed down from earlier days when it was essentially a party of the aristocracy. I have a feeling, but I may be wrong, that consciously or unconsciously the Conservative Party has some sort of constitutional theory that the Government should have a considerable degree of independence, and, though responsible to the House of Commons as a whole, should not live too closely with its back-benchers. It would follow from the theory, if I am right, that the Conservative back-benchers should be able to exercise a critical judgement on the policy pursued by a Conservative Government or by the Front Bench when the party is in opposition. At most this would be a theory, for one cannot show that it works out in practice. Their Whips keep the Conservative leaders or Ministers well aware of back-bench feeling. Revolts are infrequent and even then often carried through with a privacy that would be impossible in the Labour Party. Differences of opinion among the Conservative M.P.s do occur, but, whereas they would probably quickly 'leak' or result in a public argument in the case of the Labour Party, they are usually kept private among the Conservatives, who have a considerable capacity for safeguarding party secrets. They regard a breach of this tradition as a sin against political decorum and as ungentlemanly. Loyalty to their leaders and Ministers is strong among Conservative back-benchers and more so among the constituency associations. Discipline can be and is enforced, and from time to time the Whip has been withdrawn, though, as in the case of the Labour Party, this is avoided if at all possible.

The Leader of the Conservative Party is not appointed on a sessional basis; once elected he remains the Leader until he dies or resigns. When a vacancy occurs the new Leader is elected by a meeting consisting of the Conservative and Unionist Members of both Houses of Parliament, all prospective Conservative and Unionist parliamentary candidates in the United Kingdom, and the Executive Committee of the National Union of Conservative and Unionist Associations. If the appointment of the Leader of the Conservative Party appears to be for something like life, it would be more accurate to say during pleasure. For, if the Conservative Party sufficiently badly wanted to change its Leader, it would find ways and means of doing so.

The Leader of the Conservative Party possesses powers much beyond those of the Leader of the Labour Party. He is responsible for the elaboration of and statements on party policy. He appoints the Chairman of the Conservative Party organization at Central Office; this gives him a special authority over the party in the country. In opposition he selects the M.P.s and Peers to act with him in the so-called Shadow Cabinet. These are considerable powers which may historically have some relationship to an earlier and more aristocratic society; or they may be powers acquired and handed down by earlier Conservative Prime Ministers. Nevertheless, it is almost certain that the Leader of the Conservative Party has, in practice, to exercise these powers in consultation with his colleagues, for otherwise he would probably get himself and the party into trouble with fatal political consequences for himself. The Whips undoubtedly warn him what the party will stand and what it will not.

In spite of my theory that there is some sort of mutual separation between the Conservative Front Bench and the back-benchers, I have a feeling that their practice is probably nearer to that of the Labour Party than we know. There is a Conservative Members' Committee (commonly known as the 1922 Committee), meetings of which all their back-benchers are entitled to attend. Normally the Committee's meetings are not attended by Ministers, but party leaders can and at times do attend when the party is in opposition. If there is criticism of a Minister and the Committee want him there, he will be produced and the argument will proceed, though the secrets will have a fair chance of being kept. A Whip is, I understand, always in attendance at these party meetings (though they are not called party meetings), so that the Prime Minister or other appropriate Minister may be informed if there is trouble brewing. Moreover, the Chairman of the 1922 Committee has the right of access to the Leader of his party, whether Prime Minister or not. These meetings are powerful and notice has to be taken of them.

As a rule no resolutions are proposed and it is seldom, if ever, that any vote is taken. If the meeting feels strongly critical of its leaders on any topic, a deputation may be appointed to wait privately on the Leader of the party (or the Minister or Front Bench Member particularly concerned) and to express the views of the meeting. On other controversial matters it is left to the Chairman or the Whips to convey the general sense of the meeting to the Leader of the party or to the Minister concerned. But the responsibility and right of the Leader of the party and his colleagues to decide on matters of public policy is not questioned.

Like the Labour Party, the Conservatives have extensive Subject Groups which can examine the party's policy and actions whether in power or in opposition and can effectively request the presence of a Minister or a party leader to discuss matters when differences have arisen or are likely to arise.

My impression, therefore, is that its various traditions and some of the forms of feudal aristocratic society have persisted in the organization of the Conservative Party, but that in practice a fair degree of democratic squeeze and push has developed, particularly in the Parliamentary Party. Such pressure is patient but at times very persistent.

Party Organization in the House of Lords

Party organization in the House of Lords is not fundamentally dissimilar from that in the House of Commons, though it is probably somewhat less intensive owing to the difference in atmosphere and procedure.

Each party has its Leader and Whips—the Leader of the Government party being the Leader of the House (Lord Addison under the Labour Governments of 1945–51 and Lord Salisbury under the present Conservative Government). When the Labour Peers became the official Opposition in 1951, Lord Jowitt was elected by them as their Leader and Lord Hall as Deputy Leader. The Leader of the Liberal Peers has been Lord Samuel since December 1944. The Deputy Leader of the House of Lords under the present Conservative Government is Lord Swinton. The Conservative and Labour Parties have their junior Whips to whom groups of Peers are 'allocated'. Both the Conservative and Labour Peers are represented in the so-called Shadow Cabinets of their parties when in opposition.

The officers of the Labour Peers are appointed by the House of Lords Labour Party at the commencement of each Session. The Party has no Executive or Parliamentary Committee, though it is the custom of its Leader to call weekly meetings of his Front Bench colleagues to consider the Business coming before the House.

There are regular meetings of the Labour Peers as a whole, whether Labour is in power or in opposition. The Labour Peers, who in 1953 numbered sixty-three, have their own subject groups, the following being the list at that time:

Supply, Raw Materials
Ministry of Labour, Ministry of Fuel and Power
Home Office
Defence, Army, Navy, Air Force
Housing, Local Government and Education
Board of Trade, Transport
Foreign Affairs
Agriculture
Treasury and Economic
Commonwealth and Civil Aviation.

On Business of major importance the Labour Peer responsible in the Lords customarily consults a knowledgeable member in the Commons to promote harmony in the party in the two Houses.

The Conservative and Unionist Peers meet from time to time.

They have various subject committees or groups similar to those of their colleagues in the Commons. I do not think that the Conservative and Unionist Peers attend 1922 Committee meetings, though I gather that observers may be exchanged.

The Liberal Peers numbered forty-five in 1953. It is doubtful whether they hold meetings or whether they have a party committee. I am uncertain how Lord Samuel and Lord Rea were appointed Leader and Whip respectively, but it may be assumed that they are answerable to the Liberal Committee, a body which consists, I gather, of all the Liberal M.P.s, some of the Liberal Peers, and prominent outside Liberals, and numbers twenty persons.

Government and Party Meetings

When the Labour Party is in opposition, both the Front Bench and the back-benchers are expected to observe the decisions of the Parliamentary Party, though if a change of circumstances arises before the event to which the decision relates, revision may be necessary. This is not so, at any rate formally, in the case of the Conservative Party.

Neither party when in power would, however, accept the view that its parliamentary party could instruct or control the Cabinet. This is constitutionally correct, for it is important to maintain the doctrine that the Government is responsible to the House of Commons as a whole and, through Parliament, to the nation. If the parliamentary party of the Government, in formal meeting assembled, could control the Government in detail and determine its policies before they were announced to Parliament, certainly the most undesirable situations would arise.

In the first place, Ministers have before them departmental reports dealing with policy and administration in considerable detail. The Cabinet have before them ministerial memoranda of a secret and confidential nature. Meetings of back-bench M.P.s cannot have this detailed and confidential information, partly because it would be impracticable and improper and partly because it would 'leak'. A leakage would affect not only the Government and its party but also the public interest, for the details would be of value both to political opponents and to outside interests. The publication of the substance of Foreign Office papers would certainly cause embarrassment in our relationships with foreign powers and damage to the national interest. It is true that Ministers attending meetings with the Parliamentary Labour Party will, at times, give background information, but this is within their discretion, and the responsibility is upon them neither to evade their responsibility to the House of Commons as a whole, nor to run risks with the public interest. It would be unconstitutional, injurious to good government, and likely to lead to ill-thought-out decisions being foisted upon the Government to admit the right of the party to instruct Ministers or to receive premature details in advance of Cabinet decisions. The quality and coherence of government would deteriorate and great delays and confusion would arise. It just would not work. A Government placed in that position would not last very long either with the House of Commons or with the electorate. This is not to say that a Government is, or should be, isolated from its back-benchers. All the channels of criticism, suggestion, and information are open both to Ministers and to the back-benchers, and they would be foolish Ministers if they did not encourage their use.

Moreover, the Parliamentary Labour Party meetings were, and still are, notoriously liable to leaks; both accurate and inaccurate information about their proceedings finds its way into the press. The Opposition would have had a legitimate grievance if announcements of Government intentions, decisions, or policies had not first been made to the House of Commons as a whole. This position was generally accepted by the party as being constitutionally correct.

One notable exception was the introduction of peace-time conscription. This had not been in the party programme at the General Election and was likely to give something of a shock, not only to the Parliamentary Party, but to the Labour Movement as a whole. We therefore gave advance information of our intention, not only to the Parliamentary Party, but to the National Executive of the Labour Party and the General Council of the Trades Union Congress. The Prime Minister and the Minister of Defence stated their case for the proposal in the light of the international situation and the strength of our Forces; there were shortages in the Forces, for, happily, mass unemployment was no longer a recruiting sergeant as it had been between the wars. There was full and free discussion which resulted in a wide measure of agreement. But this might well not have been achieved if the party and the wider Movement had not been informed in advance.

With the rare exception of such an important, new, and unanticipated issue as conscription, the Government cannot anticipate its legislative and administrative decisions by disclosing them in advance to a party meeting, though once such decisions are announced they are open for discussion at such meetings.

Provided the principles of what I have written are observed, Conservative or Labour Ministers can meet the members of special groups of their party and discuss in the void, so to speak, matters which may or may not be the subject of forthcoming Government action. These discussions are for a mutual expression of views, to consider suggestions, criticisms, and ideas, to let the Government know how the Members concerned feel about a given problem (which helps to educate Ministers), and for Ministers to educate a body of Members specializing in a given subject.

The Parties and Outside Organizations

Let us now consider the relationship between the Government and its friends and political organizations outside Parliament. It is clear that if the Government cannot be the prisoner, so to speak, of its parliamentary party, or subject to its specific instructions, neither can a parliamentary party allow itself to be put in that position *vis-à-vis* its friends and organizations outside Parliament, for then all the difficulties I have indicated above will arise in redoubled form.

Conservative Party Practice

It is, indeed, accepted that the Leader of the Conservative Party is responsible for policy. The Conservative Party Conference has accepted the position, though it seems to me difficult to defend. The Central Council of the Conservative Party and its Annual Conference can express views, but they are restrained in such expressions, especially when the Conservative Party is in power. In any case it has been publicly and officially stated that the Leader of the party, responsible as he is for policy, is in no way bound by these expressions of opinion. It would not appear that the Conservative Conference (or even the Central Council) is in general of much importance in policy-making. One must, of course, take into account the traditional and historical influences which I have indicated earlier. Moreover, the Conservative Party is conservative and it does not concern itself with far-reaching proposals for change as does the Labour Party. I am not saying this as a party political argument, but as some indication of a possible explanation of Conservative Party practice.

There was, however, a notable exception in policy-making which occurred at the Conservative Party Conference of 1950. A motion on housing in general terms was before the Conference. There arose a proposal to insert figures, but this was at first resisted by the platform. However, delegates on the floor made loud and persistent demands that the resolution should incorporate a commitment to construct a minimum of 300,000 houses a year. In the end, Lord Woolton, no doubt feeling that he was going to be overwhelmed, reversed the attitude of the platform, and welcomed the amendment in cordial terms. It was accepted by a victorious Conference. The Conservative Government of 1951 in turn accepted the policy and thereby it became an aim of the Government. This was an instance in which Government policy was effectively determined by the floor at a Conservative Party Conference when the party was in opposition.

There was a different experience at the Conservative Conference in 1952, when the party was in power. A resolution was under consideration demanding heavy reductions in Government expenditure. Mr. R. A. Butler, the Chancellor of the Exchequer, in a speech which was well received, made it clear that heavy reductions would involve substantial changes in policy, and said that he was not going to be responsible for any big changes of policy which, in his view, were either radically unsound, cruel, or unnecessary. He intimated that he would not be a party to the wielding of a Geddes Axe, nor was he in favour of asking an outside committee to do the Government's job for them. He sat down amidst a burst of applause, but the

Conference nevertheless proceeded to carry its motion for heavy reductions in Government expenditure. This might be said to demonstrate the Conservative doctrine of the independence of Conservative Ministers from the back-benchers and the rank and file, and vice versa.

In recent years quite a number of policy pamphlets and declarations have been prepared and published by the Conservative Party Organisation, work to which Mr. R. A. Butler contributed much as the Chairman of its Research Department. These publications have been issued, sometimes unofficially, sometimes semi-officially, sometimes with the stated approval of the Leader of the party; but if they do not have the approval of the Leader of the party they cannot be regarded as expressing official Conservative policy.

Labour Party Practice

The standing and authority of the Labour Party Conference and the National Executive of the party in policy matters are stronger than in the Conservative Party, particularly on policy declarations at General Elections. Clause V of the Labour Party Constitution and Standing Orders, which was probably, in the main, drafted by Arthur Henderson and Sidney Webb, reads as follows:

1. The Party Conference shall decide from time to time what specific proposals of legislative, financial or administrative reform shall be included in the Party Programme.

No proposal shall be included in the Party Programme unless it has been adopted by the Party Conference by a majority of not less than two-thirds of the votes recorded on a card vote.

2. The National Executive Committee and the Executive [now the Parliamentary] Committee of the Parliamentary Labour Party shall decide which items from the Party programme shall be included in the Manifesto which shall be issued by the National Executive Committee prior to every General Election. The joint meeting of the two Executive Committees shall also define the attitude of the Party to the principal issues raised by the Election which are not covered by the Manifesto.

It is thus clear that both the Executive and the Party Conference have substantial policy-making functions. A Labour Government is committed to the general policy laid down in the Labour Election Manifesto, though no doubt it could modify, or even refrain from, the proposed action if, in the light of new circumstances or information, it was satisfied that a tight adherence to the terms of the Manifesto would be contrary to the public interest. Neither the Party Executive nor the Party Conference claims the right to instruct a Labour Government while it is in office. Nor is there anything in the Party Constitution giving the Conference or the Executive power to instruct the Parliamentary Labour Party when in opposition. Naturally, however, considerable attention and respect is given to the views of the Conference and the Executive.

An issue concerning the powers of the party outside Parliament was raised by Professor Harold Laski just before the 1945 Election when he was Chairman of the National Executive Committee of the Labour Party. In this capacity, after Mr. Churchill had invited Mr. Attlee to attend the conference at Potsdam between the U.K., U.S.A., and U.S.S.R., Mr. Laski issued a statement asserting that it was essential for Mr. Attlee to attend 'in the role of an observer only' and that the Labour party could not be committed to any decisions reached, before they had been 'debated either in the Party Executive or at meetings of the Parliamentary Labour Party'. The publication of these views gave rise to correspondence between the Prime Minister and Mr. Attlee in which Mr. Churchill made it clear that he had invited Mr. Attlee as a friend and counsellor in virtue of his position as Leader of the Labour Party. In accepting this invitation Mr. Attlee, with the agreement of his 'principal colleagues in the House of Commons', repudiated the suggestion that he should 'go as a mere observer' and added:

> I understand, of course, that responsibility must rest with the Government, but I take it that we should consult together upon the issues that arise in order to present a policy consonant with the views of the great majority of the people of this country.

The issue was discussed throughout the General Election campaign and on 2 July 1945, shortly before polling-day, further letters were exchanged by the leaders of the Conservative and Labour Parties. Writing to Mr. Attlee, Mr. Churchill accused him of not realizing 'the new position with which we are confronted'. Mr. Churchill continued:

I had no idea, during the late Coalition, that the National Executive Committee of the Labour Party possessed the powers which have now become obvious. I have never suggested that you or your Socialist colleagues have in any way made any improper revelations to them.

I was never aware of any case that had arisen in which the National Executive Committee had demanded secret information from Ministers serving in the Coalition Government, and I have no doubt that you would not have disclosed any such information without previous consultation with me. It seems therefore that during these five years of your active cooperation in the Coalition Government, the powers of the Socialist National Executive Committee have remained in suspense, and I am not aware of any complaint which could be made against you or their conduct during this period.

Now, however, an altogether new situation has arisen. These powers, hitherto latent, have been asserted in a surprising manner. When I invited you to form part of the British delegation to the tripartite conference shortly to assemble in Berlin, I did so because I believed that you were effectively the leader of your party, and would have the discretion accorded you which has been customary up to the present time in British politics. It then appeared that the chairman of the National Executive Committee had the right to state that you would go as an observer only, and that no continuity in foreign policy could be guaranteed. I was very glad that you felt yourself able to contradict him on the point of your not going as a mere observer, and we exchanged letters on this subject at the time when I saw you last.

However, far from withdrawing his original declaration, Mr. Laski has made a series of speeches emphasizing his authority and that of the committee over which he presides.

. . . .

I certainly expected as the days passed by with repeated effronteries that you would make some effort to establish your position against Mr. Laski, and that he would be in some way disavowed by his committee or by the Labour Party as a whole. Nothing like this has, however, occurred, and we are left in the position that he has given you instructions which you have personally rejected but which, nevertheless, remain the official authoritative and reiterated instructions of the Executive Committee of the Labour Party.

This manifestation of where the real power rests raised far-reaching considerations. We have learnt a good deal more than we knew before about the powers vested in the National Executive Committee, of which Mr. Laski is the undisputed chairman. It certainly appears that they are very wide in their terms and, from your silence, very real. It would appear that a Labour or Socialist Government would be subject to the directions of this committee, and that matters of foreign affairs and also, I presume, if they desired it, military affairs, would have to be submitted to them. So far as I am now informed, they have a right to be consulted and to express opinions which are binding on the Ministers of a Socialist Government or on the Cabinet itself.

If the Committee is to be consulted and to take supreme decisions of approval or disapproval in regard to Government policy, how can they be debarred from reasonable knowledge of the facts? It might not be possible for Ministers to convince the Committee of the unwisdom of any course without revealing confidential Governmental matter. Indeed, it might well be argued that, where the power lies there also should be the knowledge.

When we consider the members of this Committee of 27, and how very few are responsible in any way to the public or bound by any formal obligation to the State, I feel that the situation is extremely disquieting, and that it ought to be fully explained by you to the nation. The new fact is the demonstration of the power of the Committee and of its chairman, and that apparently you and the Labour Parliamentary Party are not able to challenge Mr. Laski's statement on behalf of the Committee, although it is evident that your public position greatly requires such action.

Mr. Churchill had certainly not minimized his interpretation of Mr. Laski's statements. Indeed he had rather freely made the most of them. However, an election campaign was proceeding. Mr. Attlee replied:

I thank you for your letter. I am glad to know that you make no suggestions against your late colleagues.

The new position with which you state we are confronted exists only in your own imagination.

The constitutional relationship between the National Executive Committee of the Labour Party and the Parliamentary Party has existed unchanged for years, and is set out in an appendix to the reports of the annual conference published every year. Neither by decision of the annual party conference nor by any provision in the party constitution is the Parliamentary Labour Party answerable to, or under the direction of, the National Executive Committee.

Within the programme adopted by the annual party conference, the Parliamentary Labour Party has complete discretion in its conduct of Parliamentary business and in the attitude it should adopt to legislation tabled by other parties. The standing orders which govern its activities are drawn up and determined by the Parliamentary Labour Party itself.

I accepted the invitation to go to Berlin as the responsible Leader of the Parliamentary Labour Party.

Naturally, there are consultations between the Parliamentary Labour Party and the National Executive Committee. No elector will be in the least surprised to hear that this is the case. These consultations are, indeed, arranged for in the Labour Party's own Constitution, the clause reading as follows:

> To confer with the Parliamentary Labour Party at the opening of each Parliamentary Session, and at any other time when it or the Parliamentary Party may desire a conference on any matters relating to the work and progress of the Party.

For instance, when I decided to advise the Labour Party to support you in forming an all-party Government in 1940, I consulted the Executive Committee before bringing it before the annual conference of the party, then in session. You raised no constitutional objection then; indeed, you were glad to have the backing of this democratically elected conference.

At no time, and in no circumstances, has the National Executive Committee ever sought to give or given instructions to the Parliamentary Labour Party arising out of the consultations. Indeed, as will be seen from the clause, it has no power to do so.

The Chairman has not the power to give me instructions, nor do his remarks to a Press correspondent constitute the official authoritative and reiterated instruction of the Executive Committee of the Labour Party.

With regard to continuity in foreign policy, it is obvious that a Labour Government will follow a policy in accordance with the principles in which it believes and on which its members in the House of Commons have been elected. This is sound constitutional doctrine. Presumably a Conservative Government would do the same.

The fact that in the late Government members of all parties were in accord on the main lines of our foreign policy does not alter the fact that the complexion of the new House of Commons will decide the course of future policy as it did before the war, when you and I both disagreed with the policy of the Conservative Party.

I am sorry that you should have been so distressed owing to your lack of acquaintance with the procedure of democratic parties in general, and of the Labour Party in particular.

On the following day Mr. Churchill welcomed these assurances, but said he was unable to accept Mr. Attlee's explanation as satisfactory. Mr. Laski, on the other hand, having described himself as 'scapegoat No. 1', pointed out that after the election 'he would be returned to the obscurity from which he had emerged. He knew his place and it was generally known.' Mr. Laski also commented: 'I agree with every word of Mr. Attlee's letter to the Prime Minister. It defines a position the Prime Minister knew perfectly well existed.'

With the approval, so far as I know, of all the Labour candidates and of the party generally, Mr. Attlee held firm to the principles of parliamentary democracy; and the constitutional doctrine set out in his letter has never been repudiated by the Labour Party. The British people expect from their M.P.s a general sense of electoral responsibility and that their Government shall be answerable to the elected House of Commons. In Communist countries things are very different. There the Political Bureau (or whatever new title it may have) of the Communist Party is, in fact, the body that determines Government policy. If in our own country committees of political parties could instruct the Government of the day, we should be losing our system of parliamentary democracy and moving towards single-party dictatorship. To the credit of our great political parties this is not the practice.

The T.U.C. in Public Affairs

The General Council of the Trades Union Congress is an industrial body. Naturally, it is concerned with governmental and parliamentary policy from the point of view of the industrial interests of Trade Unionists. The Council and the Congress from time to time make declarations on industrial matters and, indeed, on such wide subjects as foreign policy and defence. The relations between the General Council and the Labour Party are friendly. Indeed, the Conference which created the Labour Party (then the Labour Representation Committee) at the beginning of the century was summoned by the Trades Union Congress, which thus has a parental responsibility for the existence of the party, though Keir Hardie and other Socialist pioneers had conducted propaganda to that end from the 1880's onwards. The General Council and the Labour

Party Executive confer from time to time about specific questions of policy or even upon important political pronouncements. Both are represented, together with the Parliamentary Party and the Co-operative Union, on the National Council of Labour. Nevertheless, in its relations with the Government of the day the T.U.C. is not obliged to act through Labour Party channels, nor is it bound to accept the judgement of the Labour Party on industrial questions, or even on political matters which have economic implications.

After the Election of 1951 the T.U.C. made it clear that it would maintain correct official relationships with the new Conservative Government, that it would judge the Government's policies on their merits or demerits and that it would not withhold co-operation in the general interest merely because the Government was Conservative. Therefore, the T.U.C. has directly conferred with Ministers on matters of mutual interest. It is represented on numerous Government committees. It is recognized by the Government as a body of importance which has a right to be heard on industrial policy, though all this is without prejudice to the complete freedom of the General Council to dissent from Government policy whenever it thinks that that policy is wrong. The decision of the General Council in 1951 attracted considerable public interest and support. There is, however, nothing new about it, for, even in earlier days when the T.U.C. did not enjoy the high public prestige which it has since won for itself, the General Council and its predecessor, the Parliamentary Committee of the T.U.C., had access to and maintained official relationships with non-Labour Governments as well as Labour Governments and the Labour Party. That is also the position of individual Trade Unions on matters with which they are particularly concerned.

Whenever the General Council wishes to put its point of view to the Parliamentary Labour Party or if the latter wishes to seek the advice of the General Council, it is perfectly open to either side to do so. Thus, on the Conservative Transport and Iron and Steel (de-nationalization) Bills of 1952–3, joint committees of the Parliamentary Party, the National Executive of the party, the T.U.C., and the Unions concerned did useful work in co-operation. There is naturally a friendly relationship between the General Council and the Trade Union Group of the Parliamentary Party. All these relationships, however, never go beyond the principle of mutual consultation and certainly do not mean that either side presumes to possess the right to instruct the other.

Co-operators in Public Affairs

The Co-operative Union has established, as a subsidiary body of itself, the Co-operative Party, which nominates candidates for Parliament in association with the Labour Party. The Co-operative M.P.s are members of the Parliamentary Labour Party and accept its standing orders. Naturally they take a special interest in matters affecting the Co-operative Movement and are concerned to apply Co-operative principles, but they play their part in the wider issues that come before Parliament. The Co-operative group of M.P.s consults with its friends outside from time to time, but again this is for mutual consultation and not for the giving and receiving of instructions. There are joint committees of the Co-operative Union and the Co-operative Party and the Labour Party outside Parliament for the discussion of policy and political organization, and the Co-operative Union, as stated above, is represented on the National Council of Labour.

I have dealt with these matters of outside relationships in their parliamentary and governmental aspects only, for I am not dealing here with the general organization of the wider Labour Movement.

CHAPTER VIII

The House of Commons— Its Life and Problems

THE House of Commons uses a certain number of committees, though the main emphasis still remains on work in the Chamber rather than in the Committee Room. I will say something in Chapter X about the Standing Committees used for the Committee Stage of legislation. In this chapter I will be dealing mainly with other committees and in particular those concerned with finance or administration and with proposals for the possible extension of their number and work. I will also say something about the position of the back-bencher in these days.

Committee of Privileges

Perhaps the most important committee is the Committee of Privileges which in recent years has consisted of ten members. Its function is to consider complaints of breach of privilege. It is given power to send for persons, papers, and records. It has the delicate task of preserving the rightful privileges of the House without (it is repeatedly asserted) extending them, though I am not sure what would happen if circumstances arose which required an extension of privilege in order properly to protect the collective work of the House. It is important to realize that the word 'privilege' in this connexion has a relationship to the dignity and the free functioning of the House as a whole. It is not a question of the privileges of individual M.P.s, except in so far as they are related to the functioning of the House as a whole. The desire not to extend the privileges of Parliament stems from a general feeling among us that the last thing we should do would be to extend parliamentary privilege in ways which would limit the civil and democratic rights of the people. When a person who has to answer for the possibility of having committed a breach of parliamentary privilege appears before the Committee, the proceedings are judicial in character. The

Chairman has an important and delicate task, and in my experience both he and the members of the Committee take great trouble to be fair, objective, and impartial in the discharge of their duties. The report of the Committee can of course be challenged and voted upon in the House; on such occasions the Whips are taken off.

Committees on Public Expenditure

The Committee of Privileges includes leading members of the House of Commons. There are, however, other important committees concerned with the Government's administration on which most of the members are back-benchers. In particular there are the Committees of Public Accounts, on Estimates, and on Statutory Instruments.

The Public Accounts Committee deals with matters set out in Standing Order No. 90:

> There shall be a select committee, to be designated the Committee of Public Accounts, for the examination of the accounts showing the appropriation of the sums granted by Parliament to meet the public expenditure, and of such other accounts laid before Parliament as the committee may think fit, to consist of not more than fifteen members, who shall be nominated at the commencement of every session, and of whom five shall be a quorum. The committee shall have power to send for persons, papers and records, and to report from time to time.

It is assisted by the Comptroller and Auditor-General (who is an officer of the House of Commons) and examines the accounts of such public Departments as it may select from year to year. It has fifteen members and the Chairman is by convention a member of the Opposition party, usually a person who has been Financial Secretary to the Treasury.

Having the power to send for persons and papers the Committee can and does require the presence of Permanent Secretaries or other senior civil servants who are subject to verbal examination on the accounts and the work of the Departments. This examination may take several days and can be extensive and severe. The Committee can call for memoranda from a Department being examined and for departmental documents not of an internal character, but it cannot require the production of such documents as departmental files and minutes.

What it cannot do is to challenge the policy of the Government of the day (that being regarded as the business of the House as a whole). The work of M.P.s on the Public Accounts Committee is important to the House and the public, and it gives them an excellent opportunity of learning much about the inside of government. A considerable amount of work is involved. The reports of the Committee are presented to Parliament and published, and sometimes arouse considerable public interest.

Members of Parliament who have the time and the wish have another channel through which they can get behind the scenes and come closer to the inside of government, namely, by membership of the Select Committee on Estimates. The terms of reference are that 'a Select Committee be appointed to examine such of the Estimates presented to this House as may seem fit to the Committee, and to suggest the form in which the Estimates shall be presented for examination, and to report what, if any, economies consistent with the policy implied in those Estimates may be effected therein'. The Committee has thirty-six members and in this case the Chairman is usually a back-bencher from the party in power.

Whereas the Public Accounts Committee examines the financial affairs of the Departments after the money has been spent, the Estimates Committee examines the expenditure proposed, even though by the time the Committee has finished its examination much of the money may have been spent. As with the Public Accounts Committee, Permanent Secretaries and other senior civil servants can be summoned before the Committee and examined, and information and memoranda called for; but here again government policy is reserved for the House as a whole and internal departmental minutes and records cannot be called for. The Estimates Committee, for reasons of effectiveness and in order to cover more ground, appoints sub-committees who report to the main Committee.

In part, the existence of these two important Committees is desirable, because it would be difficult, if not impossible, for the House as a whole to examine the accounts and estimates in detail; committees are more effective instruments for such a purpose. But it is also true that such committees are desirable because the House as a whole, sitting as Committee of Supply, has tended over the years to use Supply days for the discussion of policy and alleged imperfections of the Government of the day rather than for the scrutiny of expenditure with a view to enforcing specific economies on Ministers. Indeed, sometimes a Supply day debate, even if it takes place on a nominal motion to reduce the vote, is used to ask the Government to spend more money. It should not be assumed that these things are necessarily wrong, since it is important that the House should have proper opportunities for challenging ministerial administration and ventilating the grievances of the people. This indeed is a major purpose of the control of supply by the House of Commons, as indicated in the doctrine of no supply before the ventilation of grievances.

Whether the House of Commons is an adequate and efficient watch-dog over public expenditure is open to question, even though it has the Public Accounts and Estimates Committees. However, the committees do excellent work and it should certainly not be assumed that they are without influence and the power to frighten Government Departments. If a Minister wishes to spend money for which his statutory authority is in any degree doubtful, one of the most effective restraints of the Permanent Secretary is to remind him that the Permanent Secretary is the Accounting Officer of the Department and that he has to answer for the Department's expenditure before the Public Accounts Committee. This is a polite way of telling the Minister that he cannot run the risk of exceeding his statutory authority and that, if the Permanent Secretary as Accounting Officer were challenged by the Public Accounts Committee, he would be compelled to inform the Committee that the expenditure had been incurred on the Minister's personal instructions, after he had been warned about it by the Accounting Officer. This is a minor illustration of how difficult it is under our system of government and parliamentary checks for Ministers to exceed their authority.

Committee on Delegated Legislation

The Select Committee on Statutory Instruments is relatively new. It deals with delegated or subordinate legislation, i.e. regulations having the force of law made by Ministers usually under specific powers conferred by various Statutes.

In 1929 Lord Hewart, then Lord Chief Justice of England, published a book called *The New Despotism*, which denounced delegated legislation with bell, book, and candle. He had been a member of the Coalition Governments of 1916–22, which were responsible for a good deal of delegated legislation—not that that should necessarily have precluded him from subsequently denouncing it. It was a readable volume, but somewhat extreme and unrealistic.

There are three reasonable arguments for Ministers having the power to make subordinate legislation. First, it really is impossible in modern conditions for Parliament to set out in an Act all the details of administration for the wide field of modern legislation, which is more complex in character than most of the legislation of the nineteenth century. Secondly, there is the very important and practical point that it is impossible to foresee in framing a Bill whether conditions will or will not change in a manner requiring modifications in detailed statutory provisions. If and when such changes in circumstances arise both Parliament and the public would be frustrated if (as would be quite likely) parliamentary time were not available to put things right, whereas delegated legislation can rapidly be revised by the issue of another Statutory Instrument. Parliament has the same rights over such a changed instrument as over the original. Finally, it should be noted that no Minister can make regulations having the force of law unless he has specific authority (usually by Statute) to do so. The Statute defines the field within which and the purposes for which the Minister can create delegated legislation, so that Parliament at the time of its detailed consideration of the Bill is in a position to limit and define his powers and prescribe his parliamentary accountability. Generally, therefore, not only must the regulations be within a purpose already approved by Parliament, but usually they are relatively (and I emphasize relatively, because they can be of importance) of limited significance, filling in the details of a Statute. The principle of delegated legislation is, I think, right, but I must emphasize that it is well for Parliament to keep a watchful and even jealous eye on it at all stages.

I have been dealing with delegated legislation in peace-time conditions. In war it is another matter, for at the outset of a great war Acts are passed which confer upon the Government wide powers to make regulations. This was so with the Defence of the Realm Acts of the First World War and the Emergency Powers (Defence) Acts of the Second World War. As Home Secretary in Mr. Churchill's War Government I have reason to know, for I had special responsibilities in this field and exercised enormous powers conferred by delegated legislation including the power of arrest and detention under Defence Regulation 18B, the power of interning enemy aliens and, of course, the power of release whether subject to conditions or not. I also had the power to suppress newspapers (Regulation 2D) in certain circumstances. I tried at all times to exercise these powers with a due sense of restraint and with a maximum regard for the high principles of civil liberty, and I am comforted by the fact that my friend Harold Laski, who was a valued champion of the cause of civil liberty, was not unfavourable in his comments on the administration of the Home Office at that time.[1] However, it was a happy day when at the end of the war in Europe I was able promptly to go down to the House of Commons and announce the revocation of practically all the regulations which in doubtful hands could endanger civil liberty.

Statutory Instruments do not have to go through the same lengthy process as an Act of Parliament before they become law. They are, however, subject to a measure of parliamentary control. With particularly important Regulations, it is customary for Parliament to stipulate that the Government cannot act under such authority until the proposed Regulations have been submitted in draft to both Houses and have been approved by affirmative resolutions. In most cases, however, the Minister can make the Regulations and bring them into force, but either House of Parliament can within forty sitting days challenge them by a Motion praying Her Majesty to annul them, and if either House passes a Motion to this effect the Regulation is null and void and cannot be further acted upon. These Motions are known as Prayers, and are quite frequently moved, sometimes to get information without the intention of pressing them to a division, and sometimes to give a straight challenge ending in a division. Regulations in a third group, quite minor ones, need only be laid on the Table and that is the last that is heard of them in the House (if indeed that is heard), unless some M.P.

[1] See *Harold Laski*, by Kingsley Martin, 1953.

raises the matter by Question and possibly on the Adjournment or otherwise thereafter.

All Statutory Instruments, therefore, are challengeable in some form or other, so that Parliament is in a position to assert itself both at the time the authorizing legislation is under consideration and at the time the Regulations are proposed or after they are made. The missing element over which argument frequently takes place is that Parliament has no power to amend a proposed Statutory Instrument, only to pass or reject it.[1]

If the two Houses of Parliament were to have the power to amend a Statutory Instrument, it would be difficult not to go through all or most of the stages of legislation again, and then all the details might just as well have been put in the Statute itself. There is more to be said for the proposal to give a Select Committee power to revise and amend, though it is difficult to see how these powers could be completely delegated to a committee without giving Parliament the right to consider and revise the revisions or to restore the Statutory Instrument to its original form on the Floor of the House (or Houses) at what would constitute something in the nature of a Report Stage. So that idea is not easy either.

The issue of the control of delegated legislation was taken up by back-benchers during the war. They put forward various arguments and proposals, including the proposal I have just mentioned, but also lesser ones together with a proposal which was ultimately accepted. I had resisted it in the earlier and more distracting and dangerous stages of the war on the ground that it would not be in the public interest for Ministers and civil servants to be diverted from full concentration on the prosecution of the war. What we ultimately did, in 1944, was to establish a Select Committee on Statutory Instruments and this is now renewed each Session. The function of the Select Committee is to consider every Statutory Instrument or draft of an Instrument laid before the House,

> with a view to determining whether the special attention of the House should be drawn to it on any of the following grounds:
>
> (i) that it imposes a charge on the public revenues or contains provisions requiring payments to be made to the Exchequer

[1] In October 1953 a Select Committee under the Chairmanship of the Liberal Leader, Mr. Clement Davies, reported against such a change in procedure.

or any Government Department or to any local or public authority in consideration of any licence or consent, or of any services to be rendered, or prescribes the amount of any such charge or payments;

(ii) that it is made in pursuance of an enactment containing specific provisions excluding it from challenge in the courts, either at all times or after the expiration of a specified period;

(iii) that it appears to make some unusual or unexpected use of the powers conferred by the Statute under which it is made;

(iv) that it purports to have retrospective effect where the parent Statute confers no express authority so to provide;

(v) that there appears to have been unjustifiable delay in the publication or in the laying of it before Parliament;

(vi) that there appears to have been unjustifiable delay in sending a notification to Mr. Speaker under the proviso to subsection (1) of section four of the Statutory Instruments Act, 1946, where an Instrument has come into operation before it has been laid before Parliament;

(vii) that for any special reason its form or purport calls for elucidation;

and if they so determine, to report to that effect.

The Committee has done excellent work and has received much valuable assistance from the Counsel to Mr. Speaker, Sir Cecil Carr, as its principal adviser.

Clearly, these Select Committees provide an important field for useful and informative work by back-bench M.P.s, to whose credit it is that there is no great difficulty in finding Members to man them, even though considerable labour is involved. The atmosphere in the Select Committees is usually good; party friction and conflict are the exception rather than the rule, for the members seek to pull together in the public interest and in a large proportion of cases produce agreed reports. Parliamentary institutions owe much to the work of the Chairmen and members of the Select Committees.

Rights of the House as a Whole

It is noticeable, however, that broadly speaking (though there can be exceptions) the function of examining and challenging important Government policy is reserved to Parliament as a whole. This doctrine has, I imagine, been preserved for two reasons: the wish of Parliament not to weaken its own powers and authority, and the desire of Governments not to become (to put it crudely) the victims or creatures of committees.

In the United States and in France things are very different. American Secretaries of Departments may be summoned to give evidence and to be examined by Committees of the Senate or of the House of Representatives in Washington, and in France the Parliamentary Committees have considerable powers over French Ministers. The result may indeed be fatal for the Minister, or what the United States calls the Official, concerned. In the United States the President's nominees for his Secretaries of Departments, Ambassadors, and even delegates to the United Nations Assembly, are subject to approval by a two-thirds majority of the Senate and can be summoned before Senate Committees and severely examined not only on their policies and capacities, but also on their past lives. Budgets and legislation are exhaustively examined in Committees of the U.S. Congress and the French Parliament, which would often appear to have even more decisive powers and influence than the parliamentary institution as a whole.[1]

I once had the experience, exceptional for a foreigner, of giving evidence before a Committee of the United States Senate, on the late Senator Wagner's Housing Bill. It was an interesting and fascinating experience: a crowded room, some seated, some standing, including local government officers who had come long distances. The Chairman of the day was evidently hostile to the Bill and he handled me with some degree of American frankness and hostility. By the time we had reached nearly the last question I was beginning to feel at home and equally frank, so that when he asked me, 'Well, Mr. Morrison, what *is* this London County Council, anyway?', I thought I had better be a little boastfully British and I replied, 'Sir, it is the greatest municipality in the world—that's what the London County Council is'. I forget whether the Chairman snorted or said, 'Uh huh'. However, it was a most interesting and, for me, happy experience. But if you ask me whether it was anything like the procedure or atmosphere of a Select Committee of the

[1] For the unhappy consequences of French practice and also the lack of balance between the authority of the French Parliament and Government, see *France under the Fourth Republic*, by François Goguel, 1952.

House of Commons or the House of Lords, the answer is in the negative.

Our own Parliament has not gone in for these procedures. I feel sure that it would regard the practice as a derogation of parliamentary authority.

Government by Committee

A somewhat different proposal was made before the First World War by Mr. F. W. Jowett, Labour Member of Parliament for West Bradford. He had been a Bradford City Councillor since 1892 and was a leading member of the Independent Labour Party. His biographer, Mr. Fenner Brockway,[1] says:

> Even before he entered the House he had been critical of its procedure as he had learned it from [Keir] Hardie and from his reading of the Press and Hansard; but actual experience strengthened his criticism tenfold. He saw Parliament just as a stage for the Party game . . . He proposed that the six hundred and seventy members of Parliament should be allocated to Committees responsible for the administration of the various Departments of State, just as members of the local authorities are distributed among committees responsible for Health, Transport, Finance and so on. He proposed that each Minister should preside over his Departmental Committee and that all legislative and administrative matters relating to that Department should come before the Committee before being presented to Parliament as a whole. He proposed that all Departmental documents and information should be available to the Committee, that nothing should be withheld. In this way every Member of Parliament could, if he desired, make an informed and constructive contribution, and the full light of democracy would be thrown on everything done (pp. 73–74).

Mr. Jowett elaborated these ideas in evidence before the Select Committee on House of Commons (Procedure) of 1913–14. He also advocated the abolition of Cabinet Government much on the lines of the Independent Labour Party resolution carried at its Bradford Conference in 1914. The resolution stated:

> That Cabinet rule, which involves the suppression of the rights of the private Member to any adequate voice in the policy of his Party, and which implies the resignation of the Ministry and the dissolution

[1] *Socialism over Sixty Years: The Life of Jowett of Bradford (1864–1944)*, 1946.

of Parliament when proposals of the Cabinet are negatived, besides making almost impossible the free consideration of proposals which have not received the Cabinet hall-mark, is inimical to the good government of the country; that, with a view to the ultimate break-up of this system, the Parliamentary Labour Party be asked to take no account of any such considerations and to vote on all issues only in accordance with the principles for which the Party stands (p. 109).

In 1926 Jowett's proposals for government by Committee were endorsed by the Independent Labour Party Conference, but not without a struggle by his opponents, including H. B. Lees-Smith, Harold Laski, and Ramsay MacDonald, who held 'the view that Cabinet co-ordination and control was the key of representative government', and that 'Departmental Committees should, therefore, be purely advisory' (p. 236). MacDonald pointed out that Jowett's responsible all-party committees would tend to make Parliament a permanent Coalition and that a Labour Government would lose all driving force.

In 1931 Mr. Jowett and Mr. E. F. Wise gave evidence on behalf of the Independent Labour Party before the House of Commons' Select Committee on Procedure on Public Business. Departmental Committees were also advocated by Mr. Lloyd George and Professor Ramsay Muir, but the Select Committee was 'not convinced that these committees would either be sufficiently representative of the House as a whole to achieve the end desired, or be a sufficient check upon Ministers and Departments to counterbalance the grave disadvantage which would, in their judgement, arise from the delays inherent in the system' (*H.C.* 129 (1932), p. xi).

Mr. Lloyd George's proposals had much in common with those put forward by the Independent Labour Party, but there were certain significant differences; for example, the Minister would not be the Chairman of the all-party Committee for his Department and the Committee would not have power to control the administration of the Department, though it could examine the Minister and his civil servants and any papers it chose to ask for. Administrative 'control must rest with the Minister, because he is responsible to Parliament, and through Parliament to the Crown. The Minister must have the ultimate say, subject to what Parliament says, but it would enable the House of Commons effectively to supervise, and not only that, but to keep itself informed' (*H.C.* 161 (1931), q. 362). Mr. Lloyd George started by drawing his analogy from the committees of local government, but as he developed his argument it became clear that what he wanted were Parliamentary Advisory Committees, which should supervise but not have control over or responsibility for the Departments of State (qq. 443–9). These Sessional Committees would have power to recommend, but not to initiate, legislation (qq. 542, 553). Non-specialist Standing Committees would continue to deal with legislation (qq. 552, 1034), and apparently both types of committees should contain not more than fifteen to twenty members (qq. 1031–2).

So far as I know there was nothing in Mr. Lloyd George's earlier career as a Minister to show that he was in favour of such ideas. However, one must make allowance for the fact that in view of the decline of the Liberal Parliamentary Party he could not expect to be Prime Minister again or even become a Minister unless it were in a Coalition Government. He was indeed offered office in Mr. Churchill's War Coalition, but he declined.

Mr. Jowett is to be praised and certainly not to be blamed for bringing forward his interesting scheme. But the proposals have hardly been heard of for quite a long time, and just as they did not commend themselves to the Labour Party as a whole so they did not win the necessary degree of general support. They appeared to be democratic, for they more effectively subjected ministerial power to the will of Parliament, and they were calculated to give to back-bench M.P.s not only greater influence over the Government but also valuable experience.

Nevertheless, there were and there remain substantial objections to Mr. Jowett's ideas. The life of the Minister would have been almost intolerable; his heavy departmental work would continue and indeed increase through the extensive labour involved in his Committee, in preparing himself to meet his Committee, and no doubt in preparing his own friends on the Committee, and possibly in seeking to placate the Opposition. Administration and legislation would be delayed because of the time taken by Committee discussions. Whilst it is a more or less accepted doctrine that the duty of the Opposition in Parliament is to oppose, it is another thing to give the Opposition a free hand in opposing and possibly obstructing current administration and the preparation of the heads of legislation not yet submitted to Parliament itself. It would have involved very heavy work for Members on both sides of the House, possibly to the detriment of their work in the House itself.

There is another objection from the point of view of the Opposition of the day itself. A persuasive Minister might well win the support of the Opposition members of his Committee, or a number of them, for his policy; when the report came to be considered by the House, the official Opposition might find its members on the Committee already committed. If they were thrown over this would be humiliating for them and would be used against the Opposition on the Floor. Similarly, if the members of the Committee from the Government side had been persuaded against the Minister by the Opposition both he and they would be embarrassed. Certainly these considerations can lead one to picture a good deal of parliamentary fun and merriment, but it would hardly be conducive to the effectiveness of either Parliament or Whitehall.

Finally, the proposals challenge the vital doctrine of the responsibility of Ministers to Parliament as a whole. We have already discussed this in considering the imposition of supervising Ministers over departmental Ministers. The objection obtains here also, for if the responsibility of Ministers were in a sense divided between responsibility to Parliament as a whole and to all-party committees it would, I think, be less democratic in practice, and back-stairs influences over government might well tend to increase. Whilst I respect the sincerity and ingenuity of Fred Jowett, I have never personally been able to accept his views. My devotion to local government is no less than my devotion to Parliament, but with an extensive experience of both I do not think it would be useful to aim at largely imposing upon Parliament the local government system any more than it would be desirable or practicable to impose the parliamentary system on local government.

Heavy Labours of M.P.s

Great as are the improvements and changes over the years in the organization and procedure of the House of Commons, and however largely effective the House is for its purpose, we must keep our minds open for possible further changes, improvements, and modifications, with a view to making our parliamentary institutions even more effective. Certainly there is a real problem in respect of parliamentary time and the amount of work and worry required under modern conditions from Members of the House of Commons. It is a hard life; for some it is more than a full-time job, for others nearly a full-time job. For myself, I think it is good for M.P.s to have something to do other than parliamentary work, and certainly to have time in which to travel at home and, upon occasion, abroad.

A House of Commons consisting of Members spending excessive hours at Westminister (which is inevitably a somewhat distracting place), and largely cut off from outside life and contact with people in industry and agriculture, is not good. The House of Commons is in danger of becoming a monastic institution, suffering from some degree of isolation and mental ingrowth. What the remedy is I am not sure. I wish I were. Maybe light will descend upon us: let us keep our minds open for it. What I am clear about is that the practice of the United States Congress and of the French Parliament, and the ideas of Mr. Lloyd George and Mr. Jowett, would add to our troubles unless we were to give up our rights on the Floor of the House—and that would not be well. Nor will Parliament help itself by adding to its labours through attempting to control in undue detail, e.g. local government and the nationalized industries. The problem is—and it is a very difficult one, for Parliament is inevitably much busier than it was a century or even fifty years ago—to lighten the labours of M.P.s without sacrificing the vital and essential rights and duties of our great parliamentary institutions.

The M.P. as an Individual

It will by now be seen how many opportunities of expression, consultation, and even agitation, are open to the Private Member of Parliament. But it may be asked, 'Has he opportunities of giving expression to his individual views in the House of Commons itself?' As a whole, the answer is yes. He can freely put Questions to Ministers either on the Order Paper or by way of supplementary Questions. He can in speeches put points of view which are his own rather than the general view of the party to which he belongs. It is true that he cannot speak in all the important debates, for there is much competition; and Mr. Speaker tends to leave a Member out of a big debate if he has recently spoken in another. Moreover, the Front Bench speakers necessarily occupy some time—back-bench M.P.s often complain that they take too much time.

Members of a party are not obliged to say exactly the same thing as each other. An M.P. can put down Motions or amendments to Motions or Bills, though in this case he would be wise to consult the Whips' Office or the appropriate Front Bench member of the party in case such action should be seriously embarrassing to the party. There is, however, something else to be said: if members of a parliamentary party are flagrantly disagreeing and are gravely at sixes-and-sevens, and particularly if they personally attack each other in public, it is obvious that the party will be damaged. A political party is a voluntary association of people who have agreed to co-operate with each other for certain general ends. To the extent that a party is democratic (and this varies), its general policy is arrived at after collective discussion in which members can participate, and decisions are reached by majority vote where necessary, though there are limits to this when the party is in power. Members of the party have certain rights, notably the right of discussion, argument, and voting at the party meeting. Having taken advantage of those rights, the general unity of the party would be imperilled and feelings aroused if members then went away and carried on as if no consultation had taken place. The man in a minority has a perfect right to seek to convert the majority, but it is desirable that the right should be exercised in a way which is least likely to damage the standing or reputation of the party. Of course, there are great occasions when the interests of the country—even in the view of a material number of M.P.s on the Government side of the House—require a change of Administration. That was what happened when the Chamberlain Government fell in 1940 on a vote on the Adjournment, even though it had a majority. In that case no dissolution occurred: Mr. Churchill took over.

There are public as well as party reasons for the views set out above. The British people rightly attach importance to a party being sufficiently coherent and united to give the country a Government not only of sound policy but of adequate strength and unity of purpose. The advice I gave, as Leader of the House of Commons, to the Parliamentary Labour Party when Labour was in power, was to the following effect: You are not all bound to say the same thing; you are free to express disagreement with Ministers; all I ask is that you will exercise these rights in a way calculated to cause the least friction and embarrassment. If, for example, you were to say, 'Mr. Speaker, the Minister is a traitor to the party, a liar and a crook', or words to that effect, you would not only be out of order: you would cause a first-class row. The better and the more effective way to put your case would be somewhat on the lines that 'I agree with my right honourable Friend about so-and-so, and I was delighted when I heard that he was proposing to do this or that but, Mr. Speaker, there is one point upon which I am afraid I do not see eye to eye with my right honourable Friend', and then state your case with clarity and courtesy. If you express your disagreement in this spirit, feelings will not be hurt, the Minister will not be provoked into a retaliatory attack, the issue is more likely to be discussed on its merits, and the good comradeship of the party will be protected.

The conduct of back-bench Labour Members under the Labour Government was generally in accordance with this advice. The result was a considerable degree of parliamentary individuality. The back-benchers did not become mechanical vocal instruments of the Front Bench, and there was variety of expression without fundamental conflict of purpose on the Government side. The House was alive, for in addition to the individual expression of view among Government supporters there were the vigorous clashes of debate between the two sides of the House.

The Free Vote

It is sometimes argued that there should be more frequent occasions when Members are free to vote as they wish, with the Whips off, particularly during the Committee Stage of Bills. Those who hold this view urge that it would give Members a better opportunity to express their opinions and feelings in the division Lobby and would indeed help them to feel a greater sense of personal responsibility for what Parliament was doing; that it is unreasonable that the Whips should systematically be put on in respect of Government Business on matters of detail or even where high moral principles of a non-party character are involved. I well understand this point of view and have been a party to taking the Whips off on a certain number of occasions. In 1930, on the Road Traffic Bill which I had introduced as Minister of Transport, the Whips were taken off in respect of a Government proposal to abolish the speed limit; and abolition was carried on the Floor of the House on a free vote. As Home Secretary in the war I brought forward, with the support of the Coalition Government, a proposal for the opening of theatres on Sundays under the same conditions as cinemas for the benefit of troops who were away from home. Nevertheless, I successfully urged the Government to take the Whips off. In this case we were defeated by eight votes—we would certainly have won if the Whips had been on. In the chapter on the House of Lords I recount the free vote which was accorded to the House of Commons on the question of capital punishment. Those favouring its suspension won in the division Lobby, but it is very doubtful whether a majority of public opinion was behind them; the subject had not been mentioned in the election programme of either party and in the end the Commons had to submit to the decision of the House of Lords to leave the subject out of the Criminal Justice Bill. On all these occasions some of the Members would have been happier if they could have had official assistance from the Whips in making up their minds. However, I hope I have shown that I am not the inveterate enemy of free voting. I must add, however, that many Ministers and parliamentarians of long experience are doubtful about its virtues and are of opinion that it should be resorted to only on Private Members' Business and otherwise on very rare occasions.

If it were left to Members to decide whether there should be a free vote of the House, parliamentary difficulty and confusion of an awkward character would in all probability arise. The merits of the question would become confused with a desire on the part of many Members for a free vote. Moreover, there could be much argument about what should or should not be eligible for a free vote. What may appear to be an issue of detail to back-benchers may not be so much a matter of detail or may at any rate involve serious repercussions which Ministers can see but which back-benchers cannot so readily understand. For example, during the consideration of the Education Bill in 1944 there was a revolt against the Government (not on a free vote) and an amendment was carried in favour of equal pay for men and women teachers. Was this a matter of detail? It could be so argued. It could be argued that women teachers have a stronger case on grounds of equal work than a good many other employed women. Alternatively, it could have been argued that here was a great matter of principle on which the House of Commons should be free to express itself and decide. Nevertheless, Mr. Churchill subsequently went to the House of Commons and made it reverse its decision as an issue of confidence, or at any rate persuaded it to do so. The Coalition Government took the view that this was certainly a matter where there would have been considerable repercussions in the Civil Service, the local government services, and, quite possibly, in private industry; and that if the principle was to be established in legislation it should not be for one calling only but after comprehensive consideration. I am not arguing the merits in this case; I mention it as an illustration of the difficulty in separating matters of detail from matters of broad public policy. And an Act of Parliament has to stand up as a coherent whole, or administrative and possibly legal trouble may well follow.

In Standing Committee upstairs, at any rate when there is a Government with a working majority, Members assert their independence with slightly more freedom than on the floor, even though it is officially discouraged. However, the Government is then in a stronger position because if fifty Members in Standing Committee upstairs out of over 600 M.P.s reach a decision opposed by Ministers the Government can, without much loss of face, accept it if it is not too great a matter of difficulty or, as often happens, it can have the decision reversed on the Floor of the House at Report Stage.

Back-bench Influence

Even occasional revolts against the Government on the part of its own supporters on the Floor, annoying as they may be at the time, are not wholly to be deplored. They give reality to parliamentary life, they stimulate public interest in parliamentary proceedings, and they may make a good many Members feel a good deal better afterwards, whether or not they have done any good, although they will make others very cross. I would, however, add that such things can be dangerous if they are too frequent, or if personal animus or motives are manifested, or if they imperil the essential unity of the party, or embarrass the Government to such an extent that it is seriously weakened. There were a number of back-bench revolts during the Labour Government of 1945–50, some of which were bad and embarrassing, but a number of which were healthy and did good. But although such luxuries could be occasionally afforded with the big Labour majority of 1945–50, they just could not be afforded with the majority of six in the Parliament of 1950–1 any more than the subsequent Conservative Government could afford them. This is one of the reasons I was sorry about the small Labour majority, for it meant that almost any revolt or abstentions could bring the Government down, and this was a responsibility which, quite understandably, nobody was disposed to take. However, it also imposed restraint upon the Government. So let the electorate remember that whilst there are objections to excessively large parliamentary majorities, there are even greater objections to a majority so small that the legitimate freedom of the M.P. is gravely limited. Reasonable unity, discipline, and good comradeship are necessary, but I should not like what may be called 150 per cent. discipline. That would mean parliamentary death.

I have dealt at some length with the rights and obligations of the individual Member of Parliament, and have explained the channels and processes through which he can make his individuality felt. What we have been concerned with is the maintenance of happy relationships between the Government and its supporters, and fair and just opportunities for the Opposition, combined with the provision of proper opportunities for the back-bencher on both sides to get consideration for his point of view. We have seen how the Whips have the double duty of promoting support for the Front Bench, but no less acting as channels of complaint and criticism from the back-benchers to the Front Bench, and even the Cabinet itself. Above all, the members of the Cabinet and other Ministers must play their part. When their business is before the House they have to lead the House of Commons and seek to get their view accepted. But if they act or speak—even in relation to the Opposition—as if they were masters of the House of Commons, they will be riding for a fall.

It may be asked whether I have not exaggerated the responsiveness of Ministers and the Cabinet to back-bench opinion and that of the House as a whole. Do the Ministers not get away with most things, in the short run at least? With most things, yes; but there have been noticeable exceptions. In the course of parliamentary history there have been a number of instances of Ministers making concessions or changes in policy following upon pressure in Parliament. Some examples occur to me. There was the case (to which I have just referred) of the free vote on the proposal to suspend capital punishment in the Criminal Justice Bill. The fall of the Chamberlain Government in 1940 was the result of back-bench revolt. The Milk Industry Bill of December 1938 was not proceeded with in view of the objections which were raised in many quarters, being postponed for further discussion and re-examination. The Judges' Remuneration Bill did not pass in the Session of 1952–3 owing to parliamentary objections to the 'tax-free' element in the Bill. The Hoare-Laval Pact in connexion with Mussolini's aggression against Abyssinia led to a parliamentary storm and Sir Samuel Hoare had to resign as Foreign Secretary.

The reader may wonder why the list is not very much longer, but he must take into account a very important consideration. That is—as has been amply shown—that there exist many channels through which Ministers are made aware of their own back-bench opinion, through debates on the Address and on other occasions. Speeches in the country and articles in newspapers and periodicals opposed to the Government provide extensive opportunities for the Opposition to make its views known. In considering projected legislation or policy a sensible Government will take all opinions into account before becoming committed, and so it is likely that modifications will have been made before the publication of Bills. This may be described as the process of concession in advance of parliamentary proceedings, though sometimes Ministers may prefer to save up concessions until Parliament is dealing with the matter. To the extent that the Government in shaping its policy has anticipated back-bench and Opposition criticisms, Ministers are entitled to the credit. Such concessions of course cannot very well be recorded in the columns of Hansard. They do, however, tend to limit the number of publicly known occasions on which concessions have been made.

Upon occasions a Government may semi-officially or unofficially consult the Opposition on policy or projected legislation, especially in cases where the matter is not sharply controversial, at any rate in the party sense. The result may affect the decision of the Government to proceed with the measure. This contact may be upon the basis of conveying information of decisions reached as a matter of courtesy, or of ascertaining and possibly taking into account the reactions of the Opposition, or of estimating whether a non-party Bill under consideration is likely to prove sharply controversial or not. These contacts or consultations are private and as a whole useful within a proper field.

If a Government has been careless in estimating parliamentary opinion and has to make an excessive number of concessions it will lose caste—it will get the reputation of a Government that does not know its mind, a Government of shilly-shally. This was indeed the case with the two minority Labour Governments, partly through their inexperience or faults, partly owing to the imperfect relations which existed between them and their back-benchers and partly because, not having a majority, they were liable to be 'pushed around' by the Conservatives or the Liberals or both. Sometimes, indeed, one of the other parties would combine with rebellious Labour back-benchers in revolt. It is, however, fair to remember that Mr. MacDonald had no previous ministerial experience and that the same was true of most of his colleagues. The minority Labour Governments gave Labour valuable experience.

One of the decisive issues upon which the minority Labour Government of 1924 was brought down was the prosecution of a Communist (Mr. J. R. Campbell) authorized by the Attorney-General (Sir Patrick Hastings) on the alleged ground that he had attempted to weaken the loyalty of the Armed Forces of the Crown. Following upon Labour back-bench pressure the proceedings against Mr. Campbell were brought to an end by the prosecution and it was wrongly alleged that the Prime Minister (Mr. Ramsay MacDonald) had sought to bring pressure upon the Attorney-General to that end. The Conservatives moved a vote of censure; the Liberals moved an amendment in favour of a Select Committee of Inquiry. Mr. MacDonald was defiant, possibly hoping that the Conservatives would vote with the Government against the Liberal amendment and that then the Liberals would vote with the Government against the Conservative vote of censure. This would have been very nice for the Government, but anticipating this possibility the Conservatives announced in the course of the debate that they would abandon their vote of censure in favour of the Liberal amendment. That settled it. The Government were defeated. Electorally the Government had severely damaged itself; its weakness pleased nobody. One beneficial result of this experience was that the majority Labour Governments of 1945–51 were scrupulously careful not to interfere with the independent judgement of the Law Officers of the Crown on judicial proceedings.

Public Opinion

One of the duties of the Government—and it is not always an easy one to discharge—is to estimate the reaction of public opinion to proposals under consideration and the extent to which those reactions should influence Government policy. We are a democracy and there is clearly an obligation on Ministers to take public opinion into account. A wise Government would not wish to bring itself into sharp conflict with predominant public opinion or, unless the public interest really required otherwise, with informed bodies of opinion entitled to respect and consideration. Such estimates of public opinion may be right or wrong. Some politicians have a valuable 'hunch' as to what the British people are or will be thinking about a given matter. Others are failures in this respect and a liability to their party as a consequence. More than once a policy has been changed after it was announced as a result of extensive public criticism, and certainly the ministerial estimate of what the public will or will not stand is a factor in the shaping of policy.

The art of judging public opinion is not an easy one. The most desirable requisite is an extensive knowledge of the outlook of the people in various walks of life and an understanding of how their minds work. It is important to have a respect and not a contempt for the general body of good citizens. It is undesirable to cultivate a vindictive relish in offending the susceptibilities (even if mistaken) of large numbers of one's fellow citizens—this is engaged in now and again by the 'suicide clubs' of both the great political parties. On the other hand, if measures which, on the face of them, will prove to be unpopular are vitally necessary in the public interest, conscientious Ministers will probably decide to go ahead confident in their ability to explain the public necessity to the generally fair-minded and not ungenerous British people. Ministers should have a human liking for the people as well as for Parliament, for it is not easy to understand either people or Parliament unless one likes and respects them.

One cannot effectively serve the people unless one likes them and does one's best to understand them and how their minds are working, even when one thinks them wrong. And as a whole the British people are a great people, well worthy of respect and of conscientious and upright service as well as frankness—even though at times it be an unwelcome and annoying frankness—from their public representatives. For there are exceptional times when the public may be swept by an emotion, possibly hatred which, for the time being, leads them to wrong conclusions, although later on when calmness has been restored their fairness and commonsense will reassert itself.

I went through such a necessary but not very pleasant experience at the hands of a large body of my fellow citizens when I released Sir Oswald and Lady Mosley from detention under Defence Regulation 18B, subject to strict conditions. In rather less sympathetic language than I am using that considerable Liberal statesman, Sir William Harcourt, put his own view of the duty of the statesman in such circumstances in his introduction to the collected edition of the 'Historicus' Letters (1863): 'To be firm when the vulgar are undecided, to be calm in the midst of passion and to be brave in the presence of panic are the characteristics of those who are fit to be the rulers of men.' He put it another way when writing to Joseph Chamberlain in

1880:[1] 'There is no danger in facing a difficulty, but much in running away from it.'

Love of the House of Commons

So it is with the House of Commons. It will respect one for standing up to it so long as one uses the language of respect for the institution, though it will be well for one to feel confident that in due course the House will come to see that one was right. But above all, if one is to be effective in the House of Commons one must love the place. The House has an uncanny capacity for knowing who really likes it and who does not. The House will forgive much in a Minister if it likes him and if it knows he likes the House. I remember an incident that shocked me during the lifetime of the 1929–31 minority Labour Government. I was sitting beside the Prime Minister (Mr. Ramsay MacDonald) on the Treasury Bench. He had been rather cruelly and harshly attacked about the mounting unemployment by Sir Kingsley Wood from the Conservative Front Bench. Mr. MacDonald had a rough time of it, but when at the end he whispered to me, 'Herbert, I hate this place', I was deeply shocked, and began to understand why in some way, considerable as he was as a writer on constitutional and parliamentary matters, Mr. MacDonald, at any rate as Prime Minister, did not achieve an effective sympathetic relationship with the House of Commons.

Nobody can play a great and enduring part in that Assembly unless he knows what he is talking about and is sincere; and a successful relationship cannot be achieved unless one respects and even loves the House. And for no Ministers is this more important than the Prime Minister and the Leader of the House of Commons. Again I quote Sir William Harcourt, who, on taking farewell of the House of Commons as its Leader, stated on 24 June 1895: 'I would ask leave to say that for every man who has taken part in the noble conflicts of parliamentary life, the chiefest ambition of all ambitions, whether in the majority or in the minority, must be to stand well with the House of Commons.'

Those are my sentiments also.

[1] *Life of Sir William Harcourt*, by A. G. Gardiner, vol. i, p. 379.

CHAPTER IX

The House of Lords

RELATIONS between the House of Lords and the Government are very different from those between the House of Commons and the Government. In earlier times the House of Lords was a very powerful Chamber; indeed, at one time, more powerful than the Commons. The Prime Minister was then frequently a Peer and so were many of his senior colleagues in the Cabinet. However, not since Lord Salisbury resigned in 1902 has a Prime Minister been in the Lords, and by common assent it is now agreed that he must be a member of the Commons. The Chancellor of the Exchequer must also sit in the Commons; not since 1767 has one sat in the Lords. The claims of the House of Commons on a Minister concerned with the liberty of the subject (notably the Home Secretary) or on a Minister discharging functions which are of extensive concern in the daily lives of the people has tended to increase and has resulted in fewer Ministers of importance sitting in the House of Lords. Mr. Churchill somewhat reversed this process during 1951–3 by drawing his supervising or co-ordinating Ministers (the so-called Overlords) from that House.

Powers of the Lords

When we came into power in 1945 the powers of the House of Lords were already considerably restricted by the Parliament Act, 1911. This Act provided that a Bill certified by the Speaker of the House of Commons to be a Money Bill should become law within one month of its having been passed by the Commons and sent up to the Lords, whether or not their Lordships had consented to it within that time limit. The 1911 Act also made it possible for any other Public Bill (except a Bill to extend the maximum duration of Parliament beyond five years) which had been passed by the House of Commons in three successive Sessions (whether of the same Parliament or not) to receive the Royal Assent despite its rejection by the House of Lords, provided that two years had elapsed between the Second Reading in the Commons in the first Session and the Third Reading in the Commons in the third Session.

Moreover, a Government defeat in the Lords does not constitutionally involve an issue of confidence in the Government as such a vote would in the House of Commons. So both practice and statutory provision have materially lessened the powers of the House of Lords.

However, we were apprehensive about what we considered to be the power for mischief that still existed in the House of Lords during the later Sessions of a Parliament. Therefore we brought in legislation to amend the Parliament Act, 1911, so as to limit further the powers of the Lords to delay the passage of Bills approved by the Commons. We proposed to reduce the three successive Sessions over a period of not less than two years to two Sessions and one year. This caused great controversy, and the Bill was passed only by the use of the 1911 Act. Mr. Chuter Ede and I had to make so many speeches to the same end about this Bill under the 1911 procedure that we (and the Opposition as well) found ourselves somewhat repetitive and a little bored by the time we had finished.

The new Parliament Act received the Royal Assent on 16 December 1949. But Section 1 provided that its amendment of the 1911 Act would 'be deemed to have had effect from the beginning of the session in which the Bill' for the 1949 Act 'originated', i.e. from October 1947. The Act also made clear that even a Bill already rejected twice by the House of Lords after October 1947, but before the Bill for the 1949 Act had received the Royal Assent, could be presented to His Majesty as soon as the new Parliament Bill had received the Royal Assent, provided that twelve months had already elapsed in the Commons between Second Reading of the rejected Bill in the first Session and its Third Reading in the second Session.

Retrospective legislation is bad, but in this exceptional case we held it to be justified as enabling the will of the Commons to prevail over the Lords. In the event, though there was talk of using the retrospective provisions to deal with the strong objection of the House of Lords to the Iron and Steel Bill, a compromise was reached which avoided the necessity for this course of action.

All this is not to say, however, that the House of Lords is

devoid of either importance or utility. The active members (and the great majority are inactive) include men of ability and extensive public experience. A substantial proportion of those who attend are former Members of the House of Commons and some others have acquired valuable experience in many walks of life. Consequently, whilst I certainly would not say that debates in the Lords are more important than those in the Commons, debates in the Lords have a character and importance of their own and are not without their influence on public opinion and Government policy. The style of speech is quieter, less oratorical, and less sharply controversial than in the Commons. Strong language and 'political knockabout' in debate are discouraged. The general atmosphere of the two Houses is in strong contrast. Former Members of the House of Commons find that it takes time to adapt themselves to the lordly style of speech.

• *How the Lords Function Together*

A remarkable feature about the House of Lords is that although they have many Standing Orders, they have few rules or Standing Orders governing debate. There are two Standing Orders dealing specifically with debate, namely, that a Peer can speak not more than once on any Motion (except that the mover can reply) and that debate must be relevant to the question before the House. In addition there are a number of unwritten rules sanctioned by custom, such as those forbidding quotations from non-ministerial speeches in the other House, or the reading of speeches; but rules of debate are few and widely interpreted. The Lord Chancellor, a Minister who is also Speaker of the House and sits on the Woolsack, has but little controlling power over debate, his duty being substantially confined to putting the question on all Motions which are submitted to the House and 'collecting the voices' or stating the results of divisions. Moreover, he freely takes part in debate, moving to the place he occupies in the House as a Peer, as opposed to the Woolsack which he occupies as Speaker. The Woolsack is technically outside the House.

Despite all this, however, their Lordships are rarely disorderly. They are probably the only Parliamentary assembly in the world in which the members collectively have to take care of their own procedure and order without a presiding officer to control and guide them. And they do it very well. They do not address the Chair, they address 'My Lords', the House as a whole. Through some 'usual channel' or other they agree the order of speakers. Tradition and a collective sense of the proprieties keep debate orderly. On controversial matters they develop warmth in their debates and even some sharpness of cut and thrust, but it is all much subdued as compared with the atmosphere of the House of Commons.

There are two groups in the House not to be found in the House of Commons: the Law Lords who function as the highest Court in the land; and the two Archbishops and twenty-four Bishops in their robes. The presence of the Bishops of the established church is another parliamentary anomaly which it is impossible to defend on grounds of formal democracy, but the Bishops make their contribution, and so long as the Lords do not exercise decisive political power I, personally, would not seek to eliminate them as members of the House of Peers, though I think their numbers might perhaps be reduced.

So here we have this remarkable institution with much diminished but responsible powers, which if irresponsibly used could still bring about real parliamentary and constitutional trouble. The avoidance of that trouble is dependent on the good sense of the House and especially of its leaders. It is fortunate that good sense has, as a whole, been in the ascendant in recent years.

• *Non-legislative Work of the Lords*

Much of this chapter will be concerned with the legislative functions of the House of Lords, but it should not be thought that the House spends all or even the bulk of its time in discharging its legislative functions. The Lords are, in general, expeditious in examining legislation; and, notwithstanding that their sittings are much shorter than those of the House of Commons, the Lords are able to devote many days to the consideration of Motions promoted by back-bench as well as Front Bench Members. Sometimes these debates are about high issues of public policy such as overseas affairs or the liberty of the subject or the economic state of the nation, and at other times they may deal with relatively small matters which, nevertheless, are of interest to sections of the public. The usual form of Motion is to call attention to a matter and to move for Papers. For example, according to the *Official Report* of the House of Lords for 29 October 1952 (col. 1091) Lord Ogmore 'rose to call attention to the political and security situations in Kenya, with special reference to the reported activities of the Mau Mau society, and to the emergency legislation lately passed in the Colony; and to move for Papers'. From the other side of the House a Conservative back-bencher, Earl Howe, on 22 October 1952 (col. 837), 'rose to call attention to the continuation of crimes of violence towards women and other defenceless persons, and to ask whether the existing penalties which the courts have power to inflict in such cases are adequate to protect the public; and to move for Papers'. The most appropriate Minister in the Lords will usually intervene to state the Government view, and it is common for Lords with special knowledge of the subject to take part in the debate. It is exceptional for a division to take place. The debate usually ends by the mover of the Motion asking leave to withdraw it, whereupon the *Official Report* records: 'Motion for Papers, by leave, withdrawn.'

One of the highlights of recent House of Lords' debates was that on the Conservative Government's intention at some future time to promote commercially sponsored television. The debate[1] was initiated by Lord Reith on the following Motion: 'To call attention to the Government White Paper on Broadcasting Policy (Cmd. 8550); and to move for Papers.' It will be noted that the Motion was neutral in its terms; it expressed no opinion, though the subject debated was very controversial. It was an impressive debate covering two days and was maintained at a high level. Extensively reported in the Press, the debate attracted a great deal of public attention. At the end the Motion was, by leave, withdrawn.

Debates and votes on Motions in the Lords may or may not affect government policy. Constitutionally no Government is obliged to take any notice of declarations, not directly involving legislation, in Motions passed by the House of Lords. A Lords' vote of no confidence in the Government of the day does not of

[1] 176 *H.L. Deb.* 1289–1448 (22 and 26 May 1952).

itself imperil the Administration. All this, however, is not to say that such debates in the Lords are without effect. That will depend upon the subject together with the merits of the debate. They can, and at times do, stir public opinion, or they may ventilate real public grievances or have repercussions in the House of Commons; so they may make the Government conscious of some failure or shortcoming. No Government, therefore, whatever its political complexion, studiously and systematically ignores the opinion of the House of Lords. Indeed, it is the duty of the Leader of the House of Lords in the Cabinet to indicate to his colleagues the feelings of his House on subjects under consideration.

Questions may be put down for oral or written answer; but compared with the Commons there are few of either. Sometimes there are no oral Questions and there are seldom as many as half a dozen. On the other hand, unlike the Commons, the Lords in certain circumstances allow short debates on oral Questions. As most Ministers sit in the House of Commons the Questions in the Lords are not directed to particular Ministers but to Her Majesty's Government. The supplementary Questions are not limited in number, at times they can run for a while and at other times there will be none. Nearly always, however, in contrast to the cut and thrust of Question Time in the House of Commons, they are polite.

• *The Lords as Legislators*

Provided that party politics are not heavily involved the Lords are usually businesslike and competent in the revision of legislation. I was impressed by the contrast between Lords and Commons during the Committee Stages of my Bill which became the Road Traffic Act, 1930. The Bill was important but politically non-controversial. It sought to bring about much-needed reforms, in the interests of safety, of road traffic regulation, and improvements in the licensing of public service vehicles. In the Standing Committee of the Commons I experienced about four months of irritating, meticulous talk and obstruction, the aim of the Opposition being to prevent another Bill (which was controversial) coming before the Committee. I found it a very tiring and exasperating experience.

There could have been no greater contrast between this and the proceedings that had taken place on the Committee Stage in the Lords, where my valued Parliamentary Secretary, Earl Russell, had been in charge of the Bill. Within a few days their Lordships had made a workmanlike job of their Committee Stage revisions. An amendment would be moved in about one-tenth of the time that would have been taken in the Commons. In many cases Lord Russell would say, 'My Lords, this amendment really will not do', and in a few courteous but plain sentences explain why. Whereupon it was highly probable that the Peer who had moved the amendment would beg leave to withdraw it. Of course there were some discussions of greater length, but the handling of this Bill in the Lords' Committee of the Whole House impressed me very much with its businesslike character and its objectivity. I fear that I could not pay these tributes in respect of the later Labour Government's controversial legislation, especially the Iron and Steel Bill; but it is right to give credit where credit is due.

All Private Bills promoted by a local authority or other outside bodies or persons have to be considered by the House of Lords as well as the House of Commons. As with the Commons, the Bills are referred to a Committee for the Committee Stage, a considerable amount of work being involved for the Members concerned. The House of Lords, like the Commons, enjoys a high reputation for the fair and just hearing of the parties and the consideration of the Bills. Unlike Public Bills, if the Lords throw a Private Bill out on Second Reading or on Preamble in Committee the Commons are powerless and so are the promoters. Private Bills may start in either House and sometimes the Committee Stage is considered by a joint Committee of the two Houses.

General Relations between Lords and Commons

The case against the Lords in past years has been that with their Conservative majority they were more considerate to the legislation of Conservative Governments than to that of Labour or Liberal Governments. This was certainly the case up to and including the Labour Government of 1929–31. The resulting difficulties were the major reason for the limitations which have been imposed on the powers of the Lords. Generally speaking, however, during the Labour Governments of 1945–51 they treated us with consideration, as indeed was our due. This was largely owing to the ability, tact, and wisdom of two men: Viscount Addison, the Leader of the House of Lords, and the Marquis of Salisbury, the Leader of the Conservative Opposition. Lord Addison, as the Leader of the House of Lords, and I as Leader of the House of Commons, often exchanged a joke to the effect that his majority, a hostile one, was in front of him, whereas my majority, a friendly one, was behind me. He was an adroit and respected Leader of the House of Lords. He would champion the proper rights of their Lordships' House in the Cabinet, as was his duty, but he would competently and persuasively champion the rights of the Government and of the House of Commons in the House of Lords. He was ably assisted by the Lord Chancellor (Lord Jowitt), the First Lord of the Admiralty (Lord Hall), the Minister of Civil Aviation and later First Lord of the Admiralty (Lord Pakenham), the Government Chief Whip (Lord Shepherd), and others. Much business which could otherwise have been difficult was amicably settled between the party leaders in Lord Addison's room, and much of the credit belonged to Lord Addison and Lord Salisbury. Lord Salisbury was, in general, anxious to avoid serious conflict between the two Houses, and he exercised a restraining hand upon his followers. Certainly the Lords, on a fair number of occasions, insisted upon making amendments to Bills against the Government's advice, but in most cases they did not insist upon their amendments when they were rejected by the House of Commons.

Procedure for Settling Differences between the Houses

I will now explain the procedure for resolving differences between the two Houses on amendments to Bills made by one or other of the Houses. I will take the case of amendments reaching the Commons from the Lords, but the procedure is much the same if amendments are made by the Commons to legislation originating in the House of Lords. When the amended Bill is received from the Lords a Paper is printed setting out the Lords' amendments. An Order for the consideration of the

Lords' amendments will be set down on the Commons Order Paper for the appropriate day, and unless exceptionally large issues are raised, the House will consider them after 10 p.m. The proceedings commence with a Minister moving that the Lords' amendments to the . . . Bill be now considered. This being agreed to, the amendments are then dealt with one by one. It is almost certain that the bulk of them are uncontentious. In this case the Motion is, 'That this House doth agree with the Lords in the said Amendment' and if (as is most often the case in such circumstances) there is no opposition, Mr. Speaker will put the question by saying, 'As many as are of that opinion say Aye; of the contrary No; the Ayes have it.' Of course, if the Opposition wishes to be troublesome it can talk on such amendments, but usually they go through without discussion, and indeed a substantial proportion will have been promoted by the Government to correct drafting or to comply with undertakings given by the Minister to the House of Commons when the Bill was being considered by that House. On some amendments, however, points of policy will arise. In that case if the Government propose to agree with the Lords there may be opposition and a division may follow. If the Government do not agree with the Lords on an amendment, the Motion will be, 'That this House doth disagree with the Lords in the said Amendment'. This, like the other Motion, is, of course, debatable, and a vote may take place. If, when all the amendments have been considered, some have been disagreed to, a committee is appointed to settle the message to the Lords indicating the reasons for the Commons disagreement. Amendments may also be made to the Lords' amendments. It is then for the Lords to decide whether or not they will insist upon the disputed amendments. If they do not, that is the end of the matter, but if they do a message comes back to the Commons from the Lords indicating their insistence upon the amendments, which are again considered by the Commons, the Motion being under a similar procedure, 'That this House doth insist on its disagreement with the Lords in the said Amendment', or that it does not insist. Sometimes an alternative amendment may be proposed. If, however, direct disagreement is registered for the second time (no alternative being offered) and the other House (whether Lords or Commons) does not give way the Bill is lost. But it is more likely that unofficial conversations will take place with a view to a compromise being agreed.

In earlier days such disagreements could be so serious that even though the Bill had not been rejected outright by the Lords on Second or Third Reading the Bill was, nevertheless, killed by the failure of the two Houses to reach agreement, in which case the Lords were usually charged with setting aside the will of the elected representatives of the people. However, at any rate for the time being, such difficulties have been reduced to a minimum, and during the Labour Governments of 1945–51 the only case in which Lords and Commons failed to reach agreement of some sort was on the proposal of the Commons to suspend capital punishment. But we had considerable difficulty in reaching a compromise over the Iron and Steel Bill.

Iron and Steel in the Lords

The proposal to nationalize the Iron and Steel industry aroused sharp controversy between the two Houses. In the end the controversy concentrated on the date on which the Bill, which ultimately became the Iron and Steel Act, 1949, should come into operation. When first published on 29 October 1948 the Bill named the vesting date as 1 May 1950 or such later date as the Minister of Supply might direct, but not later than 18 months after the passing of the Bill. The Second Reading was given on 17 November 1948, and on 9 May 1949 the Bill received its Third Reading in the House of Commons after a Motion for its rejection had been defeated by 333 votes to 203.

The Second Reading debate in the House of Lords took place on 24 and 25 May 1949 when Lord Salisbury suggested the line of action to be taken by the Opposition Peers. He recommended the House not to reject the Bill outright but to amend and improve it in Committee, and in particular to put in an amendment to defer its operation until 1 October 1950, i.e. after the latest date for the next General Election. This course, he claimed, would avoid departing from the Opposition's policy in the House of Lords of not rejecting any measure included in the Government's 1945 election programme, while still achieving the desired object of enabling the electorate to have 'another look' at the Bill. If the Government were returned, he said, nothing could stop the Bill from becoming law, and if they were defeated it would be clear that the electors rejected iron and steel nationalization. Lord Samuel announced that the Liberal Peers regarded the iron and steel industry, with its need to take risks and make quick decisions daily, as the least suitable of all industries for nationalization, and would support the amendment proposed by Lord Salisbury to postpone the date of operation of the Bill until October 1950. The Bill was then given a Second Reading without a division.

During the Committee Stage in the House of Lords, which lasted from 23 June to 4 July 1949, a number of Opposition amendments proposing important changes in the Bill were carried against the Government, the principal being a series of amendments to postpone the vesting date from 1 May 1950 to 1 July 1951, but not later than eighteen months after the coming into force of the Act. Moving the amendments on 29 June, Lord Salisbury explained that they were consequential on an amendment which would be introduced later in Committee to delay the coming into operation of the Act until 1 October 1950, i.e. until after the General Election, in order to give the electorate a chance of expressing a considered opinion on the nationalization proposals and to enable the Government, before bringing the scheme into force, to make certain they had the support of the people. The amendment was supported by Lord Samuel on behalf of the Liberal Peers. Lord Addison, the Lord Privy Seal, declared that the Government could not accept the position that an unrepresentative and unelected Chamber had a right to demand a second mandate from the people and refuse to pass Bills introduced by a Government with a large majority in the House of Commons. Nevertheless, the amendment was carried against the Government by 89 votes to 22. The related amendment, to postpone the operation of the Act until 1 October 1950, was introduced by Lord Swinton on 4 July and carried without further debate.

The Lords' amendments were considered by the House of Commons on 25 and 26 July 1949 in a continuous sitting lasting over twenty hours. Mr. G. R. Strauss, the Minister of Supply, explained at the outset that, of about sixty amendments, the Government proposed to accept twenty-eight, most of which were concerned with drafting and none of which conflicted with the Government's general intentions, but to reject the others. After debate, the principal amendment, to postpone the vesting date until 1 July 1951, was rejected by 285 votes to 137.

On 28 July the House of Lords considered the Commons' reason for disagreeing with the rejected amendments. After a protest by Lord Salisbury against the 'cavalier treatment' to which the House of Lords had been subjected after it had done its best to improve the Bill and make it workable, it was decided not to insist on any amendments rejected by the Commons, except those postponing the vesting date until 1 July 1951 and the operation of the Act until 1 October 1950. A Government Motion that the first of these amendments also should not be insisted upon was defeated by 103 votes to 29, and the House then accepted without a further division the Conservative Motion that it should insist upon the remainder of this group of amendments.

Had the situation remained thus, the Iron and Steel Bill could not have been enacted until the new Parliament Bill, with its retrospective provisions, had received the Royal Assent. However, on 15 November 1949 the Government announced the terms of a compromise proposed by them as to the dates in the Iron and Steel Bill, and amendments were tabled by the Minister of Supply on the same day which provided (1) for the changing of the vesting date from 1 May 1950, as named in the Bill, to 1 January 1951 (instead of to 1 July 1951, as insisted upon by the House of Lords); or to 'such later date, not more than 12 months later, as the Minister of Supply may by Order substitute'; (2) for the deferment of appointments to the proposed Iron and Steel Corporation until 1 October 1950 at the earliest. Since the appointment of the members of the Corporation would be the first step to nationalization, this amendment was equivalent to delaying the operation of the main provisions of the Act until 1 October 1950, i.e. until after the forthcoming General Election.

In moving the amendments on 16 November 1949, Mr. Strauss explained that when the Bill was originally introduced the Government had fixed 1 May 1950 as the vesting date because they had assumed that the measure would receive the Royal Assent before the summer recess in 1949. The Lords' action, however, had so delayed the Bill that it was now apparent that even if it became law early in 1950 under the new Parliament Act, the takeover could not be arranged for the original date without so rushing the preliminary steps as to jeopardize the successful launching of the scheme. After asserting that the House of Lords had acted contrary to all principles of democratic government by preventing a measure already approved by the electorate and passed by the Commons being carried into effect until the electorate have pronounced upon it a second time, Mr. Strauss claimed that the Government amendments would go a long way towards meeting the Lords' object of delay and at the same time preserve the important features of the Bill without making nonsense of many of its provisions. In conclusion he maintained that in putting forward the above amendments the Government were facing the realities of a situation which they were powerless to alter; and emphasized that if Parliament accepted them, the Bill 'undamaged in its structure and effectiveness', would be on the Statute Book immediately, ready to be implemented in full if the Government were returned to power.

Mr. Churchill, accepting the amendments on behalf of the Opposition, said that a careful consideration of the differences in form between them and the Lords' amendments which the Government was rejecting had satisfied him that 'for all practical purposes they mean the same thing'. After predicting that it was 'very likely' that the amendments would also be accepted by the House of Lords, he emphasized that the Opposition were 'very glad that the issue should be presented in so clear-cut a form to the electors', and declared that in 'making sure that the people are effectively consulted on the proposals' the House of Lords had once again vindicated its wisdom and sagacity and rendered the nation a service. After I had declared that the substitution of a later vesting date was entirely due to 'the intolerable interference of their Lordships with the decision of the people', the amendments were agreed to without a division.

On 24 November 1949 the Government's amendments were accepted without dissent by the House of Lords. In recommending this course of action, Lord Salisbury protested against my description of the Lords' action and claimed that the Government's decision to delay the operation of the Bill was 'a victory for constitutional procedure and . . . a complete justification of the existence of a Second Chamber'. The Bill received the Royal Assent on the same day.

Capital Punishment

The other disagreement between the two Houses apart from the dispute about the amendment of the Parliament Act, 1911, was on the Commons' proposal to suspend capital punishment. The Criminal Justice Bill enacted as the Criminal Justice Act, 1948, was introduced in the House of Commons on 31 October 1947, and as published on 4 November contained no proposal for the suspension of capital punishment. The Second Reading debate took place in the Commons on 27 and 28 November and was concluded without a division. On the question of the death penalty, Mr. Chuter Ede (Home Secretary) presented to the House certain details of criminal statistics indicating an increase in crimes of violence between 1938 and 1946. In the circumstances the Government felt that the time was not opportune for the inclusion in the Bill of provisions for the suspension or abolition of the death penalty. 'The Government', Mr. Ede declared, 'recognise that this is a matter on which very strong individual conscientious feelings are held, and on which the division does not follow the usual party lines.' They suggested, therefore, that if an amendment to deal with the death penalty was moved, this should be done on the Report Stage so that the decision should be taken by the whole House, when the Government would leave the final decision to a free vote. Mr. Osbert Peake, giving an assurance that the Bill would not be debated by the Opposition on party lines, said that capital punishment should be retained on the ground that if the Home Office thought the abolition of the death penalty would be a dangerous experiment in 1938, it would be still more dangerous now in view of the tremendous increase in crimes of violence after the war.

On 14 April 1948, during the Report Stage of the Bill, the House debated a new clause which proposed that for an experimental period of five years the death penalty for murder should be suspended and substituted by life imprisonment and that the five-year period might be extended with or without a further time limit by Order in Council on a Motion by each House of

Parliament. This new clause was tabled by 147 M.P.s of all parties, including 135 Labour Members. Winding up the debate, Mr. Chuter Ede said the Government found that they could not recommend the House to support the clause as they believed the time was not ripe for undertaking this reform. On a free vote, contrary to this advice, the clause was carried by 245 to 222 votes, a majority of 23 in favour of the suspension of the death penalty.

In the House of Lords on 27 April 1948 the Lord Chancellor (Lord Jowitt) moved the Second Reading of the Bill as amended by the Commons and declared himself personally opposed to the suspension of the death penalty as it acted as a deterrent. However, if it was repugnant to a large section of the population as had been shown by the recent vote in the Commons, he was prepared to accept that vote and to try the experiment, though with misgiving and anxiety, but also with hope that his worst fears might not be realized. Viscount Simon insisted that Parliament had no right to risk making an experiment which might put innocent lives in jeopardy, and that there was nothing to suggest that public approval had been given to the abolition of the death penalty. Both Lord Halifax and Lord Salisbury spoke on the constitutional position. Repudiating the Lord Chancellor's suggestion that the House of Lords must accept the narrow vote in the Commons as conclusive, they maintained that, having regard to the gravity of the issue, the force and power of the arguments deployed in the debate, and the fact that this was not an ordinary question of political difference between parties but one which cut across party lines, the House of Lords must decide on the merits of the case to the best of the ability and conscience of its Members. Lord Salisbury also spoke of the indications that the country as a whole was heavily against abolition, mentioning that he had received moving letters, not confined only to members of his own party, but including letters from members of the Labour Party, appealing to the House of Lords to save the country, and that all the letters without exception had been opposed to abolition. The Lord Chancellor's suggestion that they must accept the Commons' decision 'like that of an umpire' was, he maintained, entirely contrary to the Constitution, adding that it was not the Commons or the Lords that was the 'umpire' but the British people.

The Lord Chancellor, replying, made it clear that the House of Lords had constitutionally a perfect right to send the matter back to the Commons for consideration, and that his acceptance of the Commons' free vote was only his personal opinion. The House of Lords then gave an unopposed Second Reading to the Bill.

A Motion by Lord Llewellin to delete from the Bill the provision for the suspension of the death penalty was adopted after another two-day debate at the Committee Stage on 2 June by 181 votes to 28, thus reversing the Commons' decision.

On 9 June 1948 a meeting of the Parliamentary Labour Party expressed general agreement with a Government proposal to frame a compromise clause on the death penalty to be inserted into the Criminal Justice Bill. This new clause, which sought to retain the death penalty only for certain categories of murder committed with 'express malice', was debated in the House of Commons on 15 July. After discussion, the Motion to disagree with the Lords' amendment in removing from the Bill the original clause suspending the death penalty was carried by 332 votes to 196, and an amendment moved by Mr. Chuter Ede giving effect to the Government's compromise clause was carried by 307 votes to 209.

The House of Lords on 20 July rejected the Government's compromise proposal by 99 votes to 19. The new clause was severely criticized by Lord Goddard and other Judges. Lord Salisbury concluded by saying that the 'only sensible course' was 'to reject this new proposal as being both illogical and unworkable', and to allow the existing system to continue until the forces of law and order have regained power and the arguments against abolition have lost their present force. Calling it, however, 'deplorable' if the loss of the clause should lead to the loss of the whole Bill, he said that the easy way for the Government would be to introduce a separate Bill on capital punishment at a later date—a suggestion which the Lord Chancellor, in reply, agreed was feasible.

On the Motion of the Home Secretary, the House of Commons agreed on 22 July to drop the death penalty compromise clause in view of its rejection by the Lords. Mr. Ede pointed out that if the House insisted on this clause the whole Bill could not be passed that Session and would therefore be lost; that the machinery of the new Parliament Act could not be used to pass the clause into law because the latter in its amended form was not in the Bill when it left the Commons; and that they would not be acting in the public interest, nor in accordance with public opinion, if they were to lose the whole measure merely to give further expression to their disagreement with the Lords. The dropping of the compromise clause did not mean the abandonment of the issues which it raised, and the Government would explore without delay what practicable means there were of limiting the death penalty to certain categories of murder in a manner which would not be open to the objections taken against the recent compromise clause, after which Parliament could give further consideration to the question as a separate issue. Mr. Ede's Motion was carried by 215 to 34. The Bill, as amended, received the Royal Assent on 30 July 1948.

In passing it is worth noting that after the Lords' rejection of the new clause, the Government were obliged to deny to the Commons the indulgence of a free vote which they had enjoyed when the clause was first debated. In the divisions in the House of Commons on 15 and 22 July, the Government Whips were on.

Conference of Party Leaders on Reform

During the course of the great controversy over the amendment of the Parliament Act, 1911, it was agreed, on the initiative of the Conservative Opposition, to set up an inter-party Conference to consider whether agreement could be reached on the future of the House of Lords. The Conference was composed as follows:

For the Government: The Prime Minister (Mr. C. R. Attlee), the Lord President of the Council and Leader of the House of Commons (Mr. Herbert Morrison), the Lord Privy Seal and Leader of the House of Lords (Lord Addison), the Lord Chancellor (Lord Jowitt), and the Chief Whip (Mr. William Whiteley).

For the Opposition: Mr. Anthony Eden (absent through illness, his place being taken by Col. Oliver Stanley), Lord Salisbury (Leader of the Opposition in the Lords), Lord Swinton, and Sir David Maxwell-Fyfe.

For the Liberals: Lord Samuel and Mr. Clement Davies.

Without being able to commit their parties at that stage, the party leaders did agree provisionally on certain proposals.[1] It was agreed that the existing constitution of the House of Lords should be modified so as to ensure that the Second Chamber should be complementary to and not a rival of the House of Commons and that there should be no permanent majority for any one political party. On the composition of the new House it was agreed that

1. The present hereditary Peers would not *ipso facto* be qualified to attend and vote.
2. Instead new 'Lords of Parliament' would be appointed on grounds of personal distinction or public service. They might be drawn either from the hereditary Peers or commoners who would be created Life Peers. They should be paid and would be disqualified if they neglected or became unable or unfitted to perform their duties.
3. Women should be equally eligible and certain Peers of the Blood Royal, certain Lords Spiritual and the Law Lords should also be included.
4. Peers who were not Lords of Parliament would be able to vote at elections and be candidates for the House of Commons.

On one point we could not agree, and this led to the breakdown of the Conference. It concerned the powers which should be vested in any reformed Upper House, and in particular the length of time that would be reasonable for the performance of its functions. The Parliament Bill then before the House of Lords proposed to reduce the number of Sessions in which a Bill in dispute between the two Houses had to be introduced and passed by the Commons from three to two, and to reduce the time which had to elapse before the Bill could receive the Royal Assent from two years to one year between the Second Reading in the Commons in the first Session and the Third Reading in the Commons in the second Session.

In order to overcome the objection that a disputed measure which had had a slow passage through the House of Commons after its Second Reading might become law without the Second

[1] *Parliament Bill, 1947, Agreed Statement on Conclusion of Conference of Party Leaders, February–April, 1948*: Cmd. 7380 (1948).

Chamber having had due opportunity to reconsider it, the Government representatives would have been prepared, as part of a general agreement over the reform of the House of Lords, to suggest to the Labour Party that the 'period of delay' should be extended to nine months from the Third Reading in the Commons if this proved to be a longer period than one year from the Second Reading as provided for in the Parliament Bill.

The Opposition leaders regarded the 'one year's delay' proposed in the Parliament Bill as largely illusory. They looked upon the compromise proposal of the Government as unsatisfactory as, in their view, it would not allow sufficient time for reflection by the country after discussion in Parliament had been concluded and the matters at issue between the two Houses clearly defined. However, subject to a general agreement on the other issues, the Conservative leaders might have been prepared to accept a period of eighteen months' delay from the Second Reading in the Commons, and, in order to facilitate such agreement, they would have been prepared to suggest to their supporters a period of twelve months from the Third Reading in the Commons. The Conservatives were unable to agree to any further curtailment of the powers of the Second Chamber lest—so they argued—its value as a balancing factor in the Constitution should be largely nullified and the liberties of the people be imperilled by the virtual creation of single-chamber government.

The Liberal leaders objected to the insufficient suspensory period provided in the Parliament Bill and suggested that the 'period of delay' should run, not from the Second Reading, but from the Third Reading in the Commons. They would, however, have been prepared to recommend the acceptance of the later compromise proposal put forward by the Government.

Some Thoughts on the Breakdown of the Conference

On the face of it the final argument was about a matter of three months, but what was really involved—and was known to be involved by both sides—was that a non-Conservative Government's legislation would stand the risk of being upset by the Lords over the last two Sessions of a Parliament instead of the one Session in which we still stood a risk under the Labour

Government's Parliament Bill. There was not universal agreement with the proposals in the Parliamentary Labour Party, but the need for decision never arose. If it had I think the Government would have got our proposals through at that time, for most of us were convinced that an agreed settlement of the constitutional future of the House of Lords would be worth while, provided that any undue powers on the part of the Lords were still curtailed on the general lines proposed in the Parliament Bill. The scheme would have saved any energetic young man going into the Lords because of the death of his father if he did not wish to, and the proposed life peerages would have made it easier to exercise a wider choice in the creation of Peers. The two Liberal members of the Conference supported our view—Lord Samuel in particular contributing much wise counsel—but the Conservatives were firm on their line; and so agreement was not possible.

I personally was and remain keen on the admission of women to the House of Lords; indeed I would favour that in principle whether the House is reformed or not. The House is now, so far as I know, the only public institution in our country from which women as such are excluded, and I can see no more reason for excluding them from the House of Lords than from the House of Commons. It is argued by some that there are complications in connexion with the application of the hereditary principle (so long as it lasts), but I feel they could be overcome by the eldest child (irrespective of sex) succeeding to the title. On 27 July 1949 the Lords did in fact carry a Motion favouring steps to confer upon women Peers the same rights, duties, and privileges as male Peers who had seats in the House. However, I gather that most of their Lordships (as things are) are not very keen on the admission of women as members of the House, though that in itself is not necessarily conclusive.

On 3 February 1953 the Prime Minister (Mr. Churchill) wrote to Mr. Attlee (Leader of the Opposition) suggesting that the matter should again be considered at a preliminary inter-party Conference with a view to deciding whether there were grounds for continuing discussion at a more official Conference of party leaders. Mr. Churchill's letter was in the following terms:

My dear Attlee,—As you know, Her Majesty's Government have

announced their intention to invite the leaders of the other main political parties to consider the question of the reform of the House of Lords. It has long been held by the Conservative party that such a review is urgently required if the House is to play its proper part as a Second Chamber under the Constitution, and it is clear that if such a reform can be achieved by agreement between the parties, so much the better.

It was for this reason that, in 1947, during the debates on the Parliament Bill, at that time before the House of Lords, the Conservative party, with the support of both wings of the Liberal party, urged on the Labour Government of the day the desirability of all-party conversations, covering both the composition and powers of the House. The Labour Government were good enough to agree to this proposal and the conversations took place and achieved a not inconsiderable measure of success. But it was unhappily found impossible to register a sufficient measure of agreement to justify the leaders of the parties concerned, who had been negotiating *ad referendum*, in submitting joint proposals to their parties.

It appears to Her Majesty's present advisers that the time has now come to make a further attempt. I therefore write on behalf of Her Majesty's Government to invite the Labour party to take part in further conversations. Following the precedent of 1947, these would be at first of an informal character to see whether a sufficient area of agreement exists to justify the holding of a more formal conference.

I greatly hope that your party will find it possible to accept this invitation, which is sent to them in a sincere desire to achieve an agreed and enduring solution of this long-standing and difficult problem, to the advantage of Parliament and the Nation. I am also sending an invitation to the Leader of the Liberal party.—Yours sincerely, WINSTON S. CHURCHILL.

After the proposal had been considered by the Parliamentary Committee and at a meeting of the Parliamentary Labour Party, Mr. Attlee on 18 February 1953 replied:

My dear Prime Minister,—I have carefully considered with my colleagues your invitation to take part in an informal conference on the subject of the reform of the House of Lords. In view of the fact that the previous discussions in 1948 on this subject revealed a fundamental cleavage of opinion between the Labour and Conservative parties on what is the proper part to be played by the House of Lords as a Second Chamber under the Constitution, we have come to the conclusion that no useful purpose would be served by our entering into such a discussion.—Yours sincerely, C. R. ATTLEE.

Difficulties in Selection of Peers: Life Peers

A Labour Government is confronted with somewhat greater difficulties than a Conservative Administration in the creation of Peers. If a Member of the House of Lords is to do real work in that House and live he must either have a private income or, at any rate, a modest pension, for Members are paid nothing beyond travelling expenses for actual attendances. In these circumstances it is to be expected that more Conservatives will be available for service in the House of Lords than Labour people. Labour Prime Ministers and possible Labour Members of the House of Lords have had to have regard to this question of means. Even so, some Labour Peers (and indeed some Conservative Peers) are, I believe, experiencing a difficult time financially.

Another consideration liable to affect possible Labour Peers arises out of the hereditary principle itself. If there is a son to inherit the title, the parents and the son himself would normally wish to consider whether his prospects in life were such that he could 'carry it'. Moreover, if a son has ambitions to become and remain a Member of the House of Commons he may be averse to being 'pitchforked' into the House of Lords upon the death of his father. The present Lord Hailsham, when as Mr. Quintin Hogg he sat in the House of Commons as Conservative M.P. for the City of Oxford, made it publicly clear that he would prefer to remain in the House of Commons and that he considered it unjust that he must contemplate at some future time being forcibly transferred to the House of Lords. Either on these grounds of personal inconvenience or because of his democratic dislike of the hereditary principle, Mr. Ramsay MacDonald, when Labour Prime Minister, aimed in advising the Sovereign at selecting Peers without male offspring. This, however, must have limited his field of selection, especially as the question of means also had to be taken into account. Mr. Attlee did not feel himself to be so circumscribed, and I imagine that he regarded this (not unreasonably) as being a matter for consideration by the parents and the son.

It should also be noted that there is no compulsion on Peers to attend the House of Lords and indeed the great majority seldom appear there or take part in debates.

All this leads me to believe that there are considerable arguments for the merits of the proposal to institute life peerages or Lords of Parliament, especially if, on condition that they really discharge parliamentary duties, a modest salary were paid, being of course materially less than that of a Member of the House of Commons. Prime Ministers of both parties would have a wider choice; it would be a condition that if the Lord of Parliament did not or could not reasonably attend to his duties the peerage could be terminated; the question of means would no longer be important or as important; if a Life Peer resigned he could vote and stand for the House of Commons, and the political freedom of his son would not be imperilled; and, finally, it would remove the possible objection to women members arising out of the hereditary principle.

Quite a number of my colleagues in the Labour Party, however, do not agree with the idea, their main point being that it would partially rationalize the House of Lords and help to make it look democratically 'respectable'. I think this fear is exaggerated, for the assembly would continue not to be elected, either by the public or by learned professions or other interests. The bulk of Members would, I should hope and imagine, be chosen because they were good intelligent citizens, though if some of them had special knowledge useful to the community, that would be advantageous. But the assembly would not become an assembly of specialists, nor would they function in a representative capacity. A Second Chamber so modified without any increase in powers would not on the face of it look very different from the present House of Lords. The Life Peers would have no moral authority to assert their political powers unduly, and certainly such an assembly would in no way compare with the Senate of the United States of America.

Future of the House of Lords

To the foreign observer it may be remarkable that there is no great public agitation for the transformation of the House of Lords into a more democratic and representative assembly, or indeed for its abolition. The fact is that there is no widespread demand for such changes, although some members of the Labour Party would favour abolition and some members of the

Conservative Party, wishing to strengthen the power of the Second Chamber as against that of the House of Commons, would wish for reforms (including an increase in powers) which in their view would give the House of Lords a more representative and authoritative character. But most thoughtful politicians would, I think, not wish for such changes as would make the House of Lords something like the United States Senate—the Conservatives out of respect for tradition and Labour for substantial reasons of principle and expediency. The fact that the House of Lords has many irrational features is not in itself fatal in British eyes, for we have a considerable capacity for making the irrational work; and if a thing works we tend rather to like it, or at any rate to put up with it.

The Labour Government was not anxious for the rational reform or democratization of the Second Chamber, for this would have added to its authority and would have strengthened its position as against that of the House of Commons. Changes which gave the House of Lords a democratic and representative character would have been undemocratic in outcome, for they would have tended to make the Lords the equals of the Commons. We should be alarmed if our Second Chamber had the great powers of the United States Senate. Nor should we be attracted by the idea of a Chamber composed on lines such as those of the Council of the Republic in France. The very irrationality of the composition of the House of Lords and its quaintness are safeguards for our modern British democracy. Whilst willing to respect the House of Lords for the standard and value of its debates, and for its capacity as a Chamber of legislative revision, we would not tolerate from such an institution any undue interference with the will of the House of Commons or of the people. So most people are reasonably—though not wholly—happy, though for differing reasons.

Legislative Utility of the House of Lords

From Radical days there has always been the school of thought that says 'End 'em, don't mend 'em'. Some of my friends in the Labour Party still advance that slogan of earlier days. However, my own experience as Leader of the House of Commons in organizing a heavy legislative programme convinced me that it was better to limit the powers of the House of Lords so that it could do no substantial harm rather than to establish single-chamber government. My principal reasons for this are severely practical, though wider constitutional considerations would arise. I have had a fairly long experience as a Minister, both in preparing and piloting Bills through Parliament and, as Leader of the House of Commons, in organizing and time-tabling the legislative programme. It is profoundly to be desired that a finished Act of Parliament should be word-perfect. For, if mistakes are made, the Government may be involved in administrative embarrassment or confusion or, worse, the Government, and indeed the community, may be placed in grave difficulties as a result of legally correct but unexpected and disturbing decisions of the Courts of Law. The fact that these things do not very often occur is a tribute in the main to those parliamentary draftsmen to whom I have paid tribute elsewhere: they are among our most valuable 'backroom boys' and have received all too little public praise. The Civil Service deserves its share of praise too. But credit is also due to the alertness of Members in both Houses of Parliament and of all parties in looking out for imperfections in drafting and for lack of clarity. Even amendments of substance involving policy may well be the means of calling the attention of Ministers or draftsmen to the need for drafting amendments.

This business of scrutinizing the words of a Bill goes through many stages. The drafting includes consultation in and between Departments, examination by the Law Officers and by the Legislation Committee of the Cabinet. There are the subsequent departmental examination and consultations while the Bill is before Parliament, together with representations from outside interests, or even individual communications from good citizens, including men of the law who take an interest in such matters. But apart from all this there are two stages in each House of Parliament for the examination of the Bill in detail: the Committee and Report Stages. Now the outsider, or even the less experienced Member of Parliament, might well think that a Committee Stage and a Report Stage in a single Chamber should be reasonably certain to bring to light all drafting imperfections.

I assure them that they would be wrong. Indeed one or other

of the Houses has sometimes to recommit a Bill so as to get an unobserved imperfection right in a second Committee examination of the Bill. To a new Minister handling a Bill of substance for the first time it almost seems that the process of revision and the discovery of imperfections is endless. So that, whether a Bill originates in the Commons or the Lords, the further Committee and Report stages in the second House are of real value on practical grounds. From my own experience I would say that it is certain that drafting imperfections would materially increase if we relied upon single-chamber legislation. The fact that the House of Lords is a different kind of assembly from the Commons means that, except when their political blood is up, its Members set about the task of revision in a different spirit, looking at the Bill, perhaps, from a somewhat different angle; and that helps. Because it includes not only distinguished lawyers (as indeed does the House of Commons) but a number of Members who function or have functioned on the bench of a High Court of Justice, the House of Lords is a specially valuable institution in this matter of spotting lack of clarity or doubtful matters of drafting.

The single-chamber man may object, however, that as two Houses and not one have to examine legislation, the legislative output must be slowed down. Even this argument, in my experience, is not only untrue but more probably the reverse of the truth. When the House of Lords is examining a Bill which has come from the House of Commons it is not using up the time of the House of Commons. Usually it is improving the work of the House of Commons, often—indeed probably in the case of most amendments—at the request of the Government itself, whether that Government be Labour or Conservative. If that work of revision were not done in the Lords it is reasonably certain that at least one additional stage would have to be invented in the Commons in order that the work of revision could be continued. As a consequence the work of the House of Commons itself would become more congested and slowed down. There is another and equally important point. Bills can start in either House; therefore the Second Reading of different Bills and their examination in Committee and on Report can be proceeding simultaneously in the two Houses. Controversial Bills, quite properly, usually—and Money Bills always—

start in the House of Commons; but there are many Bills, including Bills of substance and especially less controversial Bills of legal complexity, which may best start in the House of Lords. This not only pleases their Lordships—and if we have to live with a Second Chamber there is something to be said for keeping them happy so long as one does not give away points of principle—but is also calculated to save time in the Commons because the Bill, when it reaches them, has already been largely and usefully tidied up. It will be seen, therefore, that this two-way legislative traffic is not only valuable in ensuring good legislative revision and in bringing two types of mind to bear upon legislation, but almost certainly saves time and is helpful in preventing legislative congestion in the House of Commons. This is true even if we take into account the fact that the Commons have to consider and decide upon the Lords' amendments. For the surprising thing is that clashes on amendments between the two Houses are not frequent; indeed sometimes the amendments may be the result of Opposition Members or others having asked that the Government should promote a desired amendment in 'another place'. Normally Lords' amendments are taken after the transaction of most of the main business of the day in the House of Commons, and their consideration does not take much time. The Labour Government's Iron and Steel Bill and Criminal Justice Bill (as regards capital punishment) were exceptions. So was the Conservative Government's Transport Bill in 1953.

British Political Genius

The fact that the Labour Governments of 1945–51, with their controversial and heavy legislative programme, managed to live with the House of Lords—not without some trouble, it is true—without reaching any final 'last ditch' irremediable crises, was an extraordinary achievement. That this happened is in itself a great compliment to British political genius.

If on practical grounds, and as one who seeks to be fair-minded, I have made some not unfriendly observations about the work and utility of the House of Lords, I should, perhaps, add that I personally much prefer the life of the more troublesome and lively House of Commons.

CHAPTER X

Changes in Parliamentary Procedure

PARLIAMENTARY procedure, like most things British, has reached the stage it has, not as a result of sudden and violent change, but consequent upon a process of adaptation, a gradual evolution based on the lessons of practical experience, together with a persistent determination to maintain, develop, and protect the rights and the prestige of Parliament.

It is important to realize that most of House of Commons procedure is not determined by Standing Orders; indeed, in 1953 there were only 112 Standing Orders governing the transaction of Public Business as compared with the 304 Standing Orders of the London County Council, though the Council's Standing Orders are by no means analogous, for many of them are concerned not with procedure but with executive administration. The bulk of parliamentary procedure is determined by the rulings of various Speakers going back for many years, and by custom and practice. Running through it all is a high degree of common sense which may surprise a number of people who regard the procedure of the House of Commons as being in many ways quaint and cumbersome. If in this book I manifest some degree of satisfaction with and admiration of this procedure it is the result of experience which has led me to that conviction, and not because of an aversion to change; indeed, as this chapter will show, I have played my part in bringing noticeable changes about.

Erskine May

The bible of parliamentary procedure is a large volume called Erskine May, which now, in its 15th edition, runs to over 1,000 pages, the full title of which is *A Treatise on the Law, Privileges, Proceedings and Usage of Parliament.*[1] It was originally the

[1] The first edition of May's *Parliamentary Practice* was published in 1844. The author was 16 when he obtained the post of assistant librarian of the House of Commons in 1831 and he continued in the service of that House until his death in

result of Erskine May, an officer of the House of Commons, setting down for the convenience of the Clerks and the Speaker a record of the rulings which had been given by successive Speakers. This useful piece of private enterprise on the part of Erskine May was continued and much developed by successive Clerks of the House, assisted by their staffs, the 15th edition having been edited by Lord Campion (Clerk of the House of Commons from 1937 to 1948) and published in 1950. The volume is highly authoritative. If a Member, in rising on a point of order, can effectively quote Erskine May as a witness in favour of his argument, he is on strong ground, as is the Speaker when he quotes Erskine May against the Member raising a point of order. This volume, which is not a product of a committee of Members of the House of Commons but of its learned Clerk, as he is sometimes called—though he is not usually a lawyer—deals with the Standing Orders, but its great value is that it embodies the customs, practice, and Speakers' rulings governing the procedure of the House. I doubt whether there is any Parliament in the world outside the British Commonwealth which has had its procedure so determined. Most of them would prefer to appoint committees of Members, who, after extensive and argumentative labours, would produce for their Parliament a large volume of meticulous Standing Orders seeking—probably unsuccessfully—to allow for every possible contingency.

It should not be thought, however, that any given volume of Erskine May is as the law of the Medes and Persians. New or unforeseen situations arise and circumstances change, and it is here that the common sense and adaptability of our procedure manifest themselves. A *prima facie* case for a change in Standing Orders may arise, but it is highly probable that what is required is a new Speaker's ruling. If the Speaker were satisfied that something had to be done to assist the House to discharge its duties in the new circumstances, either he would be asked to give a new ruling or he would himself volunteer to do so. After careful consideration he would make a statement to the House

1886. In 1838 he was called to the Bar at the Middle Temple. From 1847 to 1856 he was examiner of petitions for Private Bills and taxing master for both Houses of Parliament; from 1856 to 1871 Clerk Assistant; and from 1871 to 1886 Clerk of the House of Commons. May personally supervised the production of no less than nine revised and enlarged editions of *Parliamentary Practice.*

indicating that he proposed to make modifications in parliamentary practice on the matter in question for the general convenience of the House. Some informal discussion might ensue which would or would not cause the Speaker to change his view. If it were clear that there was not fairly general agreement, Mr. Speaker would no doubt reconsider the matter and possibly consult with party leaders through the Whips, and then give a similar or a revised ruling. But on most occasions the Speaker is so successful in arriving at a common-sense conclusion and meeting the general wishes of the House that no great difficulty arises. A revision thus established from the Chair will find its place in the next edition of Erskine May. In this way the contents and rulings of Erskine May have evolved and changed much over the years. This great and valuable, changing and living, volume is so persistent and powerful an influence in the House of Commons that I sometimes feel that the ghost of Erskine May is floating about the Speaker's Chair and the Clerks' Table or their offices in the Palace of Westminster.

Learning the procedure takes some time and Members vary in their ability to understand and use it. I will give one illustration of a perfectly sound procedure which nevertheless may not only mystify the public, but also mislead a new Member for quite a time and even cause him to vote against his intentions. When a Bill is being examined in Committee an amendment may be moved to leave out certain words and insert others. (A similar procedure is followed on Motions.) The question put is not for or against the amendment. Two questions may be put: the first being that the words proposed to be left out stand part of the clause. To the surprise of the novice, thinking in terms of voting for or against the amendment, those in favour of the amendment should vote 'No' and those opposed to the amendment should vote 'Aye', the explanation being that it is first desirable to determine whether the existing words should come out before voting on what words should replace them if the amendment to omit the words be carried. Nevertheless, it is understandable if a new Member scratches his head and thinks that he is voting upside down.[1] If the amendment to omit the

[1] Some Commonwealth Parliaments avoid this by proposing the question 'That the words proposed to be left out be left out', thus enabling those in favour of an amendment always to vote 'Aye'.

existing words is carried, the second question is then put 'That these words be there inserted', the words having been quoted by the Chairman, who may, however, to save time refer to the insertion of words as on the Order Paper. Members then vote on whether the proposed words should be inserted. It may happen that there are further proposals for words to be inserted and the merits of the various proposals will be considered in turn. It may well be asked, however, why not put the amendment as a whole and take a vote for and against? The answer is that it saves time and indeed is more sensible if the House first decides whether it wants any change at all, for if the House decides to leave the words in, well, that is that, and it must then proceed to the consideration of later amendments, for all amendments challenging the words it has been decided to preserve would fall to the ground. Thus time is saved whilst completely preserving the right of Members to determine whether or not the House wishes to consider actual changes in the wording of the clause. I have dealt with this aspect of procedure merely by way of illustration, for I am not attempting to write a chapter which would be a textbook on parliamentary procedure.[1]

The Closure

Undoubtedly in earlier days the House was unduly conservative and apprehensive about improvements in procedure by way of Standing Order modifications. There was almost a feeling that practically any change was wrong. We have to remember, however, that the work of Parliament was then much lighter, and the subjects dealt with very restricted as compared with the matters with which Parliament now deals. Perhaps it was for that reason that the House could afford the luxury (if it was a luxury) of speeches lasting for hours on end from distinguished and even undistinguished parliamentarians, or even the reading of pages and pages of books by Irish Nationalists, who achieved fame as being perhaps the most brilliant obstructionists in our parliamentary history. However, it is an ill wind that blows

[1] Among the best of the many excellent books on parliamentary practice and procedure is Campion's *Introduction to the Procedure of the House of Commons.* Her Majesty's Stationery Office publishes on behalf of the House of Commons a *Manual of Procedure in the Public Business.*

nobody any good, for they made their indirect contribution to what have proved to be reasonable reforms in parliamentary procedure and perhaps were a major factor in disturbing the theory that parliamentary procedure was sacred and should be unchanged.

For example, although there had been talk about the need to expedite business by curtailing Private Members' rights, it was only in the panic which followed the successful Irish obstruction in the 1880's that the House parted with its long preserved liberties. One of the most far-reaching of these reforms was the closure (that is to say, the Motion 'That the Question be now put'). It was first used by Mr. Speaker Brand, on 2 February 1881, who, in the course of a long debate and considerable obstruction, decided to put the question without further debate.[1] He made a dignified statement saying that he considered that a crisis had arisen in parliamentary procedure and that the tedious discussions were against the general sense of the House. He ended by saying that further measures for ensuring orderly debate must be left to the judgement of the House, meaning either that the Government must take responsibility by bringing forward appropriate orders or that the House itself must find ways and means of solving the problem. After the division the Prime Minister, Mr. Gladstone, gave notice of his intention on the following day to move certain resolutions which he read out to the House. In the course of debate on the Motions the Government proposals were altered and it was eventually decided that a 3 to 1 majority would be required for a closure in a House of not less than 300 Members. In these days such a rule appears to be distinctly timid and certain to be ineffective in a considerable proportion of Parliaments, but it must be remembered that in those days the principle of unrestricted debate was held in high esteem despite extensive obstruction by Irish Members; the idea of closure at all was no doubt looked upon as a revolutionary departure from tradition.[2] The Standing Order governing the closure today, whilst requiring only a simple majority, does stipulate that not less than 100 Members must vote for it: so if the voting on a

[1] Before the introduction of the closure Members could go on talking indefinitely.

[2] It was a foreign innovation which already existed in France and Lord Randolph Churchill always spoke of it as 'La Clôture'.

closure Motion was, for the closure 99 and against the closure 70, the Chair would declare the Motion not carried. Such a situation is very liable to arise on a Friday afternoon in connexion with Private Members' Bills or Motions.

The Speaker

The Speaker of the House of Commons is, of course, the guardian of its rights and liberties. The very name Speaker indicates that he was the spokesman of the House of Commons in its corporate capacity to the Sovereign in days when friction was likely to arise between the House and the Monarch; and the Speaker ran some risk of severe displeasure at the hands of the Sovereign. The Speaker is elected by the House of Commons subject to the final approval of the Queen. Frequently the choice, in which the back-benchers play the large part, is unanimous. But there have been on certain occasions not only contests, but also contests during which highly controversial speeches have been made. At the opening of each new Parliament, the Speaker with the faithful Commons attends the House of Lords to seek the Royal approval of his appointment. On that occasion he lays claim on behalf of the House to its rights and privileges, saying:

> My Lords, I submit myself with all humility and gratitude to Her Majesty's gracious commands. It is now my duty, in the name and on behalf of the Commons of the United Kingdom, to lay claim by humble Petition to Her Majesty to all their ancient and undoubted rights and privileges; especially to freedom of speech in debate; to freedom from arrest; and to free access to Her Majesty whenever occasion shall require; and that the most favourable construction shall be put upon all their proceedings. In regard to myself, I pray that if in the discharge of my duties I should inadvertently fall into any error, it may be imputed to myself alone, and not to Her Majesty's most faithful Commons.

These rights and privileges the Sovereign is pleased to confirm.

As the Speaker must be a Member of the House it is almost certain that up to that point he has been a member of one or other of the great parliamentary political parties, but upon being appointed Speaker he rigorously cuts off his party affiliations. He declares his honourable intention of being the impartial servant of the House as a whole and that in particular he will do his best to safeguard the rights of minorities. Motions can be put on the Order Paper criticizing or even censuring the conduct of the Speaker or his Deputy (the Chairman of Ways and Means) or the Deputy Chairman of Ways and Means. These may then be debated and may even be voted upon. Such occasions, fortunately, are very rare. The House of Commons has been well served by its Speakers.

The traditions of the office are very high and the position of Speaker in the House of Commons is a great one. He not only presides over the proceedings of the House, but he protects its liberties and rights of debate. If Guillotines are enforced from time to time that is the responsibility of the Government and not of the Chair. The Speaker is also the ceremonial head of the House: he is, in fact, Member of Parliament No. 1. He is available to Members who seek advice or guidance or who are anxious to remedy what they believe to be a grievance. He is liable to be a somewhat lonely figure in that great Chair, and I suspect enjoys very brief and infrequent chats with Members as they pass behind his Chair, provided the proceedings of the House are not disturbed. The wig and gown play their part in contributing to the authority of the Speaker and to his dignity; if you doubt this, then, if you have seen the Speaker in the Chair, go and look at the unadorned Presidents of other Parliaments. I am all in favour of these dignified decorative aids to democratic authority. They also make their wearer to a large extent anonymous and therefore impersonal.

The Speaker has no bell with which to restore order, not even a gavel. When he rises in his place and says 'Order, Order', it is rare for the House not to come to order at once. And if some Members should be noisy a large proportion of the House will aid the Speaker by crying 'Order, Order' until the noisy or disorderly ones are quietened, or a Member standing at the same time as the Speaker rises resumes his seat. One evening between the wars I was much impressed by a comparison with the French Chamber of Deputies. The occasion was exciting and the Deputies were thoroughly enjoying themselves in one of their occasional outbursts of noisy and persistent disorder. The President sat in his place ringing the bell vigorously and at length. It almost seemed that the louder he rang the bell, and the longer he rang it, the worse the disorder became. I could not help thinking, with some British parliamentary pride, of Mr. Speaker in the House of Commons.

The Chairman of Ways and Means

The next officer of the House is the Chairman of Ways and Means, who is sometimes called the Chairman of Committees and he is also the Deputy Speaker. He is nominated by the Government, but he is expected, like the Speaker, to be impartial. The Chairman of Ways and Means presides over the House when it is sitting in Committee, whether it be the Committee of Ways and Means, the Committee of Supply, or other Committees of the Whole House. He has the delicate task of selecting for debate amendments to Bills in Committee of the Whole House. He is also the guardian, so to speak, of the Private Bills of local authorities and other public bodies, in the sense that he is responsible for securing facilities for these measures to be considered. He is therefore an important officer of the House and has a considerable amount of work to do.

The Chairman of Ways and Means is assisted by the Deputy Chairman of Ways and Means, who also can function as Deputy Speaker and is nominated by the Government of the day. In the Chair of the House, functioning as Deputy Speaker, they have nearly all the powers of the Speaker, but not quite all; for example, they cannot give the closure or select amendments in the House. When the House is in Committee the Chairman and Deputy Chairman of Ways and Means can be relieved by Temporary Chairmen. These are members of the Chairman's Panel nominated by Mr. Speaker. Unlike the other three officers of the House (the Speaker, the Chairman of Ways and Means, and the Deputy Chairman of Ways and Means), they are not required to disaffiliate themselves politically, and indeed they freely take part in debates when they are not in the Chair. As a whole, the Temporary Chairmen of the House in Committee, as well as the Chairmen of the Standing Committees upstairs (drawn from the same Chairman's Panel), have a high reputation for impartiality and efficiency in the Chair.

The Clerks

The Clerk of the House and the two Clerks Assistant, wearing wigs (less elaborate than that of the Speaker) and gowns, sit at the Clerks' Table in the House and contribute also to the dignity of the assembly's appearance. They are important officers of the House; they are impartial and rightly enjoy a position of parliamentary independence. The Clerk of the House is appointed by Letters Patent by the Crown on the advice of the Prime Minister.[1] The Clerks Assistant are appointed by statute under the Sign Manual on the recommendation of the Speaker. Their duties are many. Under the direction of the Speaker they prepare the Order Paper and keep the Votes and Proceedings and Journals, recording the decisions of the House. They privately assist and advise the Speaker and Members on matters of order and procedure. They have given valuable advice to Commonwealth Parliaments, Colonial Legislatures, and frequently are consulted by the authorities of foreign parliamentary institutions. One of their most delicate duties is the handling of Questions. There are extensive rules about the admissibility of Questions, and although the Speaker can overrule the Clerks, and the responsibility is ultimately his, they have the awkward duty of privately arguing with Members about the form and admissibility of Questions. They are assisted by Committee Clerks who serve the Standing Committees and Select Committees upstairs, and other members of their staff. I have had a good deal to do with them, and have always found them, whilst quite properly maintaining their independence of the Government and the Opposition, able, courteous, and helpful officers of the House of Commons.

Parliament and Post-war Reconstruction

During the Second World War it had been clear to the Coalition Government that there would be an exceptionally heavy programme of legislation in the reconstruction period. It was important that the parliamentary machine should not break down under that burden for, in the words of the Third Report of the Select Committee on Procedure in October 1946,

> The danger to parliamentary government in this country at the present time is less likely to arise from lack of confidence in it than from the overwhelming burden which the growth of Governmental

[1] The Clerk of the House of Lords (Clerk of the Parliaments) is also appointed by the Crown on the advice of the Prime Minister.

activity places upon it. This burden has become greater, not less, with the arrival of peace, and it seems probable that it may increase. It is therefore a matter for constant vigilance to ensure that the machine is continuously adapted and strengthened to bear the new burdens put upon it.

Towards the end of the war a Committee of Ministers of the Coalition Government had discussed methods of adapting the machinery of government to bear the extra stresses and strains of the reconstruction period. In particular a scheme for the acceleration of proceedings on Public Bills had been drafted by this Committee, but it had not been approved by the War Cabinet nor were individual Ministers in any way committed to it. In August 1945 a Select Committee of the House of Commons was set up, on the Motion of the Labour Government, 'to consider the Procedure in the Public Business of this House and to report what alterations, if any, are desirable for the more efficient despatch of such business'. This Committee made three reports—in October 1945, January 1946, and October 1946—all of which were in general approved by the House. The changes made in parliamentary procedure were not drastic for it was generally agreed that a change in the basic character of Parliament was neither desirable nor necessary. In some ways the changes made did not go as far as the Government had originally suggested, but as a whole I think that they greatly facilitated the better organization and conduct of Parliamentary Business.

The members of the Select Committee under the Chairmanship of Sir Robert Young worked hard and their reports were and remain of great value. The reports cover much ground but I propose to confine myself to the more important changes considered.

In their First Report the Select Committee examined the draft war-time proposals which had been forwarded by the new Labour Government as a useful basis for discussion. This scheme is published as an appendix to the First Report. The Government did not think it right to commit itself at that stage, but felt that the proposals were eminently worthy of consideration, conceived as they were to meet the special circumstances of the post-war period and to enable the major reconstruction Bills to pass with reasonable expedition through Parliament.

The Select Committee emphasized that the Government proposals were experimental and could be amended by the House in the light of experience. The Government memorandum was concerned mainly with improving the procedure for the Committee Stage of Bills. This, it was felt, was the stage at which the larger economies in time could be made.

Committee Stage in Standing Committee or on the Floor?

All Bills in whichever of the two Houses they are introduced go through the following stages: First Reading (which is formal); Second Reading, when a broad debate on the Bill takes place; Committee Stage, when the details of the Bill are examined and amendments considered; Report Stage, when the result of the Committee Stage is reviewed and amendments are considered; and Third Reading, when the Bill can be debated only within its existing limits, although in the House of Lords amendments can be moved at this final stage. Obviously the Committee Stage is an important one and on a substantial Bill can last a considerable time. It was to this stage, therefore, that particular attention was devoted, particularly on the question whether the Committee Stage should be taken on the Floor in a Committee of the Whole House or whether it should be dealt with by a smallish Standing Committee upstairs.[1]

The Government's main proposal was that substantially all Bills should be referred to Standing Committees, and that as a consequence certain changes should be made in the number and size of these Committees and in their procedure. This proposal involved no more than a more extensive application of the procedure already provided for in Standing Orders. S.O. No. 46[2] required that all Bills (except Bills for imposing taxes, Consolidated Fund and Appropriation Bills, and Bills for the confirmation of Provisional Orders) should be committed to a Standing Committee unless the House otherwise ordered. This order had been in operation since 1907, but it had been the practice of previous Governments to retain on the Floor of

[1] 'Upstairs' signifies that the Standing Committee meets in a Committee Room on the floor above the Chamber; so the phrase 'sending a Bill upstairs' is commonly used.

[2] See S.O. No. 38 (1953).

the House 'the great measures of the Session', as well as certain short Bills and Bills urgently required.

The Government proposed that the practice of keeping politically controversial Bills on the Floor of the House should be abandoned. All Bills should be sent upstairs, i.e. to a small Committee of the House of Commons, except:

(i) Those Bills already excepted under S.O. 46 as mentioned above;

(ii) Any Bill which it might be necessary to pass with great expedition;

(iii) 'One clause' Bills not requiring detailed examination in Committee; and

(iv) Any Bill of 'first-class constitutional importance' (e.g. the Bills for the Parliament Act, 1911 or the Statute of Westminster, 1931).

The Government would retain the right to move that the Committee Stage of any important Bill should be taken on the Floor of the House if special circumstances made it desirable to do so. 'But, with the exceptions indicated, the Government would for their part make a practice of refraining from moving in that sense, and of opposing such a motion if moved from another quarter.' The Select Committee recommended this proposal.[1]

A debatable aspect of this part of the Government's scheme was the suggestion to send 'politically controversial' Bills upstairs at all, while keeping 'constitutionally important' Bills on the Floor of the House. But even this was in no way revolutionary. The practice of past Governments in keeping contentious measures on the Floor of the House had been based mainly on considerations of expediency. They felt it was safer to keep contentious Bills on the Floor of the House because they had greater control over their own majority there. Several witnesses before the Select Committee contended that politically controversial Bills were, *ipso facto*, constitutionally important. My own view was that only matters which involved 'a material change in the working of the Constitution' were of first-class constitutional importance.

When the First Report was debated in the House on 15 November 1945, this was one of the major issues discussed. Mr. Anthony Eden (Conservative) accepted the general principle

[1] First Report, p. xi, § 5, and p. iv, §§ 6–7.

that more work should be given to the Standing Committees, but suggested that in retaining 'Measures of first-class constitutional importance' on the Floor of the House the Government should bear in mind 'the inter-relation of economics and politics'.[1]

> I am not sure but that a Bill which affects the whole economic life of the country is not just as important as a Bill which raises even a grave constitutional issue.

The same point was made, with rather more partisan vigour, by other Members.

I do not agree—and I opposed the view at the time, both in the House and in evidence before the Select Committee—that Bills which provide for considerable economic change *ipso facto* raise first-class constitutional issues. I do not agree that Parliament is changing the Constitution if, upon the advice of the Government, it transfers the ownership of a private industry to the public. The desirability of such a change may well be politically debatable; but the change does not involve important constitutional issues. It is a matter of deciding that an industry or service shall be owned and managed one way instead of another.

It seemed to me that Members who were arguing that Bills which provided for considerable economic change were necessarily of first-class constitutional importance were falling back on an earlier, and now outmoded, view. This view was that anything which in any way impaired the free working of the capitalist system of production and distribution involved revolutionary constitutional doctrine. But this view is patently wrong. An argument about how best a nation can get a living within the system of parliamentary democracy does not involve revolution in any way. It involves issues about which there may well be argument. They are of real importance. But *ad hoc* Bills on such matters hardly raise large constitutional issues.

Number of Standing Committees

Under Standing Orders in 1945 the maximum number of Standing Committees including the Standing Committee on

[1] 415 *H.C. Deb.* 2354 (15 Nov. 1945).

Scottish Bills was five. Clearly if a substantial number of large and controversial Bills were to be referred to Standing Committees this number would be inadequate. The Government, therefore, desired that the number should be increased 'to secure the passage of the volume of legislation which is likely to be required during the reconstruction period'. For two reasons we also felt that a reduction in the size of the Standing Committees might be necessary. One was that it might be difficult to find the Members to man a substantial number of Committees and to give the necessary time to their work, for regular attendance in Standing Committees is very necessary both to Government and Opposition. The other and perhaps more important reason was that, with Standing Committees of sixty or seventy Members, as the general practice had been, the membership was so large that it was more difficult to develop the committee atmosphere, with the shorter and more business-like speeches, which was to be desired. There can be occasions when big issues arise in Committee and speeches of substance are appropriate. But a large number of points arise, limited in scope and more detailed in character, and long speeches or orations about them are out of place and time-wasting.

The Select Committee recommended that 'as many Standing Committees should be appointed as are necessary expeditiously to dispose of the Bills coming up from the House'; that the permanent nucleus of Standing Committees (other than the Scottish) should be reduced to twenty; that not more than thirty Members should be added in respect of a Bill, and that the quorum should be fifteen.

These changes in procedure were, in themselves, not enough to ensure that the Committee Stage worked with full efficiency. What was really needed was a change in attitude towards the Standing Committees themselves. For the Government's scheme to work successfully it was necessary for the Committees to accept the view that they must do something like a real day's work when required instead of just a few hours. It was necessary to develop the doctrine and practice that the House should split up into Committees to carry through Bills which would otherwise have occupied the full House with a smaller output. Unless Standing Committees took this view any attempt to develop them into useful parts of the legislative process, instead of mere time-savers, would break down. What was needed was a change of habit and a change of outlook; that the Standing Committees should talk and act like Committees. That was the view I urged in evidence before the Select Committee.

The main difficulty in exciting the enthusiasm of Members for Committee work had been that, owing to the nature of the Bills which had normally been sent upstairs, it lacked the colour and conflict which naturally marked proceedings on the Floor of the House. But our practice of sending important and controversial Bills upstairs did much to improve things. Members increasingly realized the importance and interest of the work. Indeed often there was competition to get on the Committees.

Application of Guillotine in Standing Committees

The Government's memorandum also contained a number of other proposals designed to accelerate procedure in the Standing Committees. The Select Committee accepted these in general, recommending a few minor modifications, one of which, at least, constituted to my mind a distinct practical improvement. There was, however, one very controversial innovation—the power to guillotine Bills in Standing Committee. If large controversial Bills go to Standing Committee the power to guillotine there logically follows, though it should be avoided if possible. In only three cases was this done; the Labour Government did not exercise this power in the case of the Gas Bill and we had a severe experience of day and night obstruction upstairs as a consequence.

The power was needed, however, to ensure that the Standing Committees worked efficiently if obstruction should arise. We did not know how much obstruction we would have to face, but experience of the Labour Government of 1929–31 showed that it could be serious. Though we worked the Committee system harder than most Governments had done hitherto, we were still badly held up on our programme of legislation. For instance, I was 'stuck' in a Standing Committee for about four months with the Road Traffic Bill of 1930, which was not controversial at all, politically speaking. When I complained to Opposition Members I was told—'It is not your Bill we are worrying about. It is the one that is coming after.'

Despite the need for it, the Government were reluctant to use Allocation of Time Orders (Guillotines). Personally, I thoroughly dislike the Guillotine. It is justified in conditions of real obstruction and national emergency; but unless there is genuine co-operation and fairness in its application, the Guillotine can make a mockery of the legislative process. We hoped that by removing control of the Guillotine within the overall time limit from the Government and placing it in the hands of a 'neutral' Committee, we would take part of the political edge off the Guillotine and make it less objectionable to Members. If it was necessary to have a Guillotine, what the Government wanted was a fair Guillotine.

Alternative methods were considered. In the end it was decided (on the recommendation of the Select Committee) that where the Government wished to prescribe a time limit in a Standing Committee, the Allocation of Time Motion should take the form of naming a date by which the Standing Committee should conclude its proceedings on the Bill and report to the House. The detailed allocation of sittings of the Standing Committee to parts of the Bill should be the work of a Sub-Committee of the Standing Committee itself, consisting of the Chairman and seven other members nominated by Mr. Speaker.

There remained the question of the allocation of time within the overall limit for the Committee Stage of Bills taken on the Floor of the House and the Report Stage which is always considered by the House as a whole. We thought this could best be done by an inter-party Business Committee of the House itself, and put this view forward in a second memorandum. But the Select Committee in their Third Report declined to reconsider the question.

However, we were anxious, as the Home Secretary (Mr. Chuter Ede) pointed out in the House, 'that when the Guillotine procedure has to be followed, both sides should have an opportunity of making an effective contribution towards setting up the Guillotine which is to be operated'.[1] We therefore persevered with our proposal and successfully introduced a new Standing Order[2] to put it into effect.

[1] 443 *H.C. Deb.* 1736 (4 Nov. 1947).

[2] See S.O. No. 41 (1953).

The Select Committee rejected our proposal that Committee Chairmen be empowered to disallow debate on the question 'That the Clause stand part' if, in their opinion, the principle of the clause had been discussed adequately in debate on amendments.[1] We doubted whether the powers which Chairmen already possessed were adequate, and unsuccessfully asked the Committee to reconsider the point.[2] Eventually, in November 1947, we introduced and carried a new Standing Order to give effect to our wishes.[3]

Report Debated in the House

In the debate on 15 November 1945 it was questioned whether the proposals as a whole were going further than was justified by the legislative needs of the reconstruction period. On this a number of party hares were started by Opposition Members[4]—and a few of them were pursued by enthusiastic Government supporters. But certain restrained doubts were also raised about the general effect of the proposals on the function and character of Parliament.

My Labour colleague, Maurice Webb, urged restraint in extending the Committee system lest the House should be turned into 'some sort of exalted town council'.

> I think we should be ill-advised to destroy the central function of this House as the great forum of debate on public policy, and a general clearing house for the people's aspirations. We must preserve that at all costs and adjust our extension of Committee activity to it without destroying that central function.[5]

Other Members expressed fears that the proposed changes would go further than the mere prevention of senseless obstruction—that they would impose limits on the opportunity for reasonable opposition and on the rights of minority groups within the House.

The Government was always sympathetic to these fears. In replying to the debate I tried to make it clear that we were de-

[1] First Report, p. viii, § 19.

[2] 415 *H.C. Deb.* 2349–50 (15 Nov. 1945). Third Report, p. xix, § 60.

[3] See S.O. No. 45 (1953).

[4] For example, Major Guy Lloyd: 'There is really no indispensable legislative burden. . . . I think that it is a mere excuse . . . to get through this mass of legislation in their revolutionary programme'. [415 *H.C. Deb.* 2374 (15 Nov. 1945).]

[5] 415 *H.C. Deb.* 2370–1 (15 Nov. 1945).

termined to preserve the character and freedom of the House. It had always been my view that one should not attempt to restrict the political rough-and-tumble in debates on the Floor of the House, that first-class disputations were the staple of Parliament. But Committee work required its own atmosphere and conditions. Long orations in Committees upstairs are inappropriate. And it was our view that the proposals embodied in the Select Committee's First Report would secure that higher degree of co-operation and mutual tolerance necessary for the Standing Committees to work efficiently.

During the debate I made a special appeal to Ministers and Members on the Government side of the House to recognize that in Committee under a Guillotine the Opposition had most right to consideration.

> It is their liberty of unrestricted opposition that is being limited. They are being somewhat fettered in their style in the discharge of a duty, because the Opposition have a duty to be critical, and I think that on balance the Opposition are entitled to somewhat more consideration than the majority. If the Committees will try to handle the matter in that spirit, and the Opposition will try to conduct themselves in Committee style, I believe that, under this new era, we can build up Standing Committees that will work on business lines, leaving the rather more free-for-all controversies for the Report stage and Third Reading on the Floor of the House.[1]

The Select Committee's First Report was approved by the House without a division, and the procedural changes in the form of Sessional Orders were voted with minor amendments.

Divisions and Questions

The Select Committee's Second Report dealt with two separate aspects of parliamentary procedure—Divisions and Questions.

The Committee failed to find any acceptable scheme which would reduce the amount of time spent on Divisions in the House. A method of mechanical voting was suggested, but the Committee felt it would be 'neither so convenient nor so accurate a means of counting votes and recording names as the present method'. In general I agree with this view. Anyway, moving through the Division Lobbies is a useful and pleasant social occasion.

[1] 415 *H.C. Deb.* 2397–8 (15 Nov. 1945).

Their recommendations with regard to Questions were brief, but their Report drew attention to the right to put Questions to Ministers as 'one of the most important possessed by Members'.

> The exercise of this right is perhaps the readiest and most effective method of parliamentary control over the action of the executive. They [the Committee] would therefore deprecate anything which tended to diminish the effectiveness of this right. On the other hand the very powerfulness of the right imposes upon Members a proportionate responsibility in its use. The Departments very properly accord a high degree of priority to the answering of parliamentary Questions. It is important therefore that Questions, especially oral Questions, should only be put down when other and less formal methods have failed to produce a satisfactory result, or when some information or action is urgently desired.[1]

Originally the number of, and time for, Questions was unlimited. Since 1902 a limit has been set to the time during which oral Questions can be asked. This cannot be less than three-quarters of an hour and in practice is usually about one hour. The number of oral Questions that an individual Member could ask on one day was limited to eight in 1909, and reduced to three in 1920. The Committee discovered that on an average, half the Questions put down for oral answers were not reached and the Members asking them had to be content with written answers. They therefore considered whether it would be desirable further to reduce the daily ration of Questions from three to two to enable more Members to get an oral answer to a Question each day. They decided not to recommend a further reduction on the grounds that the right had already been severely curtailed and that 'there are many occasions when a Member may fairly require oral answers to at least three Questions'. However, the Select Committee on Nationalised Industries reported on 29 October 1952 in favour of a reduction from three to two, but up to the time of writing no change has been made.

Procedure in Committee of Supply

One of the main fields with which the Third Report of the Select Committee dealt was concerned with the control of policy and administration. Their main recommendations were

[1] Second Report, p. iii, § 3.

directed at the reorganization of procedure in Committee of Supply. Both the Select Committee and the Government recognized that, by the process of slow evolution, the proceedings in Committee of Supply had come to be given over almost entirely to the consideration of Government policy; they had lost their purely financial significance; and points of administrative detail were rarely discussed. On the basis of Sir Gilbert Campion's proposals, supported largely by the Government, the Committee made a number of recommendations, the object of which was to enable Supply days to be spread more evenly through the Session, and to be used, on occasion, for debates of a less restricted character than had been previously permitted. The new and amended Standing Orders[1] which the Government introduced on 4 November 1947 gave effect to the recommendations except on two points. They allotted twenty-six instead of twenty-eight days to Supply Business and proposed that debates on moving Mr. Speaker out of the Chair should occur on any of the allotted days provided that the necessary motion was moved by a Minister.

Considerable time and effort were spent in debate on these points in trying to show that the Government was deliberately endeavouring to prevent Members from having an adequate opportunity of discussing matters of interest to them. But the main object of these amendments was to ensure that debate on the issues of general policy did not become too extended and did not become even further removed from financial issues.

Control of Finance

Another aspect with which the Third Report dealt was the control of finance. With regard to the control of taxation, the Committee examined a proposal submitted by the Government to avoid duplication in debate by shortening proceedings on the Budget Resolutions and the Finance Bill.

We pointed out that there was a double duplication in this field: first, between the Committee Stage of the Budget Resolutions, when a general debate takes place, and the Second Reading of the Finance Bill, when there is another general debate, and secondly, between the Report Stage of the Resolu-

[1] See S.O.s Nos. 16 and 17 (1953).

tions, when they were examined individually, and the Committee Stage of the Finance Bill. As the least complicated solution to this difficulty we proposed that the Report Stage of the Budget Resolutions should be 'formalized'—that the questions should be put without amendment or debate, the right to challenge divisions being preserved, and any points of detail which Members desired to raise left over for the Committee Stage of the Finance Bill. The Select Committee rejected this proposal on the grounds that the duplication was more apparent than real, and that the number of days devoted to control of taxation was already small. Nevertheless, we felt that too much time had been occupied with tedious repetition in this way, and introduced a new Standing Order[1] to give effect to our view relating to Budget Resolutions.

Nearly two hours were spent in debating this proposal. The view expressed by the Government was that, if the House was going to save time at all, it should save it where it had been most wasted. No great constitutional innovation was involved in amending a procedure which had allowed the House or a Committee to debate the same points with the same arguments on six different occasions, i.e. the Committee and Report Stages of the Budget Resolutions, and the Second Reading, Committee, and Report Stages, and Third Reading of the Finance Bill. To reduce the number of opportunities to five did no real harm to the Constitution.

Private Members' Time

The other main procedural problem examined by the Select Committee was that of Private Members' Business.[2] Its recommendations in this field were, of necessity, less immediate in their effect. Private Members' time was not restored until 1949.

The Committee recommended that the facilities for Members to initiate legislation should be restored 'as soon as possible'. It proposed that steps should be taken to improve the distribution of Private Members' time and recommended that:

(*a*) The first twenty Fridays after the debate on the Address should be Private Members' days, Motions and Bills to be taken on alternate Fridays.

[1] See S.O. No. 86 (1953).

[2] Third Report, pp. xvi–xviii.

(*b*) The first six *Bill* Fridays should be for Second Readings, the last four for Report Stages and Third Readings.

We accepted the recommendation and proposed that when Private Members' time could be restored the scheme should be put into operation. This was done and the scheme now operates.

Value of the Reforms

In the discussions[1] which took place in the House after the publication of the Select Committee's Third Report, the Government was criticized for not introducing a Motion accepting or rejecting the Select Committee's Report as such, and for pressing certain reforms which the Committee had rejected. Much of this criticism, though well-intentioned and reasonable, ignored the legitimate and proper view-point with which we had approached the whole problem. In their memorandum to the Select Committee the Government had made it clear that they 'must be constantly mindful of their legislative requirements, and proceed with the main objective of facilitating the passage through Parliament of legislation which the Government regard as necessary for the well-being of the nation.'[2] This view governed the proposals which the Government submitted to the House. In introducing them I said:

> It is commonly said that changes designed to economise time are dangerous, because they encroach upon the opportunities which the House must have for criticising the Government. That is true, up to a point. But there is another danger which is often overlooked—that the essential functions of the House may be neglected, if time is frittered away on matters of inessential detail and vain repetition. The Select Committee have steered a careful course between the danger of over-simplification of procedure on the one hand, and over-adherence to tradition on the other.[3]

It was in that spirit that the Government brought its proposals for procedural reform to the House.

The work of the Select Committee was of high value and the amendments to the Standing Orders which the House accepted on the recommendations of the Government constituted, I think,

[1] See 435 *H.C. Deb.* 29–32 (17 Mar. 1947) and 443 *H.C. Deb.* 1547–1790 (4 Nov. 1947).

[2] Third Report, p. 97.

[3] 443 *H.C. Deb.* 1547 (4 Nov. 1947).

real and useful improvements in parliamentary procedure. The value of its work is shown by the fact that Parliament carried a heavy post-war legislative burden without resort to any drastic schemes involving a basic change in its procedure and a departure from its tradition of gradual development.

To carry through a large legislative programme not only is parliamentary procedure needed which enables work to be done with reasonable speed and efficiency, but also Government organization which can plan the preparation of Bills and Parliamentary Business so that Bills are ready when Parliament needs them. I now turn, therefore, to the preparation of the legislative programme.

CHAPTER XI

The Legislative Programme

THE passing of a Bill through Parliament to the Statute Book enables things to be done, but does not of itself effect physical change or executive action. The considerable work of implementation comes later and will involve the Ministers concerned in much labour. It is for this reason that the size of a legislative programme should allow adequate time for Ministers to implement new Acts. If Ministers are too heavily involved in legislation they will find themselves unduly rushed in the preparation of later Bills and the implementation of the new Acts for which they are responsible.

Legislation and Administration

The Parliament of 1945 came at the end of a great war and the legislative programme was bound to be heavy. The electorate had decided for forward-looking, positive, social and economic change, rather than merely dismantling the war machine and going back to the pre-war order of things. But the consequent legislative burden was heavy upon Ministers and upon M.P.s. We took the view—the Opposition held that we were doing too much—that our legislative programme was approximately right in the circumstances, though heavier than was desirable in more normal times. Indeed, it was the general view, not only of Ministers but of Labour M.P.s, that if we were returned with a working majority in 1950 the legislative programme should be lighter, leaving more time for improvements in organization and administration and for parliamentary debates other than on legislation. The need for substantial time for the study and improvement of administration and organization affected many aspects of Government and public policy. Work in connexion with economic planning, including trade overseas and the balance of payments, and the stimulation of industrial productivity at home; improvements in the organization of the extensive social services developed under a series of important Acts of Parliament; the promotion of a high public spirit in industry; and the close study of the working of the publicly owned industries—all these matters required careful attention free from excessive rush and strain. It was not a question of abandoning all progressive legislation providing for further change; it was a question of recognizing that the legislative programmes of 1945–50 were abnormal, that somewhat less time should be devoted to legislation and more for administration and general parliamentary debates and review. Governments and Parliaments do not live by legislation alone. The House of Commons should have enough time to discharge its undoubted responsibility for critical examination of the work of the Government and the Public Corporations and to debate public policy generally, including foreign and Commonwealth affairs.

Before the election I had presided over a sub-committee of the Labour Party Executive charged with the responsibility of drafting an election manifesto and programme. In due course this was approved at the Labour Party Conference at Blackpool in 1945 and was sold in large numbers under the title of *Let Us Face the Future*. For myself I had sought to make the programme bold, relevant, sensible, and capable of implementation within the lifetime of a single Parliament of approximately five years possessing a sufficient Labour majority. It was on the basis of this policy document that the majority Labour Government of 1945 set about shaping both its legislative programme and the work of administration, which was no less important.

Supervision of the Programme

It is my belief that the Labour Governments of 1945–51 organized their legislative programme and Parliamentary Business more thoroughly than any previous Administration. It would not be fair to make comparisons with the War Government, for war upsets everything and in any case diminishes legislation except on the first day when a whole series of war measures are likely to go through without discussion or, as we say, 'on the nod'. Certainly there was an enormous improvement in the organization of the legislative programme in 1945–51 as compared with the minority Labour Government of 1929–31.

Of course, the first Parliamentary Session of a new Government cannot be as well planned as succeeding Sessions, though even there it may have valuable guidance from its election documents if they have been well and responsibly drafted.

If the legislative programme was to be well arranged, suitable Cabinet Committee organization was necessary, assisted by a competent Secretariat provided by the Cabinet Office. We continued a Legislation Committee with Mr. Arthur Greenwood in the Chair. This Committee was attempting the double task of shaping the programme for the Session and examining Bills as they came up for approval. We soon came to the conclusion that there were two difficulties about the composition and scope of this Committee. First, it was very difficult to settle which Bills should go into the sessional programme with all the Ministers competing for places present (and there were a fair number). Secondly, it was desirable to separate the task of shaping the legislative programme from the work of examining actual Bills. At an early stage, therefore, we set up a Future Legislation Committee under my Chairmanship to deal with the sessional programmes, preserving the Legislation Committee for the examination of Bills and important Statutory Instruments. A little later it was found that co-ordination would be the better promoted if both Committees had the same Chairman, and the Prime Minister decided that as Leader of the House of Commons I should preside over them. The Home Secretary (Mr. Chuter Ede) became Chairman of both these Committees in March 1951, when he succeeded me as Leader of the House of Commons upon my becoming Foreign Secretary.

Experience had shown that departmental Ministers should not be members of the Future Legislation Committee because all of them were possible competitors for a place in the programme. And it was also desirable that the Committee should be very small. The Future Legislation Committee was therefore designed as a small and impartial planning tribunal and included Lord Addison as Leader of the House of Lords and Mr. William Whiteley as Chief Whip. After hearing the representations and arguments of what one may call the 'promoting' Ministers (who naturally had arguments between themselves as to relative priorities) and after putting appropriate questions and obtaining further relevant information, we would deliberate quietly among ourselves and try to reach a fair judgement on the sessional legislative programme to put forward to the Cabinet for decision.

We kept in the forefront of our minds three important factors:

(i) That both Houses of Parliament should have fair opportunity for the examination of the proposed legislation on the assumption that old-style leisurely obstruction would not take place;

(ii) That subject to unforeseen circumstances we would seek to implement the legislative aspects of *Let Us Face the Future* within the lifetime of a single Parliament; and

(iii) That the selection of the Bills should be determined by the public interest in the first place and the party interest in the second place. The more legislation can pass both tests the better. It is easy to forget the first and to remember only the second, but from two points of view it is a mistake so to proceed. A Government is entitled to take into account what is politically advantageous to its party, but it must never forget that it is responsible to the community as a whole for the well-being of the country as a whole. In the framing of the legislative programme, as in other matters, it is morally wrong and in the end politically suicidal to forget that the public interest comes first.

Programme for the Parliament

With our large majority we could afford to plan on the assumption that barring some quite unforeseeable event we were likely to be in office for nearly the full five years, which is the statutory maximum life of the House of Commons. We thus had to settle the spread of the major and controversial legislative proposals over the probable five Sessions and the order in which they were to be introduced.

The first Session was the most difficult, for having only just become the Government we had to start almost from zero. However, there were some necessary Bills more or less ready and fortunately one big and controversial measure, the Supplies and Services (Transitional Powers) Bill, had been substantially drafted under my supervision as Home Secretary in the War Government. So that was ready at a fairly early date; and indeed it was urgent in order to have appropriate authority for that economic planning and control which we regarded as vital if we were to achieve a successful transition from war to peace. Of the socialization measures we regarded coal as the most urgent basically because of the importance of coal in the national economy and the necessity for securing the goodwill and understanding co-operation of the miners and avoiding industrial disputes in the industry. Another Bill of a controversial character which we put in the programme for the first Session was the Trade Union Bill, which had the simple purpose of repealing the Trade Disputes and Trade Unions Act, 1927. It may be argued that this Bill hardly passed the test of national as against party interest and, of course, the Labour Party was very keen on the Bill from the Trade Union point of view. Apart from this, however, we held that the public interest, especially at that time, required that there should be goodwill and close co-operation between the Trade Unions and the Government and that the likelihood of industrial disputes should be reduced to the minimum. In these circumstances it seemed to us that, having regard to the strong feelings of the Trade Unions against the Trade Disputes and Trade Unions Act, 1927, an Act which they had bitterly opposed and to which they had never become reconciled, it was desirable to repeal it in the interests of industrial goodwill, peace, and co-operation. There were also the three big social service measures mentioned below. These, then, were the major Bills for the first Session—a big programme—but we had not yet reached, nor could we have done, the stage of planning comprehensively the programme for the Parliament.

This we now proceeded to do. We had to keep in mind two things: first, completing the programme during the full lifetime of the Parliament and, secondly, settling the programme for each Parliamentary Session.

On the first aspect we sought to arrive at a general view without completely committing ourselves in detail on the spacing of the major controversial measures over the Sessions. These included such great social service measures as National Insurance, Industrial Injuries, and the National Health Service—all in the

1945–6 Session; and the large and complicated Town and Country Planning Bill in 1946–7. As for the socialization measures, urgency had settled coal for 1945–6 and this was a big and difficult Bill to draft; electricity and gas followed in 1947 and 1948; transport, a big complicated measure, was taken in 1947; steel came last (1949) because it opened up complex problems of organization and policy for the consideration of which substantial time was necessary. A Representation of the People Bill was required because we had been committed in the War Government to the view that redistribution of seats was necessary (even though on balance it was to our electoral disadvantage) owing to the serious inequalities of constituency electorates, and, as we ourselves wished to introduce certain changes in electoral law, a large and comprehensive Bill had to be provided for. For some Bills the balance of considerations might be settled by the degree to which the Departments were ready. In any case we arrived at a general idea, subject to revision, about the order in which the big Bills would be taken. We were conscious, however, that our overall plan might be upset. One Minister might be quicker with the preparation of the heads of a Bill than we expected, or another might be later. Moreover—most important of all—unanticipated problems or crises might arise and then we should have to be ready to modify our provisional conclusions in the public interest.

Departmental Preparations

Before we examine the processes by which each sessional programme was collectively determined, it will be well to consider the processes through which the departmental Ministers went before their proposals were submitted to the Future Legislation Committee. They had all been urged to keep in mind that we were planning a programme with a view to settling it (apart from measures of unforeseen urgency) well before the Session began. So they had to remember that they should not be leisurely and that if they were they might damage their legislative prospects. They also had to observe certain guiding rules and principles and remember that the actual drafting of Bills could not proceed until the necessary approval had been given, including approval of the general policy to be followed. We were determined to avoid the old evil—a last-minute scramble just before the opening of a Session. It was no less our wish that the work of the parliamentary draftsmen should be spread as evenly as possible over the years. In March 1948 the Treasury issued to Departments a most useful guide to the preparation of Bills, setting out the various stages.

So now let us enter the individual Department and look at the work of a Minister and his officers involved in legislation, or who seek to be so involved. The Minister will have noted which, if any, of the legislative projects in *Let Us Face the Future* will have to come from his Department. At the same time his civil servants may well have placed before him legislative projects which the Department had in mind before the Minister took office. Here, if wise, he is careful and cautious, for he, no less than the Government as a whole, has to consider first of all what is desirable in the interests of the nation and, secondly, what is desirable in the interests of the party; and he may prejudice these considerations if he swallows too many Bills from the departmental archives. Some of such projects may well be urgent and important in the national interest, in which case the Minister will give them favourable consideration. But he has to be on his guard (sometimes Ministers can be a little innocent in such matters) against being persuaded to accept projects which do not conform with the principles I have indicated and which may well be the product of the understandable, but in the circumstances misplaced, enthusiasm of the Department or even the result of a civil servant having a bee in his bonnet. He may be told, 'Minister, this has the makings of a nice little Bill, not terribly exciting but useful and will cause you to live in history.' Now we all like to live in history; but if the proposed measure is not relevant to the circumstances at the time and if it needlessly adds to the huge task with which the Government as a whole is faced in getting through the measures to which it is committed, the Minister will be wrong to accept such advice. He will experience heavy cross-examination at the Future Legislation Committee and probably go away without the necessary permission to proceed. So he will examine all the projects, consider the spacing over the Sessions, and then decide what he will go for in the following Parliamentary Session, possibly adding one or more eligible Bills to the list, realizing that he will probably not get them in the next Session but that it may help him to get them in the Session after. Having selected the Bill or Bills he will seek to promote in the following Session, he will arrange to discuss the policy of them with his officers and the Parliamentary Secretary. Detailed reports will be called for and further meetings held, as a result of which conclusions on policy and scope will be provisionally reached.

It is almost inevitable that the interests or work of other Departments, particularly the Treasury, will be involved. So, although some discussion may already have taken place, the next stage will be consultation on the official level between the interested Departments. This is a rule of procedure. Ministers must never forget that there is such a thing as H.M.G.—the Government as a whole. In most cases the Minister will circulate to the appropriate policy Committee of the Cabinet a memorandum setting out his proposals and the scheme of the projected legislation. Should the proposals be rejected, that is the end of the matter unless the Minister insists on taking the exceptional course of appealing against the Committee to the Cabinet. If the proposals are approved, then to that extent the Minister's position will be strengthened when he reaches the Future Legislation Committee, for he will be able to say that he has the support of the appropriate policy Committee of the Cabinet.

The Sessional Programme

In order that discussions should not be rushed and that Bills should be ready in good time, including quite a number by the beginning of the following Session, I arranged that the consideration of a sessional programme by the Future Legislation Committee should begin months before the Session concerned opened; indeed, not very long after the previous Session began. Here we would have before us an outline of the parliamentary time-table for the Session ahead.

It has become the practice to open the new Session before Christmas (usually in November) and programmes are generally plotted up to the end of July or before the August Bank Holiday. The aim is usually to have business pretty well finished by this date, but naturally, as the Session proceeds, it may be found necessary to have an autumn spill-over of short or substantial duration in order to finish off the legislative programme. Such an extension of time might become necessary if a large number of Bills reached the Lords late and they had insufficient time to clear them before the Summer Recess. The less there is left over to the autumn the better.

There can be another reason for leaving some business over to the autumn—deliberately. If Parliament is prorogued because the Session ends at the Summer Recess, there will be slightly more delay in recalling Parliament in an emergency than if it has merely been adjourned. As crises of one sort or another are liable to arise during the long Summer Recess, the House of Commons has tended to prefer adjournment to prorogation.

The Claims of Essential Business

A substantial part of the time of the Session is not available for Government legislation. Time for other essential business must be provided. It was necessary at an early stage for the Chief Whip to produce a picture of the forthcoming parliamentary time-table. Indeed, the time-table had to be re-examined on a number of occasions during the Session in the light of changing events. Among the claims on parliamentary time to be taken into account are the following:

- The debate on the Address in reply to the Gracious Speech from the Throne.
- Provision for essential legislation and Supply, including:
  - Budget and Finance Bill.
  - Army and Air Force Annual Bill.
  - Supply days as required by the Standing Orders and the Consolidated Fund and Appropriation Bills.
  - Certain minor measures, including the Expiring Laws Continuance Bill, the Isle of Man Customs Bill, &c.
- Opposed Private Bill Legislation.
- Private Members' time.
- Days set aside for the consideration of the work of the Public Corporations.
- Debates on delegated legislation.
- Debates on the Adjournments for Recesses.
- Contingencies.

All the foregoing are essential business in the sense that they must be provided for before the time available for Government legislation can be ascertained. A brief explanation may be needed of those items which are not self-explanatory and have not already been discussed.

Opposed Private Bill Legislation

During the Session a large number of Private Bills—that is to say, Bills promoted by local authorities, statutory companies, &c.—come before Parliament, sometimes starting in the House of Commons and sometimes in the House of Lords. Most of them go through 'on the nod', that is to say the Chairman of Ways and Means moves by slightly rising from his seat, the question is proposed and if there is no objection the Motion for Second Reading goes through and the Bill is referred to a Committee. If there is opposition a Member will call 'Object', whereupon the Chairman of Ways and Means will name another day. In the meantime the Member will probably have been seen by the Parliamentary Agents promoting the Bill and his objections may have been removed or undertakings may have been given that an amendment or amendments which remove the Member's objection will be made. Unless some other Member takes up the chase the Bill will be allowed to proceed next time. But the objection may be persisted in, and then the Chairman of Ways and Means names a day at 7 p.m. for the debate. Time may thus be required for a debate on Second Reading, or on a Motion to instruct the Committee to strike out a clause or clauses if the Second Reading Motion has been carried. If the opposition is strong, further time of the House may be needed for the consideration of amendments on Report or for the Motion for Third Reading. It is not easy to estimate the time required for the consideration of opposed Private Bills, but some provision has to be made.

Private Members' Time

Provision has also to be made for Private Members' time—Public Bills and Motions. Twenty Fridays are now given for this purpose during the Session, ten of them for Bills and ten for Motions.

Debates on Socialized Industries

When a number of socialized industries came to be established under Public Corporations, it was natural and right that both sides of the House should wish to debate their work, though debates would not necessarily take place on every publicly owned industry each Session. I therefore undertook on behalf of the Government to provide three days each Session for debates on the socialized industries, normally on a Motion taking note of the Annual Report of the Public Corporation concerned. I held that if more days were required by the Opposition for this purpose they could take a Supply day formally, and then devote it to debate on such a Motion, taking one or two industries as desired. I had it in mind, however, that as the pressure of legislation decreased we should increase the amount of Government time available for such debates, for the publicly owned industries cover a wide field and it is right that Parliament should have adequate opportunity for the discussion of their affairs. As shown in Chapter XII there are other opportunities of discussing the work of the Public Corporations.

Debates on the Adjournment

On the eve of the Adjournment of the House for Recess—that is to say, the Recesses for Easter, Whitsun, the summer (unless Parliament is prorogued and not adjourned), and Christmas—it is the established practice of the House to devote the day to a debate on the Motion for the Adjournment; the initiative is usually accorded to back-benchers, there being of course suitable ministerial replies. Members give notice to the Speaker of the subjects they wish to raise and the Speaker has the not very enviable task of selecting from them the subjects to be discussed and the allocation of time between them. Provision therefore had to be made for these days.

Another possibility has to be faced, namely half-days for debates on a Motion for the Adjournment of the House under Standing Order No. 9, namely, to call attention to a definite matter of urgent public importance. Naturally these are not freely accorded by the Speaker, and if there is any opposition the support of not less than forty Members is required; but such debates are likely to occur from time to time and the time-table must take account of the possibility. However, since an amendment to the Standing Orders, this is not now so important, for the time occupied by debates on the Adjournment under Standing Order No. 9 is compensated for by the House continuing to sit beyond 10 p.m. for the number of hours so occupied, unless the Government should move to adjourn.

Contingencies

There remain contingencies—what are these? On Supply days the subjects of debate are under the control of the Opposition. In addition it is customary and proper for the Government to respond to Opposition demands which arise from time to time for days on which to discuss important matters arising during the Session. The debate may take place on a Vote of Censure, on a critical motion which is not a full Vote of Censure, or on a motion for the Adjournment of the House. In Committee of Supply or in a debate for the Adjournment of the House, legislation cannot be discussed, so sometimes a neutral Motion such as 'That this House takes note' of a Report or a White Paper or a ministerial statement would be put down in order that the House should not find itself cramped in the course of debate. Naturally, when the Opposition claims days for debate out of Government time the Leader of the House will often say that this is a suitable subject for debate in Committee of Supply, which is a polite way of indicating that the Opposition should use its own time for the purpose. This sometimes leads to argument on the Floor or to keen bargaining between the Whips. In the case of a two-day debate—often demanded, for example, on foreign affairs—it may be that one day will be taken out of Supply time and that the Government will give the other day. In any case, a certain number of days will have to be allocated for special debates, either freely provided by the Government or conceded by them as a result of Opposition demands; so provision for a certain number of such days has to be made in the time-table. Such are contingencies.

Finally, it is desirable for some provision to be made for unforeseen events which will require discussion even if not the passing of legislation. The Conservative Government's Bill following the unanticipated serious floods early in 1953 is a good example.

Time available for Government Legislation

What I have called essential business is likely to take 80–85 sitting days. The days available for Government legislation, assuming that Private Members' time is allowed, may vary between 60 and 70, depending upon the length of the Session.[1] One way of increasing the time available to the Government is by suspending the provision for Private Members' time. In our first Session (1945–6) we had to find time for two Budgets and two Finance Bills and, notwithstanding the well above average length of the Session, if Private Members had enjoyed their usual facilities to bring forward Bills and Motions we would have had only about sixty days for our legislative programme. This was totally inadequate. We had our mandate from the country to carry out a considerable programme of post-war reconstruction, and the transition period from war to peace was likely to throw up problems requiring legislation at any moment. For these reasons I asked the House of Commons to assist us as we found it necessary to take the whole time of the House for Government Business. We had also to reduce the length of Recesses and to prolong the Session beyond its normal length in order to complete our programme. Private Members' time also had to be taken in the two succeeding Sessions.

Time taken by Bills

Having determined the time required for essential business or business calculated to be inevitable, we were left with a certain number of parliamentary days, account having been taken of the probable length of Recesses. Each Bill then had to be looked at from the point of view of the time the Second Reading would fairly occupy, which might vary between a small part of a day or half a day, and one day or two days. The length of the Committee Stage is affected by a number of factors. If, as was the case with many Bills from 1945 to 1950, they

[1] The length of a Parliamentary Session may vary quite considerably. The length of the Sessions and the use of the time of the Parliaments of 1945–50 and 1950–1 are shown in Appendix A.

were to be taken in Standing Committee upstairs, no time on the Floor needed to be allocated to this stage, though the time in Standing Committee had to be estimated. We had a large majority in 1945–50 and it was therefore safe to send a substantial proportion of the Bills upstairs. There were some Bills of constitutional significance which were kept on the Floor of the House, e.g. the Supplies and Services (Transitional Powers) Bill, the Representation of the People Bill, and the Ireland Bill. The estimate of the time needed for the different stages on the Floor would depend on the size of the Bill and the degree to which it was controversial, so that the time required for the Committee Stage on the Floor was not easy to estimate. The time needed for the Report Stage was rather easier to calculate and the time required for Third Readings was fairly straightforward. Time also had to be allocated for the consideration of Lords' amendments and this, of course, depended upon what amendments the Lords had made, but in the case of most Bills little time was needed;[1] indeed, a large proportion of the Lords' amendments were likely to be drafting amendments promoted by the Government itself and concessions to the Opposition.

With the Chief Whip's report indicating the limits of the practicable, the Future Legislation Committee met a roomful of clamant Ministers persuasively arguing the case for the inclusion of their Bill or Bills in the next sessional programme. These were interesting though sometimes trying meetings. The Ministers gradually learned the principles and standards by which the members of the Future Legislation Committee judged eligibility and made the most brilliant efforts to prove that their proposals conformed. Their sincerity was not in question, but always more legislation was sought than there was parliamentary time available for its consideration. The argument and the questioning would proceed between the members of the Committee and the other Ministers and, indeed, between the other Ministers themselves. It was inevitable, however, that many Ministers were disappointed. After the departmental Ministers had departed, or on another day, the little band of Ministers

[1] The circumstances surrounding the Lords' amendments to the Conservative Transport Bill in 1953 were exceptional. They took some days for the Commons to consider, finishing in a Vote of Censure debate. I deal with this controversial point at the end of this chapter.

who constituted the Future Legislation Committee—who had little or no direct interest in legislative projects—would fairly consider the claims and do everything they could to meet the requests of their colleagues. Some we had to exclude from the considerations of the sessional programme for lack of merit or because there just was not time, whilst others we would include in the list for introduction if time should permit. In any case it was necessary to get into our minds a picture of the sessional time-table as it would be if all the requests were met and another picture or pictures of the situation after pruning had been engaged in. So a document was prepared surveying the ground and embodying a list of Bills for the Session classified under the following heads:

(i) Essential Bills (e.g. Expiring Laws Continuance, Finance, Army and Air Force Annual).
(ii) Major Bills.
(iii) Medium-sized Bills.
(iv) Minor Bills.
(v) Bills to be proceeded with if time permits.
(vi) Consolidation Bills.

There is no argument about a place for essential Bills: they have to proceed anyway, but they, like the others, are subject to collective examination and approval before presentation to Parliament. Major Bills constitute the highlights of the Session and are almost certainly controversial. Medium-sized Bills can be controversial. Minor Bills are in most cases uncontroversial. The inclusion of a Bill among those to be proceeded with if time permits is a consolation prize. Consolidation Bills are Bills which exclusively consolidate or do not materially amend the existing law and usually occupy very little parliamentary time, having received an exhaustive examination by a Joint Select Committee of both Houses of Parliament which is set up for the purpose each Session. They are, however, valuable to the Courts, to the lawyers, and indeed to the citizen, for they give the law up to date on a given subject in one statute. The Governments of 1945–51 expanded and systematized work on Consolidation Bills; and this work owed much to the persistence of Lord Jowitt, the Lord Chancellor.

Having re-surveyed the ground it was likely that the Future

Legislation Committee would again meet the Ministers seeking approval for the introduction of Bills, and we would do our best to conciliate those who were disappointed, carefully explaining the reasons for our decision. An appeal could be made against us to the Cabinet but that was not very often done even though there may have been substantial argument at this definitive meeting of the Future Legislation Committee.

The work of the Future Legislation Committee involved a 'slaughter of the innocents', but it is better to slaughter the innocents at the beginning of the Session so as not to be publicly committed to the legislation, than it is to have to be forced to slaughter them at the end of the Session, when it would probably be a confession of parliamentary mismanagement and would cause disappointment not only to Ministers but to the parliamentary and outside supporters of the measures which failed to reach the Statute Book; if they had been partly dealt with, that time would have been wasted. It has been urged that Government Bills uncompleted should be carried over by resolution to the next Session. This was considered and rejected. It would make Governments careless about planning the programme and would not be good for Parliament. Governments should plan well and, if they fail, take the consequences.

By a process of realistically estimating and organizing the time-table we knew pretty well what we were doing, and if in the process we had to kill for that Session a number of measures, the Ministers concerned had the comfort that they had been fairly heard and that they knew the facts. They could also make another attempt when the programme for the next Parliamentary Session was framed, or they might obtain the additional comfort, which sometimes turned out to be a reality, of having their Bills allocated to the list headed 'Bills to be proceeded with if parliamentary time permits'. Anyway, we had the facts, facts which could be argued about but were substantially unalterable, and therefore we could proceed to our decisions realistically. The ministerial argumentative battle would then proceed on the relative importance of the proposed Bills in the non-essential classes.

It will be seen that the proper organization of the parliamentary time-table in the legislative programme is a difficult business, but not so difficult if pains are taken to set out essential factors. It involved a special responsibility on me as Leader of the House and Chairman of the Cabinet Committees concerned, with a risk that I might upset respected colleagues in the process. The Leader of the House of Lords, Lord Addison, was another key man, much valued in these deliberations, and not less important than either of us was the Chief Whip with his large day-to-day responsibilities for the work of the House of Commons. Fortunately, Mr. Whiteley had the assistance of a very able Private Secretary who possessed long experience of the parliamentary machine. We also had the invaluable service of the Cabinet Secretariat who, together with the Whips' Department and others concerned, saw to it that the Committee had all the relevant facts before it.

Before leaving the Future Legislation Committee I should add that apart from settling, subject to the Cabinet, a legislative programme for the Session, it met from time to time during the Session in order to receive progress reports and to consider whether revision was necessary.

Drafting the Bills

When a Minister obtained the approval of the Future Legislation Committee to a Bill and was authorized to proceed with the drafting, the Department then set to work on what is known as the heads of the Bill. This is a document setting out in fairly precise terms the powers which it is sought to have embodied in the Bill. The heads of the Bill would be forwarded to Parliamentary Counsel (he and his colleagues often being known as the draftsmen) for drafting and probably to the other Departments concerned so that observations might be received and considered. A number of meetings with the draftsman would follow. The draftsman might well have a considerable number of points to raise: possibly constitutional points; the practicability of getting a proposal into due parliamentary form; the general legislative presentation. He would also want to know whether delegated powers should be sought by an affirmative resolution of the Houses or by providing that a negative resolution could be moved against them, or merely that they were to be laid upon the Table. These decisions about subordinate legislation largely depend on precedents and relative importance or how far it is likely to be controversial. Many matters of detail must be discussed between Parliamentary Counsel and the officers of the Department. In due course the first draft of the Bill would make its appearance so that it might be examined by the promoting Department and looked at by other Departments from the view-point of their interests. Another draft or drafts—perhaps many drafts—would follow (for the aim is to be word-perfect), and in due course the Bill would be submitted, not to the Future Legislation Committee, which has included the Bill in the programme, but to the Legislation Committee, which has the responsibility of examining the form and detail of the Bill before its presentation to Parliament.

As illustrating the heavy work of drafting and redrafting (at any rate in the case of important Bills) the number of drafts made in five of the Labour Government's Bills before they were presented to Parliament were:

Coal Industry Nationalisation	13
Transport	21
Electricity	15
Iron and Steel	12
Town and Country Planning	23

Parliamentary Counsel are important people even though they are almost unknown outside Government circles. We were well served by them. They carry a heavy load of responsibility, for if drafting mistakes are made, two worrying consequences may follow. The Government may well be made a fool of in Parliament and a tangled parliamentary situation may ensue. The House of Commons never enjoys itself better than when the House has got Ministers into a state of confusion; indeed the House can be equally happy if it has (even without need) itself got into such a confusing situation that Members do not know where they are, even though the Government does. The draftsmen therefore deserve sympathetic consideration, and at times the protection of the Chairman of the Committee; for sometimes when Departments are charged with being late in the production of their Bills they will unjustly imply that the fault is with the draftsmen. It is dangerous for these men to be caused to work under excessive pressure. Drafting a Parliamentary Bill is not like writing a novel—every word matters and has to stand up to examination in Parliament and the Courts. Charles Dickens's Mr. Bumble in *Oliver Twist* declared the law to be an ass, but so far as drafting is concerned this is not often the case, and the credit mostly belongs to those quiet hard-pressed men, the draftsmen.

The Legislation Committee

So we now come to the work of the Legislation Committee. This was a larger Committee than the Future Legislation Committee. It included the Leader of the House of Commons (in the Chair after 1947), the Leader of the House of Lords, the Lord Chancellor, the Law Officers of the Crown, the Chief Whip, and a limited number of departmental Ministers. The Ministers concerned with Bills were also present and Parliamentary Counsel would be in attendance. So, although larger than the Future Legislation Committee, it was one of the smaller of the Cabinet Committees.

The Committee would examine a Bill not normally from the point of view of policy but from the standpoint of general structure, proper legal wording, fairness, good sense in carrying out the intentions of the Government, and general acceptability as a workable measure. It was at this stage that special consideration would be given to the power to make Regulations.

We improved the Government machinery for considering delegated legislation, and the Legislation Committee gave systematic consideration to important Statutory Instruments. When Instruments were of importance or likely to be controversial, and certainly when any principles of liberty were involved, we required them to be submitted to the Legislation Committee for examination as if they were Bills. The authority to make them was of course contained in Acts of Parliament, but there was at times considerable argument, for we were rightly on the watch lest the Departments went too far or in case the proper rights of the subject were impaired.

After it was passed by the Committee the road was clear for a Bill to be presented to Parliament, though in some exceptional cases Bills were examined by the Cabinet either before or after they had been to the Committee. At times Bills were also examined from the policy angle by the policy Committee concerned.

The Committee on Legislation or the Leader of the House and the Chief Whip would have to decide whether the Committee Stage of Bills should be taken on the Floor or upstairs. Another question for consideration would be whether the Bills should start in the Lords or the Commons. Hitherto their Lordships had frequently complained that they did not get enough legislation submitted in the early months of a Session, and that as a result chunks of legislation were thrown at them for unduly quick digestion towards the end of the Parliamentary Session. Our legislative planning much improved matters in this respect, and the Lords were appreciative. Quite a number of important Bills started in the House of Lords and thus tended to save parliamentary time, for its Members can be dealing with the Second Reading and Committee and other Stages of one Bill while the House of Commons is dealing with another. Money Bills and Bills of a constitutional character, or indeed controversial Bills of major importance, could hardly start in the House of Lords. But other Bills could and were much improved by the time they reached the House of Commons, and the labours of that House were to that extent lightened. This arrangement also diminished the number of Bills which had to be sent to the House of Lords from the Commons towards the end of the Session.

After the Legislation Committee had examined and passed a Bill the question of publicity had to be considered. Some Bills explain themselves, and others which have on the face of them an explanatory memorandum will often be sufficiently clear to the newspapermen. But in a number of cases it might be difficult for journalists to explain the meaning of a Bill without some assistance and guidance—and I am here concerned with understanding and not propaganda. In the case of certain Bills therefore, after presentation to the House, it was found desirable for the Minister concerned to have a Press Conference at which the journalists were given notes explaining the clauses and the Minister expounded the general purpose of the Bill and submitted himself to questioning. Care had to be taken about these Press Conferences, for Parliament is jealous of its rights. If the Press were in possession of Bills before Parliament had got them there might well be trouble. The time-table therefore had to be carefully worked out, the chief consideration being to know at what time the Bill would be available to M.P.s in the Vote Office. Once that was ascertained the Press Conference could be summoned to meet shortly after, or even at that time.

Notice appears on the Order Paper for the presentation of the Bill to the House. At the commencement of Public Business the Minister nods after the Clerk at Table has read the short title of the Bill, which is thereby automatically read the first time and ordered to be printed. A date is then given for the Second Reading so that the Bill can appear amongst the Orders of the day. It remains for the Leader of the House and the Chief Whip, in consultation with the Minister, to settle the actual date for the debate on Second Reading, and after Second Reading, the Committee Stage, Report Stage, and Third Reading. The Bill then goes to the second House for similar consideration, followed by the Royal Assent.

Achievement of the Programme

I have now told the story of the shaping and passing of what must be the most extensive and significant legislative programme in the history of our great Parliament. The table on p. 242 sets out the result in volume, comparing the Sessions of 1945–51 with the pre-war Sessions of 1932–8. It should be noted that there were General Elections which interrupted parliamentary work in 1935 and in 1950. In the Sessions of 1950–1 the Labour Government had an overall majority of six and therefore we denied ourselves the luxury of controversial legislation.

It will be noted that the average number of pages of legislation passed per Session was just under 1,113 in the six pre-war Sessions as compared with 1,558 in the six post-war Sessions, and that the average numbers of Acts passed per Session were respectively 59·3 and 68·8, so that the contrast in the number of Acts is less noticeable than the number of pages. A number of our Bills were, of course, unusually large. The work of consolidation added to the number of pages of the Statute Book, since all Consolidation Acts are long, and the Labour Government tackled this problem more systematically than previous Governments. So the table is subject to a number of qualifications.

The Volume of Legislation between 1932–3 and 1937–8 as compared with that between 1945–6 and 1950–1 illustrated by statistics of the Public General Acts

Session		Chapters*	Pages	Pages per chapter
1932–3	23 & 24 Geo. V	53	1,047	19·8
1933–4	24 & 25 Geo. V	59	664	11·3
1934–5	25 & 26 Geo. V	47	1,076	22·9
1935–6	26 Geo. V, 1 Edw. VIII	54	1,900	35·2
1936–7	1 Edw. VIII, 1 Geo. VI	70	1,039	14·8
1937–8	1 & 2 Geo. VI	73	950	13·0
Average per Session		59·3	1,112·7	19·5
1945–6	9 & 10 Geo. VI	83	1,390	16·7
1946–7	10 & 11 Geo. VI	55	1,941	35·3
1947–8	11 & 12 Geo. VI	67	2,035	30·4
1948–9	12–14 Geo. VI	103	2,327	22·6
1950	14 Geo. VI	39	947	24·3
1950–1	14 & 15 Geo. VI	66	708	10·7
Average per Session		68·8	1,558	23·3

* i.e. Acts of Parliament.

I should be among the last to argue that mere legislative output is conclusive evidence of the virtue of a Parliament or a Government, and my readers will have varying views on the quality of the legislation passed by the pre-war and post-war Parliaments. However, that argument is in the field of controversial party politics which are not within the scope of this volume. What I think I can fairly claim is that we much improved the planning and examination of legislation by the Government and that we showed that Parliament was capable of a materially increased legislative output consistent as a whole with proper parliamentary consideration, and the discharge of its other duties.

Use of the Guillotine

Unfortunately, we had to use the Guillotine on three occasions. These occasions were:

1946–7	Town and Country Planning Bill	One Motion including the two Bills.
,,	Transport Bill	

1948–9 Iron and Steel Bill.

There were, however, precedents for the Guillotine; and the Conservative Government used it three times within eighteen months in the Parliament elected in 1951.[1] These were:

1951–2 National Health Service Bill.
,, Licensed Premises in New Towns Bill.
1952–3 Transport Bill.

It can indeed be argued that this Conservative Government used it on four occasions, though what I would call a fourth Guillotine was supplementary to the original Allocation of Time Order on the Transport Bill. It involved both a Motion and the application of a principle which had never before been applied. The House of Lords had made many amendments to the Transport Bill after it left the Commons. This is not unusual, but among these amendments were a number of changes and innovations of real substance promoted by the Government which had not been examined hitherto in the House of Commons. When these amendments were debated in the Commons the Opposition strongly opposed the supplementary Allocation of Time Order on the grounds:

1. That a Guillotine Motion on Lords' amendments was unprecedented, and was additionally objectionable as it followed the main Guillotine which had limited debate in the Commons before the Bill went to the Lords.
2. That as these amendments included new and important matters, the Commons were being denied their legislative rights, and to that extent single-chamber legislation by the Lords was being imposed.
3. That the Order was so tight that many of the Lords' amendments and proposed amendments to them would be carried without debate or even separate divisions.
4. That some of the Lords' amendments involved Commons' privileges and the House would not be able to decide whether or not to waive them.

The Government answer was that the Opposition was taking up too much time and that Ministers must protect themselves.

[1] In Appendix B I set out two Allocation of Time Orders, both of which cover the whole of the proceedings on the respective Bills. The first deals with the Labour Government's Iron and Steel Bill, 1948–9, and the second with the Conservative Government's Transport Bill, 1952–3.

It was revealed that in discussions between the Government and the Opposition 'behind the Chair' the difference about time had been reduced to one parliamentary day. The Guillotine saved that day for the Government, but the Opposition proceeded to lose it for them by requiring a Vote of Censure debate on the matter the following week.[1] A new precedent was created and it will be for future Governments and Parliaments to decide whether the precedent should be followed.

The Parliament of 1945–50 achieved great things; it demonstrated that Parliament could be a workshop as well as discharging its necessary functions as a talk-shop. It was shown that legislative programmes could be planned in good time for the Session, and over the Parliament as a whole. The quality and merits of the achievements are for history to judge.

[1] For the Government and Opposition arguments the reader is referred to 514 *H.C. Deb.* 1565–1610 (23 April), 1769–1820 (27 April), and 515 *H.C. Deb.* 214–343 (5 May) 1953.

ADMINISTRATION

CHAPTER XII

Socialization of Industry: Public Control and Accountability

At the General Election of 1945 the Labour Party published its statement of policy, *Let Us Face the Future*, in the preparation of which I had played a leading part as Chairman of the Executive's Policy Committee. We included in this document proposals for the transfer from private to public ownership of the following undertakings or industries:

The Bank of England.

The Fuel and Power industries, namely, coal, gas, and electricity.

Inland Transport, comprising transport services by rail, road, air, and canal.

Iron and Steel.

In addition, the following other public concerns were set up during the 1945–50 Parliament:

Cable and Wireless.

Raw Cotton Commission.

Colonial Development Corporation.

Overseas Food Corporation.

Cabinet and Committee Consideration

It was clearly desirable that the various schemes should be subjected to careful collective ministerial examination and discussion. The Prime Minister set up a Committee of Ministers under my Chairmanship which included what we may call the socializing Ministers, and certain others dealing with industry, finance, and labour. We were served by a similarly chosen committee of officers to whom were referred from time to time, for consideration and report, matters of detail or awkward problems which had to be sorted out prior to ministerial consideration. We discussed the general principles upon which it was desirable to proceed. Ministers, seeking authority for the drafting of legislation, would submit memoranda embodying their proposals for the organization, structure, and finance of the new public concerns; the basis of compensation; the powers of the Minister; the channels of complaint for the consumer; the rights of labour; and so on. These memoranda would already have been the subject of inter-departmental consideration at the official level. They would be considered by Ministers at a number of meetings and reports submitted to the Cabinet. Thereafter the preparation of legislation could proceed and discussions with the interests concerned be entered into. The Bills when drafted were submitted to this Committee on Socialization of Industries, to the Legislation Committee, and, in some cases, to the Cabinet.

It will be seen that apart from the heavy labours of the promoting Ministers and the Departments directly concerned, extensive and responsible work was involved for the Committee of Ministers. All this, however, was worth while. We were launching big changes and engaged upon responsible tasks; it was vital to do everything we could to assure ourselves that we were proceeding on the right lines.

The Public Corporation

At one time it was generally assumed that socialization meant running an industry as a Government Department with a Minister at its head and a staff of civil servants. But during the inter-war period the Labour Party and the Trade Union Movement had put a good deal of thought into the possibility of developing the Public Corporation as the form of management best suited to large-scale concerns of a commercial and industrial character. As Minister of Transport in the Labour Government of 1929–31 I had the good fortune to be able to make an important contribution to the development of this idea by the establishment of the London Passenger Transport Board, even though my Bill was altered for the worse (as I thought) by the 'National' Government which finally put through the measure. In 1933 I published a book, *Socialisation and Transport*, in which the case for the Public Corporation was set out. I think this influenced Labour thought and perhaps even the wider circle of those who foresaw that certain major measures of nationalization were inevitable. Naturally there were some differences of view on details and there was one major difference on the constitution of the Boards—certain Trade Union leaders thought that some of the members of the Boards should be directly nominated by the Unions as representatives of the workers in the industry. However, the T.U.C. came round to my way of thinking on this point.[1] When we took office in August 1945, therefore, we knew that the Public Corporation would be the form chosen for nationalization unless a detailed study of the circumstances of a particular industry should indicate that another form was more appropriate.

What is a Public Corporation? Its characteristics can only be described in general terms, for, though the Labour Government adopted certain common features for the management of the industries it nationalized, there were nevertheless some differences, largely depending upon the character of the industry and its history. Moreover, we should remember that some of the features are adaptable in the light of experience. This is obviously desirable.

The National Coal Board, the British Electricity Authority, and the other corporations established to manage the nationalized industries are bodies corporate in which the assets of the industry are vested. The Board of the corporation is appointed by the appropriate Minister who is answerable to Parliament for the appointments. In general the Minister is required by statute to appoint the members from among persons appearing to him to be qualified as having had experience of, and having shown capacity in, industrial, commercial or financial matters, applied science, administration, or the organization of workers. That is the statutory provision governing the appointment of the National Coal Board. Most of the other Acts follow suit, except that in the case, for example, of the electricity and gas Boards, experience of the specific industry is also mentioned as a qualification which can be taken into account. For the Colonial Development Corporation the requirement is materially different:

persons appearing to him [i.e. the Secretary of State] to be qualified as having had experience of, and having shown capacity in, matters

[1] See T.U.C., *Interim Report on Post-War Reconstruction*, 1944.

relating to primary production, industry or trade, finance, science, administration, organisation of workers or welfare, and in making such appointments the Secretary of State shall have particular regard to the need for securing that adequate experience of those matters obtained in colonial territories is at the disposal of the Corporation.

Some of the members of the Boards are full-time and some part-time.

The Board has both powers and duties. Its main duty is to operate and manage the industry in the public interest, and to this end it is given all the necessary powers by Parliament. Thus the coal-mines of the country are vested in the National Coal Board and it is the Board and not the Minister of Fuel and Power which has statutory authority to employ the miners, buy machinery, and do all that is necessary to obtain the coal. In carrying out these important managerial functions the Board is required by the Act to perform certain important statutory duties. Thus the Board is charged with the duties of:

(*a*) working and getting the coal in Great Britain, to the exclusion . . . of any other person;

(*b*) securing the efficient development of the coal-mining industry; and

(*c*) making supplies of coal available, of such qualities and sizes, in such quantities and at such prices, as may seem to them best calculated to further the public interest in all respects, including the avoidance of any undue or unreasonable preference or advantage.

Whilst the primary and statutory responsibility for operating and managing the industry is thus placed on the Board, the appropriate Minister is given certain important powers of control and direction. In particular:

The Minister may, after consultation with the Board, give to the Board directions of a general character as to the exercise and performance by the Board of their functions in relation to matters appearing to the Minister to affect the national interest, and the Board shall give effect to any such directions.

The approval of the Minister of Fuel and Power, for example, is required for the lines on which the N.C.B. frame their programmes of reorganization or development involving substantial outlay on capital account and exercise their functions of training, education, and research. It is also usual for the appropriate Minister to appoint the auditors of the Board's accounts and to prescribe the form which these accounts must take. The Board must also submit an Annual Report and Statement of Accounts to the Minister, who is required to lay them before Parliament. The Act nationalizing the industry thus prescribes the statutory powers and duties of both the Board and the Minister.

In view of some of the subsequent criticisms of this form of management it is worth noticing that our legislation gave the Minister, and therefore Parliament, much more power of control over the Boards than did the legislation which set up the pre-war Boards. In the case of the pre-war Central Electricity Board and the London Passenger Transport Board, for example, the Minister was given no power to issue general directions, nor to concern himself with their programmes for capital development, research, and training. Very rightly in the case of the British Broadcasting Corporation special care was taken to establish the independence of the Governors. So long as the Governors and the administration of the B.B.C. act fairly there can hardly be argument about this, for it would be very wrong if sound broadcasting and television were to become the instruments of the Government of the day. We felt, however, that the pre-war ministerial powers over the public industrial undertakings were insufficient if the Boards were to be made properly accountable and if they were to conform to the Government's economic and social policy.

We appreciated, however, that the choice of the public corporation even with this greater degree of ministerial control did leave the precise character of the public accountability of these Boards to be worked out in the light of experience. There was a problem—the problem of getting the best of both possible worlds—the world of vigorous industrial enterprise without the restrictions imposed by civil service methods and Treasury control, and the world of public service and accountability. Had we chosen the ordinary ministerial Department there would not have been any new problems of accountability, though other serious problems would have arisen.

The Ministerial Department

Apart from not infrequent allegations of bureaucracy and parliamentary evasion, State departmental management solves the problem of public accountability. The Minister is answerable to Parliament for every detail of the work of the Department of which he is the head; and, of course, there is no doubt about his responsibility to the nation as a whole. Questions on quite small as well as on large matters can be put in Parliament. During the war, when the Minister of Transport was temporarily responsible for the management of the railways, Questions were put down asking why a particular train was *x* minutes late at *y* station on a particular day, and Questions are occasionally put down to the Postmaster-General to ask why Mr. So-and-So of Such-and-Such has not had his telephone installed. It is but fair to add, however, that a large proportion of Questions in Parliament do raise issues of importance. The estimates of any socialized undertakings vested in a State Department could be scrutinized by the Select Committee on Estimates from time to time, members of which might decide to visit the undertaking, or parts of it, and examine the management and work on the spot. The Public Accounts Committee and the Comptroller and Auditor-General would have a full and definite responsibility to examine their accounts.

Establishment and finance (including prices, charges, and income) would be subject to Treasury control, and from time to time other inter-departmental discussions would arise. The staff (including manual workers, if the practice of the Royal Dockyards were followed) would be civil servants and their numbers, pay, and conditions would be subject to Treasury approval. It would follow that these matters could be debated and voted upon by the House of Commons. As we shall see there are considerable opportunities for parliamentary debate on the work of the public corporations; but if the undertakings were managed by State Departments with the Minister at the head, not only could the general management be discussed on Supply days but also any particular issue of commercial or other practice could be challenged on a division by a Motion to reduce the Minister's salary.

In the case of ordinary Government Departments, including

even the Post Office, all these things work pretty well and there is full parliamentary accountability. But it would be a very different matter in the case of highly commercial industries or services. So the use of the public corporation method in many instances, though by no means all, is justified. If we take coal-mining, the extensive complexities of inland transport, home and overseas civil aviation, iron and steel, and raw cotton, we are dealing with lively commercial businesses which cannot and ought not to 'run on rails'. Day-to-day and even hour-to-hour decisions have to be taken on the spot, and fixed rules and precedents should not slavishly govern the management. I do not wish it to be thought that State Departments are incapable of rapid action in cases of emergency. They can and do so act from time to time; but normally decisions must be based on the minutes and memoranda of the civil service organization, and whilst there is no doubt—often rightly—some routine of this kind in the public corporations and large-scale private concerns, it would tend to become normal if the great publicly owned commercial undertakings were managed by State Departments. But commercial success requires quick and even risky decisions to be taken on business issues which come from out of the blue.

The public corporations are, for the most part, free from direct parliamentary pressure and the indirect pressure of the constituents of M.P.s. On salaries, wages, and conditions of labour they can negotiate with the trade unions concerned with much less likelihood of being subject to political pressure.

The level of salaries would present another difficulty if the socialized undertakings were run as ministerial Departments: either they would not be able to pay more than the civil service scales, or if they did there would be friction inside the Civil Service. What salaries should be paid is a question for argument, but the managerial brains of these great commercial enterprises need to be not less able than those employed in private enterprise. Unduly low salaries like unduly low wages would put the undertaking at a disadvantage and might be, in the long run, a costly affair. Even so, having regard to their responsibilities, the salaries of the Board members are, in general, lower than those paid in comparable privately owned concerns, some of which in my view are rather luxurious. Of course, there may well also be difficulties about wage standards.

From time to time the question is raised whether Parliament is not overloaded. Certainly the work of M.P.s is heavy nowadays and their hours of labour are considerable. It is difficult to fit into the parliamentary time-table all the matters which should be considered, though at the cost of much effort we succeed pretty well. Already Parliament has had to delegate a number of functions which might normally have been discharged by Ministers and therefore subjected to parliamentary examination and control. The Assistance Board is an example. If the Government were to take on the management of the undertakings of the public corporations which now exist, the added burden on Parliament would be considerable and probably excessive. Moreover, much as I admire our great parliamentary institution, modesty compels me to admit that I do not think it is suited for the management of complex economic undertakings such as coal-mines, transport, &c., even though its general debates on the public corporations are of the highest value.

If the considerations set out above carry weight it is necessary to avoid meticulous parliamentary accountability for every action taken.

It can be fairly argued that the management of the Post Office by a Government Department, with complete civil service organization, and notwithstanding the Postmaster-General's meticulous accountability to Parliament, is successful. No doubt the Post Office, like every other governmental activity, is open to criticism in certain respects. We hear from time to time complaints about the telephone service and the standard of courtesy behind the Post Office counters which may or may not be justified in particular cases. As a whole, however, I think it will be generally agreed (certainly by all Postmasters-General of all parties) that the Post Office serves us well. The General Post Office has a wide variety of functions: the collection and delivery of letters and parcels, telegrams, overseas cables and wireless; it is involved, with the B.B.C., in complicated technical problems relating to sound broadcasting and television; it manages a Savings Bank; and it discharges a considerable variety of functions on behalf of other Government Departments, particularly in the payment of allowances and pensions. This extensive and varied business is carried on with a high degree of reliability and not without profit to the Exchequer.

Another, but much smaller, State trading undertaking is the State management of public houses and hotels in Carlisle and district and in a limited area of south-west Scotland. This was instituted during the First World War by Mr. Lloyd George when Minister of Munitions in an effort to combat alleged excessive drinking among munition workers. The Home Secretary and the Secretary of State for Scotland (though they are assisted by Committees) are answerable to Parliament for every glass of beer, or lemonade, or cup of tea that is sold, and for accommodation and meals provided in the public houses and hotels vested in their Departments. Possibly it is in part owing to the limited scale of the operations, but what surprised me when I was Home Secretary was the fewness of Parliamentary Questions put to me about this interesting experiment. The State management scheme has a very peaceful existence and is a success. The Royal Ordnance Factories owned and managed by the Minister of Supply are another example of direct management by a Minister and the Civil Service.

The Problem of Accountability

There are, however, such obvious and generally admitted advantages in the public corporation form of management that it would be unwise to throw them away because it raises new issues of accountability. We must find the best working methods to overcome them.

When, as Minister of Transport in 1931, I submitted to the House the London Passenger Transport Bill, Sir Philip Cunliffe-Lister criticized the measure on the ground that:

> ... throughout this Bill you find the Minister mentioned on every page, and the control of the Minister goes all through this Measure [250 *H.C. Deb.* 80 (23 Mar. 1931)].

This was something of an exaggeration, for the ministerial powers under that Bill were small as compared with those conferred under the 1945 Labour Government's socializing laws. Since then I have had the experience that the very M.P.s who were most critical of any idea that Ministers and other politicians should be given the opportunity 'to play ducks and drakes' with the practical problems of publicly owned industries were, later on, most indignantly complaining because a Parliamentary Question to a Minister about some detail of a Board's management was not accepted by the Speaker or the Clerks as being in order. It is, of course, a firm parliamentary rule and tradition that a Minister is accountable to Parliament for anything he or his Department does or for anything he has powers to do, whether he does it or not. That is to say, if the action or possible action is within the field of ministerial power or competence the Minister is answerable to Parliament. But the principle of parliamentary accountability does not hold the Minister responsible for things which Parliament has already decided he is not responsible for, and which are therefore outside his power and competence. Yet this was exactly what some Members on both sides of the House of Commons were in danger of doing in respect of the work of the public corporations. For in setting up these socialized Boards Parliament had placed many duties and responsibilities directly on the Boards and not on any Minister.

The Parliamentary Question

This well-established parliamentary doctrine that Ministers are not answerable to Parliament for matters not under their control or direction or which Parliament has delegated to other bodies has been repeatedly laid down by the Chair. For example, on the 16th of May 1917 Mr. Billing raised a point of order with the Speaker because a Question had been refused at the Table in which he had sought to ask the Prime Minister whether his attention had been called to a recent riot at Gillingham; whether any action had been taken against the rioters; and whether the Government had any information about the reasons for the riot. He asked the Speaker why the Question had been refused. The Speaker replied: 'The hon. Member should ask the Watch Committee of the district. The great boast of England is its system of local self-government.' This ruling was given although the local Watch Committee, as police authority, received a substantial grant from the Exchequer. Nevertheless, the Speaker of the day was, if I may respectfully say so, right in ruling the Question out of order in that form on the ground that Parliament had conferred responsibility on the Watch Committee and not on a Minister. If, however, the Member had put his Question in the form of asking the Home Secretary to withhold the grant on the basis of an allegation that the Watch Committee had proved incompetent I should imagine that his Question would have been accepted and he might possibly have succeeded, up to a point, in getting away with supplementary questions embodying the point of the Question which had been ruled out of order. Even so the Home Secretary would probably have denied responsibility and the Chair could hardly have helped Mr. Billing if he had protested.

Another instance of Parliament delegating its responsibility is that of the National Assistance Board. In the House of Commons on 3 March 1948 Sir John Anderson argued that 'the Ministers concerned made it perfectly clear that the responsibility was going to rest on the Board, to the exclusion of the responsibility of Ministers. That was accepted, and, moreover, the functions in question were in the nature of judicial functions, which have to be exercised in a judicial spirit in regard to which it would not only be wrong, but an outrage, for the Minister to interfere.' It is indeed the case that the Act specifically precludes the Minister from dealing with individual cases, despite the fact that the expenditure on national assistance is wholly met by the Treasury and the Assistance Board is staffed by civil servants. In the same debate I quoted from the Romanes Lecture, given at Oxford in 1946, by Sir John Anderson, who had stated the issue in the following way: 'The extent of Ministerial control should be defined as clearly as possible in the instrument constituting the authority. In regard to matters falling within the Minister's powers of control, he would be liable to be questioned in Parliament in the usual way. On the other hand, in regard to all matters declared to be within the discretion of the authority, the Minister would be entitled and, indeed, bound, to disclaim responsibility.'

It is characteristic of the elasticity of our parliamentary procedure that when a difficulty of real substance or magnitude arises we try to find a way whereby the difficulty can be met. This kind of situation arose as a result of an extensive breakdown in electricity supply at the end of May 1948. Questions about this important occurrence were refused at the Table on the ground that the Minister of Fuel and Power had no power to act. Very rightly, as I think, the Speaker decided to go into the matter, and on 7 June 1948 he made a statement. He recalled that Erskine May's *Parliamentary Practice* laid it down that Questions addressed to Ministers should relate to the public affairs with which they are officially connected, to proceedings pending in Parliament, or to matters of administration for which they are responsible. He further said that the rule requiring ministerial responsibility has had the effect of excluding a certain number of Questions about nationalized industries, but not very many, since the responsibilities of Ministers under the relevant statutes are very wide so far as obtaining information is concerned. It was, however, the rule against the repetition of Questions (which excludes Questions repeating in substance those already answered or to which an answer has been refused) that had had the largest share in excluding Questions. Mr. Speaker Clifton Brown added that his consideration of this difficulty had led him to the conclusion that the 'strict application of this Rule might operate more harshly than either Ministers or Members generally would wish' and that whilst he proposed to leave the rule which exludes Questions on matters outside ministerial responsibility unchanged, he was prepared, if it was generally approved, to exercise his discretion to direct the acceptance of Questions asking for a statement to be made on matters on which information had previously been refused, provided that they were of sufficient public importance to justify the concession. He added that 'public importance' was one of the tests for the Motions for the Adjournment of the House under Standing Order No. 8,[1] which in his experience was a not unduly difficult test to apply.

As Leader of the House I thanked the Speaker for his consideration of the matter and indicated that as far as His Majesty's Government were concerned we would accept the decision he had reached and were prepared to try out this new method of handling of Questions about the nationalized industries. Naturally, there were a number of supplementary Questions from Members of the House who were not completely satisfied, but I think I can say that eventually Mr. Speaker's statement

[1] See S.O. No. 9 (1953).

was accepted as a sensible way out of an exceptional difficulty and as calculated to meet any outstanding grievance of substance.

On 4 December 1951 the House of Commons appointed a Select Committee on Nationalised Industries 'to consider the present methods by which the House of Commons is informed of the affairs of the Nationalised Industries and to report what changes, having regard to the provisions laid down by Parliament in the relevant statutes, may be desirable in these methods'.

The Committee, under the Chairmanship of Mr. Ralph Assheton, examined various witnesses and their First Report issued on 29 October 1952 dealt with Parliamentary Questions. Their conclusions, which would appear, as a whole, not to conflict with what I have said, are set out in paragraphs 14 to 18 as follows:

14. Your Committee are aware of a strong desire in some quarters to make the Nationalised Industries as generally subject to Parliamentary Questions as the Post Office and all the other Civil Departments. Certain points, however, must be borne in mind in considering the advantages and disadvantages of such a policy.

15. The public corporations which control the Nationalised Industries were constituted on different lines from the usual civil departments. The public corporations were established as independent entities, with statutory obligations to meet their expenditure by their own revenue. Their activities involve commercial transactions on a large scale, and it is desirable that they should not be unduly hampered by external interference. On the other hand, it is urged that the nation has become the owners of the enormous assets involved in those industries, and it is widely felt that there should be means of enquiry and criticism.

16. There are various other means of criticism and enquiry open to Members of Parliament, such as debates on the annual reports and statements of accounts of the various corporations. Your Committee intend if reconstituted in the next session to consider whether additional machinery ought to be established to meet this problem.

17. The basic feature of the Parliamentary Question is that it is answered by the Minister ultimately responsible for the decisions about which he is questioned. Under their existing constitution, the Nationalised Industries are not subject to any direct control by Ministers in individual matters of detail. Your Committee therefore feel that without altering the terms of the statutes under which the public corporations are constituted, which they are not empowered

to recommend, Questions on matters of detail in the Nationalised Industries are inappropriate.

18. On the other hand, Your Committee are convinced that the present method of placing the onus of determining in the first place whether a Question which is not obviously ruled out under paragraph 17 above should be placed upon the Order Paper should not rest upon the Clerks at the Table. Where the identical Question, or the same Question in slightly different terms, has been previously asked, the Clerks at the Table are clearly obliged to refuse it. But in the case of questions which are not obviously matters of repetition or matters of detailed administration the questions should be allowed to appear on the Order Paper and the Minister would have to answer or refuse to answer on the floor of the House.

Having shown that the constitutional doctrine on the eligibility of Parliamentary Questions is supported by Erskine May, by Mr. Speaker, and from various political quarters, let us now consider the opportunities which are open to Parliament for Parliamentary Questions and debate on the work of the socialized industries.

The Ministers appoint the members of the Boards of public corporations, determine their salaries and conditions of service, and have the power to terminate their appointments. It is clear, therefore, that Questions can be put about the suitability of the appointments or even asking for the removal of a member or all the members of a Board. Salaries could be questioned either upon the basis that they are too high or too low or that an individual board member in view of his abilities and record is not worth the salary that is being paid to him. I assume that a Question would be in order alleging that the management of a Board is incompetent or contrary to the public interest and asking that the Board should be removed and a new Board appointed.

Borrowing by the Boards and capital investment require ministerial approval so that Questions can be put to the appropriate Minister urging either that capital expenditure should be disapproved or suggesting that favourable consideration should be given to capital expenditure which would enable the Board to embark upon developments or improvements desired by the Member putting the Question.

The Minister appoints the auditors of the accounts of the

Boards, and the form of the Accounts and Annual Reports are subject to his approval. This opens the possibility of a wide range of Questions not only about the general form of the accounts and the arrangements for auditing but also, for example, asking whether additional information should not be provided or questioning the character of the Annual Reports and suggesting that additional matters should be dealt with in them.

The Minister has to approve programmes of research and development. This responsibility of the Minister clearly gives M.P.s the right to put forward suggestions about research and development on a wide variety of matters. The same rights exist for schemes of education and training, as these are subject to ministerial approval or consideration.

Pensions schemes for staff require the approval of the Minister. Questions should be in order asking whether the Minister has had schemes submitted to him, and if so what he has done about them, and (more doubtfully) whether he would give his approval if the Board were prepared to put a certain scheme forward. Another subject that requires ministerial approval is compensation for displacement. Certain Questions about this would be in order.

The Minister has considerable powers in relation to Consumer Councils which would appear to make possible Questions on matters dealt with in the Reports of the Consumer Councils and even suggestions that he should refer points to the Consumer Councils for consideration and report.

These important examples show that the opportunities for Parliamentary Questions are very wide. I take the view that it is desirable for Ministers to be helpful within the rules rather than obstructive in such matters. When Lord President I gave the House positive advice about the field within which Questions could be put. Nevertheless I am doubtful whether M.P.s have yet shown their customary ingenuity in framing Parliamentary Questions that would be in order, but I shall be surprised if they do not learn as the years pass. It is perhaps significant that with the passage of time the controversy about the eligibility of Parliamentary Questions has tended to diminish.

Questions in Parliament are not the only means whereby Members can get information or ventilate grievances on behalf of their constituents about the nationalized industries. Arrangements were made whereby letters from M.P.s to the Chairmen of the Boards would receive proper consideration and replies. The Boards very rightly go to considerable trouble to see that Members are adequately catered for in this respect. For example, the Chairman of the British Transport Commission, Lord Hurcomb, told the Select Committee on Nationalised Industries in 1952 that his average correspondence with Members was about 1,700 letters a year. I imagine that very often M.P.s will receive in the form of letters fuller and perhaps more satisfactory information than could be condensed into a parliamentary answer.

Other Opportunities in Parliament

Other substantial opportunities for the consideration of the work of the publicly owned industries are open to Parliament, largely free from any restriction on the subject-matter.

At the end of every House of Commons Sitting day a subject or subjects can be discussed for half an hour on the Motion for the Adjournment. This is a valuable facility which is used very fully by Members to raise issues of policy or grievances on all manner of subjects. In earlier days the half hour was not always available, but I inaugurated a Standing Order whereby that facility was guaranteed to Members. It can, and has been, used by Members to raise matters connected with the socialized industries, and the rules that limit the scope of Questions do not apply.

Debates can take place on the Annual Reports of the Boards which Ministers are required to present to Parliament. These extensive debates can take two forms. They can occur in Committee of Supply on the estimates of the appropriate Government Department or during the Government's time. In Committee of Supply the critics can, if they are so minded, on a Motion for the reduction in the Minister's salary, register disapproval of the work of publicly owned industries. It was not, however, fair to the Opposition that they should be required out of their Supply days to find all the time for such debates, and I therefore undertook that we would give three days of Government time for debates on the Reports of the socialized industries. In some Parliamentary Sessions these three days may be enough, but if that should not be so the Opposition could find extra days out of Supply. It is not essential for the work of all the Boards to be debated each year, so that by and large this arrangement has proved to be satisfactory, not that we should exclude the possibility of additional days. The form of the Motion is usually that the House takes note of the Report and Accounts of the public corporation concerned. This enables questions of legislation to be raised and the Opposition to move an addition or an amendment criticizing the Government or the work of the Board concerned. On the days set aside for these debates anything can be raised whether relating to day-to-day management or not. Whether on such a Motion or in Committee of Supply the debates can occupy half or the whole of a day. They have, I think, been valuable. They were rather highly charged with party fireworks in the early years but except when real issues of controversy arise they are, I think, tending to become more objective and less partisan, which is a good thing. After all there is in general no more to get red in the face about in discussing the work of the publicly owned industries than the work of the publicly owned Post Office unless some issue of genuine controversy should arise.

Certainly if and when the number of nationalized industries increases a case will arise for increasing the number of Government-provided days for debate. They are useful and are valued by the Boards not less than by Parliament. If some grave happening raised issues of urgent public importance in connexion with the work of nationalized industry it is quite likely that the Government would find it necessary to give facilities for debate in addition to the established arrangement.

From time to time Private Bills may be promoted by a Board. Up to now this has only been done by the British Transport Commission and the British Electricity Authority. If the Second Reading of the Bill is objected to at the commencement of public business, part of a day is fixed for a debate on Second Reading. The contents of the British Transport Commission's Bills have enabled fairly wide debates to take place on the work of the Commission.

There are four other opportunities for parliamentary discussion. Following the Queen's Speech opening the Parliamentary Session a full-dress debate occupying several days takes place on the Address in reply. Debate on an amendment to the Address would be in order, criticizing the work of the socialized industries or the Ministers' relations with them. The second opportunity would be in Private Members' time when opportunities to move Motions are balloted for by back-bench M.P.s. The other two are in debate on a Bill to amend the original nationalization Act and on a Motion to approve or annul a Statutory Instrument made by a Minister under one of the nationalization Acts.

Ministers and the Boards

Clearly it is desirable that the Minister should keep himself familiar with the general work of the Board or Boards with which he is concerned. It is wise for him with his Parliamentary Secretary and principal officers concerned from time to time to meet the Chairman and, indeed, the members of the Board, to discuss matters of mutual interest either formally or informally. On such occasions both the Board and the Minister will be conscious of their legal rights: the legal right of the Minister to give general directions or to withhold approvals, and the legal rights of the Board within the field of day-to-day management; but it is also desirable that such discussion should be free, frank, forthcoming, and co-operative. It is well that the Minister should have a sympathetic understanding of the difficulties and problems of the Board and should not wish needlessly to harass or humiliate them, otherwise he might unduly damage the Board's sense of responsibility to the nation which is an obligation upon them and a public asset. Similarly, the Board has to understand that the Minister may have to answer criticisms in Parliament and that he is not bound to defend the Board unless he understands its position and thinks that it is right. Therefore, these informal discussions between the Minister and the Chairman frequently take place and in themselves are good. It is very necessary, however, that the Minister should not be drawn into acquiescence in policies which he would find difficult to defend in public, and that a Board should not take a course which it believes to be wrong and against the interests of the undertaking or the public merely because the Minister asks it to oblige him. The Board has a perfect right to say to the Minister, 'Give us a general direction in writing which will be published and we will obey, but otherwise we are sorry that we cannot act as you would wish.' What is wanted is friendly co-operation without prejudice to the rights and responsibilities of either the Minister or the Board.

It may be that in the opinion of the Board the Government is restricting them unduly on matters of development and capital expenditure, or that controlled materials of some sort are not being made available to them by the Government. The Minister should never resent them putting their case to him with frankness and vigour, and if he is convinced they are right he should urge their case to the appropriate authorities. If the public corporation is being criticized because it cannot do things, and Government policy is the cause, it might even be right for it to give a frank explanation to the public without becoming involved in vicious controversy with the Government of the day. On the other hand, the Minister, who has to answer for the general work of the Boards in Parliament, must (without taking over the essential duties of management) have the right to question Boards on aspects of policy or management about which he is apprehensive and to urge appropriate action. These matters involve subtle relationships, for whilst the rights and responsibilities of the Boards have to be respected, their Chairmen must not become arbitrary Emperors of Industry. These vast public undertakings must not become economic empires resenting ministerial criticism or inspiration any more than the Minister should take a line that the Boards have no right to question such aspects of Government policy as affect them, or publicly to explain that some of their difficulties are the consequence of Government restrictions. After all, these are rights which should and do exist in the private sector of industry.

The Consumer

Most of our public corporations are very large undertakings (so large that the possibilities of decentralization and delegation of authority within proper limits should not be overlooked). Within their sphere, they are wholly or to a great extent public monopolies, so it was inevitable and right that careful attention should be given to the protection of the user or consumer.

In the case of a public concern, whether a monopoly or not, the consumer does, I think, start with certain advantages. The very fact that the Board is a public authority appointed by a Minister responsible to Parliament should, and I think does, give it a special sense of public responsibility and therefore of the rights and interests of the consumer. It does not aim to provide high profits for investors. Moreover the Board is, and knows it is, more likely to be shot at in Parliament and in the Press than is a private undertaking. There is much more public argument about increases in charges and prices by a public than by a private undertaking. And because they hold a public trust as publicly appointed members of a public authority the members of the Board would wish to be well spoken of and regarded as doing their best for the consumers. It is of course possible that they could go wrong and develop unduly thick skins which might be encouraged if they are subjected to irresponsible or biased and malicious criticism unworthy of serious consideration. Generally speaking, one would expect public concerns to be more consumer-conscious than similar undertakings not publicly owned. Certainly they should be.

Whatever may be thought about the foregoing considerations they are not enough to warrant our not providing special machinery for considering the complaints and ventilating the needs of the consumers.

In the case of the British Transport Commission we extended and adapted the old Railway Rates Tribunal under the new name of the Transport Tribunal. The Rates Tribunal was set up under the Railways Act, 1921, when the hundred or so railways of the country were merged into four companies. Its duties were to hear proposals by the railway companies for fares and charges, to hear objections by the users, to take into account the requirement to provide the Companies with a standard revenue, and after hearing the parties, by counsel, expert witnesses, and otherwise, to come to a fair and judicial decision. It had a difficult and complex task as well I know, for I appeared before it some years ago as an amateur advocate on behalf of National and London labour organizations when I was treated with much fairness by the Tribunal, and a welcome courtesy by eminent counsel appearing for various parties. In urgent cases the Tribunal can be used by the Minister as an advisory or consultative committee. It is not easy for the full hearings to take place in every case, for the procedure is lengthy, and it may well be that before the hearings have ended and a decision has been given, new wage increases or other additions to costs have come about which already make the decision out of date.

This special form of judicial machinery which, largely for historical reasons, exists for transport, does not exist for other publicly owned concerns, or private concerns either. The establishment of such bodies in other cases was considered, but thought hardly appropriate. We established Consumer Councils under different names and in different forms. There is, for example, a Consumer Council for each of the Area Gas and Electricity Boards, and the Chairmen of these Councils are members of those Boards with a special responsibility for watching consumers' interests.

It is best for the consumer first of all to make his complaint direct to the management, and in most cases courteous consideration will be forthcoming even if the outcome is not wholly to the consumer's liking. Where the consumer is dissatisfied with the decision of the Board or its responsible local organization, complaint should be made to the Consumer Council. The Councils provide machinery by which the views of consumers can systematically be brought to bear on the Boards and before the Minister. Where appropriate the Minister can issue directions to the Boards to remedy defects to which the Councils have drawn attention.

But if the Consumer Councils are to succeed there must be active public participation. They will not have sufficient life and vigour if the consumers fail to make proper use of them, for it is not easy for the Councils to take up complaints of which they have never been informed. It is desirable that the necessary particulars about the Councils should be widely known.

I do not think we have yet reached perfection in this matter, though I gather that somewhat greater use is now being made of the Councils. Their weakness is partly due to insufficient experience during their short lifetime and to inadequate public knowledge of their existence or procedure. Although most

Councils include members of local authorities we should perhaps make better provision to establish local authority organization as a channel of public criticism or complaint. I feel sure that there is room for improvement, and it is in the interests of everybody, including the public corporations, that suitable improvement should be effected.

Public Relations

Another form of public accountability is the preparation and publication of the Annual Report and Accounts. It may be said that the Report of the Board of Directors of a limited liability company, together with the speech of the Chairman at the shareholders' meeting, discharges a similar obligation on the part of a privately owned undertaking. The comparison is, however, hardly valid. The Reports of Boards of Directors are usually fairly brief documents, and the speeches of the Chairmen are by no means adequately informative to shareholders and public. Sometimes a fair amount of the speech is devoted to the giving of views on wide matters of public policy, or attacking the Government or the Opposition of the day. And although the shareholders can question or discuss the Report, such meetings are in general ineffective for this purpose. The Reports and Accounts of the public corporations are full and informative. They are written for Parliament and the public. They record the work of the Boards and give a comprehensive survey of the facts. They deal with public criticisms and apprehensions, indicate the action to be taken, or if in the Board's opinion no action is possible, proceed to explain why. These Reports are available to all M.P.s, can be bought by the public, and are extensively noticed and, if it is thought right, criticized in the Press. They are debated in Parliament from time to time. The preparation and publication of these Reports is a very real element in the process of public accountability; the fact that the Boards have to prepare them is conducive to a sense of public accountability on their part.

The Reports are also of value in the work of public relations. Public relations work at its best is really part of the process of public accountability. The public relations department constitutes an information service. Its primary duty is to give information, to answer questions, to look out for public discontents and criticisms, and to see that they are considered by the appropriate department of the undertaking or brought to the notice of the Boards themselves. Indeed, the Boards should not only listen to troubles and criticisms when they arise, but should even look for them. At all times they should be watching and listening for criticism or unhappiness on the part of their customers. To anticipate these things before they break out into public controversy constitutes a considerable achievement of management and is good public relations. From time to time the Boards might well utilize the Central Office of Information's Social Survey in order to ascertain public attitudes and the wishes of the consumer. It is not the business of the public relations or information department to deceive the public, and it will fall down on its job if, as a systematic act of policy, it tries to do so.

The draftsmen of the Annual Report will be wise to see that the public relations department is given the opportunity to examine the draft and suggest modifications in the presentation or wording to make the Report more readable or more easily understood. It is, I think, customary for the Chairman of the Board to hold a Press Conference at the time of the publication of the Annual Report and Accounts. No doubt a fair summary of the Report is prepared for the assistance of the Press and distributed at the Conference. At the Press Conference the Chairman will make a statement on the work of the Board and the outstanding facts of the year's operations; he will also subject himself to the questioning of the journalists who will try to elicit further information and get the Chairman's comments on what they conceive to be weak points in the Report. Some Boards have published a much shortened popular edition of the Annual Report suitably illustrated; this is of value to the public who are unlikely to read the whole of the official Annual Report, and also for distribution amongst the workers employed by the undertaking. For there is public relations work to be done inside as well as outside these vast businesses. The more the staff and employees understand the work of the concern as a whole the better it is for morale and the development of a healthy team spirit. The more it is possible for them to develop a legitimate sense of pride in the work of the undertaking the better. They should give of their best in energy and quality of work in the public service.

The relations between the Board's employees and the public with whom they come into personal contact are matters of the greatest importance. Discourtesy, impatience or a mere shrugging of the shoulders in response to the inquiries, troubles, or criticisms of the consumers or users of the service are most undesirable and are likely to do the business great harm. However humble the position of a person employed by the Board may be, when he or she comes into contact with a customer he or she to that customer *is* the Board. Customers may not understand how an account is made up; the commodity or service supplied may not be giving satisfaction; something may be repeatedly going wrong with a gas or electrical appliance which may be the fault of the appliance or the undertaking, or it may be clumsiness on the part of the user. Whatever the cause may be, even if it is the consumer's own fault, patience, courtesy, and simplicity of explanation are desirable. In fact, the consumer should feel that the visitor from the public corporation is never so happy as when he is helping that customer out of his or her troubles. All this is public relations, for the man who has called about the trouble stands in a personal relationship between the customer and the undertaking. The public relations department, in co-operation with management, should take a hand in helping the employee to have the right relations with the public and also in keeping him informed about the work of the corporation, so that he will at any rate understand it in general terms.

One of the best forms of public relations is public speeches. The appropriate Minister and the Chairman of the Board should make public speeches from time to time, dealing with the work of the industry generally or with some particular aspect of it. For example, if an interesting scheme or programme of development and research is on foot it might well form the subject of a public speech or a Press Conference. And provided they are objective and interesting, not partisan and not too frequent, broadcasts on the work of the public corporations can usefully be given from time to time. These speeches or broadcasts should not be a collection of dull officialese, but clear, simple, and human expositions, having the purpose of giving, and honestly facing up to, the facts, rather than using the occasion for some tendentious propaganda. Some Ministers under-estimate the importance of public speeches, and somewhat begrudge time given to their preparation and particularly to their revision. In the days of Gladstone and Disraeli ministerial speeches constituted about the only form of public relations that then existed. These two famous party leaders took plenty of trouble about their speeches, and were given much more rest and made much more fuss of before and after they made them than are we busy politicians nowadays.

Inevitably, the Government Departments concerned with the publicly owned industries become involved in a wider sense in the relations between the public and the socialized industries. The information divisions of the Ministries can bring to the discussion of their public relations a point of view somewhat different from that emanating from inside the corporations. Many criticisms and suggestions come to the Ministers from the public, from M.P.s, and in the course of Parliamentary Questions, which themselves are a form of public relations. We therefore arranged for periodical meetings between the information officers of the relevant Government Departments and the information departments of the public corporations. I am sure that this is desirable and should be continued.

From what has been said above, it is clear that public relations is not merely a matter of persuasive advertisements and the courteous answering of newspaper inquiries, but goes much deeper. Moreover, as we said about the Parliamentary Whips, it is a two-way traffic: public relations officers have just as much a duty to convey public unhappiness, criticisms, and complaints to the Boards and their management as they have to interpret the working policy of the Boards to the public at large.

Of one thing we can be sure about the future of publicly owned industry: it is that it must not get into a rut. It cannot and will not be allowed to stay put. Tendencies towards isolation and excessive bureaucracy will receive short shrift from Parliament, the Press, and the public; so management must be alive and very adaptable, ready to change its mind and its policies in the light of experience, criticism, and public needs. By the means already indicated, the public corporations will be happy in the public service, which is a good thing. If their public is happy, they should be happy. And Parliament, public, and the Press should for their part help to make the Boards and their employees happy by generally giving them credit where credit is due, and trying not to nag at or abuse the Boards without fair and reasonable cause.

Comments and Suggestions

It has been shown, I think, that the field of public accountability of the public corporations is fairly extensive, but the matter is so important that we must not be complacent any more than we must allow ourselves to be merely irritating to the responsible management of these great public organizations. I will therefore offer some comments and suggestions.

It is clear from what I have written that I would not wish a Board of a public corporation to become either officially or unofficially the creature of the Minister and the Department concerned with it. On the other hand, it is my own view that the 'parent' Minister appointing the Board and his Department can be somewhat too restrained and conservative in their attitude to the public corporation. Where a Minister has *prima facie* grounds for believing that something is wrong, either in the service to the public or, maybe, in the number of supervisory administrative and technical staff, then, provided he does it in the right spirit, I think he has the right and the duty to require the relevant information to be produced, to examine the Board about the facts, and to ask for satisfaction on the matters which are giving him concern. Certainly this process requires tact and handling in a friendly co-operative spirit calculated to be helpful and to preserve good personal relations, but a Minister ought not to drift into a position whereby he becomes an automatic apologist for the Boards in Parliament, and there is certainly no obligation upon him to defend things which he is not convinced are right. It would not be right for Departments to regard the public corporations as so distant and autonomous as not to act as I have suggested, or that there should be a bias towards leaving the Boards isolated to the greatest practicable extent. The Boards must be allowed time to settle down but the period should not be excessive.

If this work of probing, warning, encouragement, and inspiration is to be done—and I say again that it must be done with very great tact and reasonable restraint even though with firmness—the number of watching, technical, and administrative staff needed to assist the Minister in this field must be considered. There is one danger which must clearly be avoided: the danger of a large-scale duplication in the Ministries of the supervisory, technical, and administrative staffs of the public corporations. What the 'parent' Ministry needs is a quite small, brainy, constructive branch which studies the work of the Boards, examines their statistics, takes note of parliamentary, press, and public criticisms, and so on. It is desirable that these men should be on friendly terms with the staffs of the Boards and vice versa, for if bad relations and bickering between them arise the job cannot effectively be done. It is for the Minister and the Chairmen to see that good relations are maintained, for everybody should be intent on furthering the public interest. The branch should bring problems to the notice of the Minister from time to time together with the observations of the Board and their own comments. It would not be for the branch to assume that they could give the full and authentic answers; nor should they attempt to 'boss' the Boards: their big job would be to help the Minister to put the relevant questions intelligently. To some extent no doubt such branches exist, but I am not in a position to say how far they are properly organized and staffed for the purpose.

Parliament and the public wish to be satisfied that these industries are efficiently and economically managed. To some extent a judgement can be given on the basis of the Annual Reports and Accounts but these are not conclusive. It is not within the duties of the chartered accountants who audit the accounts to comment upon the efficiency and economy of the management: their business is to verify the accuracy of the accounts and to draw attention to any inaccuracies or imperfections in methods of account keeping and presentation.

It was very necessary that the Boards, no less than the Government, should realize that Parliament and the public could reasonably ask to be satisfied that everything possible was being done to ensure the general efficiency of these great economic undertakings. We therefore opened up discussions with the Chairmen of the Boards on the problem. I imagined myself sitting as a member of one of these Boards seeking and getting reports from departmental chiefs on matters which were giving us concern; possibly getting satisfaction and possibly not. If one was worried, what could one do?

I had, from conversations with industrialists in private enterprise, been much impressed with the successful work of industrial consultants in specific cases. One has to be careful in choosing them, for some are very good and others are not so good or may even be bogus. There is certainly room for expansion and improvement in this field. However, the Board of Trade has associated with it the British Institute of Management and it should be possible for this body to provide a panel of reliable and able industrial consultants available for the use of the corporations. This proposal was advanced with the assent of my colleagues.

I had another idea which we also put forward for consideration, namely, that the Boards themselves *collectively* might create an industrial efficiency unit of their own, which would be available to any of the Boards for the investigation of 'headaches'. Each Board, of course, has within its organization some means of investigating results or difficulties which give it concern. We were inclined, however, to think that a somewhat independent efficiency unit, nevertheless created by the Boards themselves, instructed by them, responsible to them and at their disposal, would be of high value in collaborating with the units of management and the workers or Trade Unions concerned. With a good co-operative spirit on both sides it could seek a solution and present reports and recommendations to the Board concerned. In general, however, the Chairmen did not like this idea; wrongly, as I think. The common efficiency unit would have been a collective creation of the Boards and it would be for them to set it to work in any particular case, but they took the view that it was a reflection upon the ability and efficiency of the Boards themselves. To this day I cannot follow the force of this argument, for what I was seeking was an instrument which, though created by the Boards themselves, would not be so closely identified with the day-to-day departmental management of particular undertakings that it could not bring to bear the fresh mind of an objective investigator. Such an instrument should be helpful not only to the Boards themselves but also to their officers. I did not wish to impose on the Boards an external commission of industrial investigation, for healthy co-operation was desirable; but some efficiency organization is necessary. At that early stage in the history of these bodies, however, we were not disposed to force the idea.

Naturally we left the Boards completely free to advance alternative proposals calculated to satisfy Parliament and the public that efficiency was being properly taken care of. The Boards declared their anxiety continually to increase the efficiency of management in their industries and assured us that they were ready to utilize the help of outside consultants from time to time—the Airways Corporations have done so with advantage—and that they were or would become members of the British Institute of Management. But they did not agree to the proposed common efficiency unit. Some progress was made, though I am sure that the last word has not been said upon this vital matter. The Boards will be wise not to be obstinate or complacent, for if Parliament gets the bit into its teeth it may go farther than is desirable.

Apart from specific questions of working efficiency, there is much to be said for a periodical inquiry into the structure and layout of the Board's organization and a somewhat general investigation into its operations.

In the case of the British Broadcasting Corporation it is the established practice before each renewal of the Charter and Licence to appoint a committee of inquiry. There have been two under the Chairmanship respectively of Lord Ullswater and Lord Beveridge since its establishment in 1927. In advising the Prime Minister on the composition of the Beveridge Committee, the Postmaster-General (Mr. Ness Edwards) and I sought, whilst avoiding the specific representation of interests, to draw the membership from intelligent, public-spirited persons of varied experience, living in various parts of the country, and including, as before, a limited number of M.P.s. It is wise in the appointment of all committees to consider the inclusion of M.P.s, for this gives them valuable experience and ensures well-informed contributions to parliamentary debate.

With the assent of my colleagues I put this idea of a periodical inquiry to the Chairmen of the public corporations, and I am glad to say that the result was happier than in the case of the proposed common efficiency unit. It was agreed between the

Government and the Chairmen that from time to time somewhat similar committees should be appointed to inquire into broad questions of policy and structure affecting particular corporations; one or more such committees should by now have been appointed, but up to the time of writing none has been. On the face of it these may not appear to be questions of public accountability but in the widest sense they are, because the public would wish to be satisfied that the Government and the Boards are doing everything to maintain and improve efficiency in the public service of these great undertakings.

Proposed Select Committee on Nationalised Industries

I have referred earlier to the First Report from the Select Committee on Nationalised Industries which dealt with Parliamentary Questions and did not recommend any material change in the existing rules and practice. A Second Report from the Select Committee was published on 23 July 1953, in which the Committee summarized its recommendations as follows:

(*a*) There should be appointed a Committee of the House of Commons by Standing Order, to examine the Nationalised Industries, with power to send for persons, papers and records, power to set up sub-committees, and to report from time to time;

(*b*) The Committee should direct their attention to the published Reports and Accounts, and to obtaining further information as to the general policy and practice of the Nationalised Industries established by Statute, whose controlling Boards are wholly nominated by Ministers of the Crown, and whose annual receipts are not wholly derived from moneys provided by Parliament or advanced from the Exchequer;

(*c*) The object of the Committee should be that of informing Parliament about the aims, activities and problems of the Corporations and not of controlling their work.

(*d*) The staff of the Committee should include an officer of the status of the Comptroller and Auditor General who should be an officer of the House of Commons, with high administrative experience; at least one professional accountant, and such other staff as required;

(*e*) The statutory auditors of the corporations shall, in preparing their annual reports, give such information in addition to that now provided by them as may be of use to the Committee and of interest to Parliament.

The Committee proposed that the staff of the new Select Committee should be as follows:

There would necessarily be a Clerk to the Committee supplied from the staff of the Clerk of the House in the normal way. Then there would be a permanent official of a status roughly equivalent to that of the Comptroller and Auditor General or Mr. Speaker's Counsel. He would work with the assistance of at least one professional accountant, and such other staff as the Committee may deem useful, and would examine the reports and accounts of the Nationalised Industries in order to direct the Committee's attention to matters requiring examination. If the Committee so desired, the Minister in charge of the Department responsible for the general oversight of the industry whose affairs were under review should be invited to send a senior official to assist the Committee in the examination of evidence.

The Committee added that 'as the proposed Committee would have to deal more with contemporary and future matters than is the case of the work of the Committee of Public Acounts, the permanent official would have a different approach from the Comptroller and Auditor General'.

In his evidence before the Committee Mr. Hugh Molson, M.P., then Parliamentary Secretary to the Ministry of Works (who was careful to explain that he was expressing his personal views only and not necessarily those of the Government), opened up a possible programme of work for the proposed Select Committee which seems to me to have been somewhat far-reaching and in conflict with the concept of the public corporation upon which Parliament has deliberately embarked. He mentioned the following possible subjects for investigation:

Capital investment in the railways as compared with other capital expenditure;
Types of aircraft purchased by the airways corporations;
Welfare and pensions schemes; and
Costs and the fixing of prices.

He also thought that the Committee should make reports at a time to enable the House, if it thought fit, to stop a certain policy.

In the course of questioning Mr. Molson, Sir Herbert

Williams recounted one of his experiences as a member of the war-time Select Committee on National Expenditure which he evidently liked. In asking question 371 he said:

> . . . In Lancashire we went to one large factory, then to another factory, and finally to one of the Royal Ordnance factories. It was out of that visit that I think we produced the report to which you made reference. When we went there we had not a thought in our minds, just the idea to give them the 'once-over'. We took all our evidence in secret from the superintendent, and then we said 'Have you got a workers' committee?' He said he had, and we said we would like to see them in private. We had that works committee, thirty of them. They had never been before a Parliamentary Committee before. We were looking for what we could find; we did not know what to look for; but as a result of asking questions of the men and women who were doing the jobs in various departments we discovered an amazing amount of information. We were 'fishing'. Several inquiries were made, and a lot of information was received. This was a pure 'fishing' inquiry, but I considered it was a most successful one. Do you think that a select committee, if one is set up, ought to do a certain amount of 'fishing'?

Whilst not wholly rejecting the idea Mr. Molson did not appear to be enthusiastic about it as an extensive practice. However, when he was asked by Sir Herbert at q. 372, 'You would not object to what I call an occasional "fishing" expedition?' he answered 'No'.

I should point out that the Royal Ordnance Factories are under the Minister of Supply and there is, therefore, full parliamentary accountability. Nevertheless, the war-time Government was not happy about these 'fishing' visits. Certainly the idea of subjecting the public corporation to them is something which is in conflict with the intentions of Parliament when the public corporations were established.

Another Minister who gave evidence was Captain Harry Crookshank, Lord Privy Seal and a member of the Cabinet, but he again pointed out that he was explaining his own views. He favoured a joint Select Committee of Lords and Commons on the ground that the House of Lords 'has got a fund of members from whom one could draw, with business experience and who look on these matters in a less partisan way than we do in this House' (q. 939). The idea of a joint committee, however, did not commend itself to the Select Committee. At q. 940 Captain Crookshank said:

. . . I think a standing joint committee, without going into meticulous detail, could quite well look at current policies on general issues, and if it found it wanted a specific inquiry on any particular aspect, for example, like the one going on now with regard to London Passenger Transport, then it would be possible for the standing joint committee to recommend to the Government that should be done by a Departmental Committee and that certain functions should be undertaken, rather than do it themselves. That is the sort of way in which my mind has been groping about it.

I am inclined to the view that the conclusions of the Select Committee are against the weight of the evidence.

The Times in its leading article of 13 August 1953 concluded:

The truth is that the Select Committee on Nationalized Industries was faced with an impossible task. The real problem is to discover how Parliament can make better use of the information it already gets rather than to devise ways and means for it to acquire more. Can it be said that even those debates that there have been on the nationalized industries have themselves been as fully used as possible? Further, if Parliament is going to preserve the relative independence of the industries—and on this their efficiency will to a very great extent depend—it cannot devise new instruments which are really the creatures of distrust. Finally the pursuit of pure efficiency is a will-o'-the-wisp. The idea that any committee can assess it, report on it, and in the last resort lead Parliament to do anything about it, is one of the illusions of the managerial state. There is still in this country, in spite of all the factors against it, a wealth of talent, of capacity, of leadership, and of devotion willing to give of its best in whatever activity it undertakes. This is true of the nationalized industries as it is of private enterprise. Real efficiency will be got neither by nagging nor by exhortation. It will be got by the appropriate Minister appointing the best Boards, by those Boards appointing the best people they can, and by the organizations then being allowed to get on with the job. If things go badly wrong they will not stay hidden for long. Then accountability to Parliament, which is properly always there, will powerfully come into play. To discharge that broad responsibility Parliament has all the machinery and powers it needs. Such a long-range vigilance and wise forbearance will stimulate not only efficiency but also enterprise. Under the proposed arrangements both will wither.

The Observer of 16 August 1953 said in its leading article:

> A body of this kind could no doubt furnish the Commons with a good deal of miscellaneous information, but one cannot see how its existence would appreciably alter the relations between Parliament and the Boards. The members of the Committee, except on the accounting side, would be amateurs, and experience has shown that a Parliamentary committee cannot readily find out much more about a complex enterprise than its managers want to reveal. Moreover, the Committee would have five industries to examine—coal, electricity, gas, railways, and air transport, with the possibility of steel and road transport returning later to the list—and to study thoroughly and frequently this enormous field would be an immense task, imposing an intractable new burden on the time and energies of the M.P.s concerned.

The T.U.C. General Council came to the conclusion that there was no real case for the setting up of a Select Committee to examine and report on the administration and activities of the nationalized industries. They thought that adequate information about these industries was already available in the Annual Reports of the Boards and that it would be more valuable if the Government and M.P.s directed their attention to ways of improving parliamentary discussion on these Reports.

The National Executive of the Labour Party concurred in this view, as did the Parliamentary Committee of the Party.

I have a high regard for the House of Commons and its Committees but, just as I think that the day-to-day management of highly commercial undertakings is better done by public corporations under a Board of hand-picked competent persons rather than political Ministers and civil servants, so also I must confess that I am not persuaded that a Committee of the House of Commons is the appropriate organ, even with the assistance of officers to advise them, to investigate and pronounce judgement on the business organization and commercial operation of these great undertakings. Select Committees of the House render useful service looking into the estimates and accounts of Government Departments. But the large-scale commercial organization and operation of public corporations are very different from the ministerial and civil service administration of Government Departments. The nation owes much to its M.P.s and the House of Commons as a corporate entity; it is indebted to them for the competence with which they carry out their parliamentary duties, but a Select Committee of the House could hardly pretend to be authoritative in the detailed investigation of and reporting upon the operations of these large-scale business undertakings.

There are other objections. Few of the members of the Boards responsible for the management of these industries have had parliamentary experience. Indeed, Members of the House of Commons are legally debarred from becoming Board members. Members of the Boards are largely drawn from one side or the other of industry. They and their managers might well find it tiring and nerve-racking to be put through the mill at the House of Commons or during visits to various parts of the undertaking by a body of politicians, and might well be annoyed by the injustices which would inevitably be inflicted on them from time to time, however unwittingly. Moreover, if they are to anticipate this possibly annual, or even biennial, gruelling, lasting for days or even weeks, they may well in their day-to-day job of making decisions on a wide range of important managerial matters lose their nerve if any such decision may be subjected to hostile examination or hostile reports from a Select Committee. They may become frightened or over-cautious; they may, indeed, develop that very sense of safety first which is (often unfairly) alleged to be the characteristic of the Civil Service, because Government Departments are meticulously responsible to Parliament. So here again the point really is that if there be a case for putting an industry or service under a public corporation then there is no good case for treating it as if it were a Government Department and in effect making the men who are running the undertaking civil servants.

Nevertheless, as stated earlier in this chapter, an inquiry of a different and broader character to look into the affairs of each Board at periods of roughly seven years would be another matter.

However, if and when such a Select Committee is appointed, it is possible that some of my apprehensions will not eventuate. Much depends on the terms of reference, which it would be for Government and Parliament to determine. In the case of the Public Accounts and Estimates Committees Government policy cannot be challenged. It may be that the proposed Select

Committee would in practice be more restrained than Mr. Molson visualized. Possibly—though the temptation will be very real—the anti-nationalizers and the pro-nationalizers will be objective and avoid using the Committee for the purpose of discrediting public ownership on the one hand or, on the other, seeking to show that the work of the Board is perfect. We do not know.[1]

Facing the Essential Issues

In any case the extreme advocate of parliamentary accountability really must face up to the essential issues involved. If he wants the Minister to be answerable in Parliament for every detail, if he desires the public corporations to be run as if they were departmentally managed undertakings, if he wishes Select Committees of Parliament to exercise functions of investigation and cross-examination of witnesses as if the concerns were run by a Ministry, then he must logically advocate that the socialized undertakings should be managed by a Government Department and not by a public corporation. What he is not entitled to do is to say: 'Well, let the business be vested in and managed by a public corporation, and let us hold the members of the Board responsible for efficient management, but let the public corporation be treated as if it were a Government Department.' This is not a fair proposition. It would not be fair to the eminent men who undertake the responsibility of management as members of the Board, nor would it be fair to the Minister, who in these circumstances could not reasonably be expected to answer for every detail of management. The fact has to be faced that if we decide for the public corporation then certain limitations on parliamentary accountability must inevitably follow. If we establish the public corporation, it must be for certain reasons. What are they? They are that we seek to combine the principle of public ownership, of a broad but not too detailed public accountability, of a consciousness on the part of the undertaking that it is working for the nation and not for sectional

[1] The Second Report was debated in the House on the 8th February 1954, when this book was at too advanced a stage of printing for account to be taken of the points made. The Lord Privy Seal (Mr. Harry Crookshank) said the Government accepted the idea of a Select Committee in principle but with limited terms of reference and without a permanent officer of the status of the Comptroller and Auditor-General.

interests, with the liveliness, initiative, and a considerable degree of the freedom of a quick-moving and progressive business enterprise. Either that is the case for the public corporation, or there is no case at all. It is perfectly legitimate (indeed, it is the great art of public administration) to seek the best of both worlds, but what is not fair when one has made a deliberate departure from part of one world is to expect that all the characteristics of that world will survive. Therefore, the decision should be made after foreseeing and accepting the consequences; and one of the consequences of plumping for the public corporation is that the carefully chosen members of the Board should have the right of independent action in the field of day-to-day management, for which they should feel a sense of social responsibility, but for which they cannot in detail well be held responsible to Parliament. We are imposing upon these men, even thrusting down their throats, as I said in *Socialisation and Transport*, responsibility for commercial success or otherwise. It is desirable that we should do so, for otherwise there is no point in constituting these Boards.

If they are to have a sense of responsibility, if they are to be saddled with the responsibility, then we must give them a reasonable and frankly recognized sphere of managerial freedom. Otherwise we should run a grave risk of irresponsibility—nobody being responsible for anything. Those who want detailed parliamentary accountability must plump for State departmental management; those who favour publicly owned industry being vested in a public corporation must be prepared to face the consequences, namely, some limitation on detailed parliamentary accountability.

Variations in Collective Enterprise

It would be a mistake to assume that the Public Corporation is now the exclusive model for the conduct of publicly owned industries and services. Much depends on the nature of the industry. Is it reasonably straightforward or is it complex and highly commercial? For example, water is already largely a local government service; if it were made wholly public the national aspects of the business might well be the functions of a State Department, though I should hope that distribution to consumers and local administration would be local government functions.

We should not rule out direct management by Government Departments or local authorities in appropriate cases. It is certainly a matter of some concern that the functions of local government have tended to diminish in a number of respects, and that local authorities are increasingly subject to control and instructions from Whitehall. Gas, electricity, hospitals, public assistance, and valuation have been taken from local government. If it cannot be helped, taking account of the larger public interest involved, well, that is too bad. Nevertheless, there is a duty upon all of us to consider most carefully, and with the desire to keep local government vigorous, independent, and healthy, any possibility of preserving and developing the useful and legitimate functions of local government to which our democracy owes so much.

I am not too happy about the working of the hospital scheme under the National Health Act. Responsibility is difficult to apportion and define. Though carrying on what is essentially a local service, the Regional Hospital Boards and the Hospital Management Committees are appointed nationally. Of course, laboratories and research are difficult for the local authorities (except possibly the largest) to conduct adequately, and a similar problem may arise with hospital supplies. It is also important to have regard to the need for different kinds of specialist hospitals, and for this some central planning and direction are required. It might be right for Whitehall to retain such functions; but if that were done I incline to the view that the local management at the hospitals could be the responsibility of elected local authorities suitable for the purpose. The local authorities have tended to feel that they are suffering from what some of their members have described as 'death from a thousand cuts'; this may be overstating the case, for after all their work, e.g. in housing and town and country planning has much increased. But I was nurtured and trained in local government; I have spent many years of my life in local authority service; and I understand—how well I understand—how the local authorities feel about it all.

Another agency of collectivist economic activity is our very large consumers' Co-operative Movement with round about eleven million members. This represents a form of social ownership. They do not work for private profit, for their surpluses are returned to the members in relation to the amount of purchases in the form of what is somewhat misleadingly called dividend. The Co-operative Societies are extensively engaged in production and their retail trading operations are very great. Moreover, in addition to the productive activities of the Co-operative Wholesale Societies and the Co-operative Producers' Societies there is a tendency for co-operative practice of a somewhat different nature to be applied in agriculture. Certainly the Co-operative Movement cannot and should not be ignored as a factor in communal economic services and as a possible instrument of extended service to the community.

We should not be tempted to think, therefore, that social ownership and enterprise can only take one form. The public corporations are still new. We have much to learn about them and they have much to learn about themselves. There is a considerable variety of structure and organization among the public corporations which was deliberately provided for in the statutes that set them up. Even so we should not rule out other possible forms of social and economic enterprise; we can make our choice when we set them up. Let us do so after careful thought and with due deliberation.

CHAPTER XIII

Economic Planning and Controls

Whilst it will contain passing references to them, this chapter does not set out to be a treatise on economic problems or economic policy. It will indicate the changing attitude of the State to economic affairs over the years; and it will show how the methods and machinery of economic planning and control evolved under the Labour Governments of 1945–51.

Earlier Views on the Functions of Government

In the nineteenth century the view was generally accepted that the less the Government had to do with economic affairs the better. It was believed that if private industry were allowed to function freely the vigorous competition thus promoted would stimulate industrial efficiency, and thus the consumer would be served in the most effective and economical way. There was a belief, not confined to the wealthier classes, that the poor, so to speak, lived upon the crumbs that fell from the rich man's table, and that, therefore, the better off the rich were the more employment and security among the working people there would be. That was another reason advanced for non-intervention. It is true that substantial unemployment occurred and that there was considerable poverty, but it was believed that this was inevitable and indeed stimulating; that it was Utopian to think that it could be avoided; and that in many cases the poverty and unemployment were in large part caused by laziness and incompetence or other imperfections on the part of many of the poor themselves. Such were the arguments: I profoundly disagree with them.

All this is not to say that the State did nothing. Lord Shaftesbury, Richard Oastler, and others conducted a great campaign for protecting women and children in particular from unsuitable work or excessive hours of labour. In due course State intervention in social and economic affairs extended, even though the reforms were modest by present-day standards.

Various economic developments and new forms of private enterprise caused Parliament to intervene in industrial matters. The Private Bills required by gas, water, railways, and other public utility undertakings gave Parliament the opportunity to insist on provisions for the protection of the public, and faced it with the need to restrict competition in order to avoid not only the duplication of the large capital investment, but also the public inconvenience of having the roads taken up frequently for the laying and repair of competing cables and pipes. As municipal corporations became powerful they, in many cases, secured powers for the conduct of tramway, gas, electricity, and water undertakings. The powers of local authorities were also extended to education, public health, and housing. However, all these developments were particular: they involved no widespread or general fundamental challenge to the nineteenth-century doctrines described above. Even with the development in the twentieth century of health and unemployment insurance, old age pensions, and certain other social services, there was no acceptance of the general responsibility of the State to see that industry functioned in a way calculated to promote full employment, or of the principle of priorities and the control of the use of the nation's resources, or of general economic planning. Indeed, the years between the two world wars saw poverty persisting as did large-scale unemployment. Governments and the majority of the population accepted these misfortunes as inevitable. However, an increasing number of people were not inclined to accept the inevitability of these social miseries even even if their ideas on the remedies were often wrong or vague.

The Need for Planning

It would be untrue and unfair to give the impression that the outlook of the Conservative and Liberal Parties in these matters has stood still, even though their economic and social philosophy has remained materially different from that of the Labour Party. The war-time Coalition Government, composed of Conservative, Labour, and Liberal Ministers, presented to Parliament in May 1944 a White Paper entitled *Employment Policy* (Cmd. 6527). This is not a party political book and it would not be appropriate here to argue which Ministers played the major part; but this Paper went a long way in affirming the responsibility of the Government for employment and economic well-being. Naturally it was a compromise document, some thinking it did not go far enough and others probably thinking it went too far. Nevertheless, the White Paper was an historic document. It was a pointer to the Civil Service and an indication that they would have to face up to extended peace-time functions.

The main objectives of post-war Government policy were set out clearly and can be summarized as follows:

(*a*) The maintenance of a high and stable level of employment was accepted as one of the primary aims and responsibilities of future British governments.

(*b*) Any government during the transition from war to peace would have to take steps to guard against inflation, to secure the production and equitable distribution of essential supplies, and to avoid balance of payments difficulties.

(*c*) The approach to the maintenance of a high and stable level of employment was to be by way of the maintenance of total expenditure. This would involve not only the continuation of the war-time practice of officially measuring the national income and expenditure, but also of operating on its various components, e.g. investment and government expenditure, to secure the right overall level.

All this, together with experience gained in the War Government of 1940–5, contributed not only to the economic policies of the first majority Labour Government of 1945, but also to a quickening of public opinion. There was a widespread desire to achieve a smoother and more successful transition to peace than occurred after the First World War.

The Conflict of Priorities

At the end of hostilities the country was faced with severe economic and financial problems, many of which were the direct result of the war. In the course of the war it had been necessary to dispose of part of our overseas investment and, despite that and lend-lease, we also had to borrow from abroad. Thus, whereas before the war our net income from overseas investments was enough to pay for over one-fifth of our imports, after the war it has in most years been enough to pay for only one-fiftieth. Soon after the return of the Labour Government the United States Administration, which had come to the conclusion that the law under which lend-lease was administered expired with the end of hostilities, notified us of its discontinuance, and this sudden and serious change added considerably to our troubles. The war had enormously damaged our overseas trade which had to be built up again. Many of our public utilities and factories had been damaged by enemy bombing and great numbers of houses destroyed or damaged. There had been large shipping losses. Our industrial machine had been geared to a war economy for five years and we had to face widespread problems of reconstruction and adjustment in the transition from war to peace.

All these special problems made economic planning more difficult but also, in our view, made it more necessary. It was clear that if everybody were allowed to do as they liked, if there were no imposed priorities in the use of the nation's resources, a grave and chaotic situation would ensue, which would damage our well-being for many years to come. This was what happened after the First World War when an unhealthy boom was followed by an equally unhealthy slump. These things we were determined to avoid.

The object of economic planning is to develop and use the national resources in the best interests of the nation as a whole. The problem was to settle the allocations and priorities within the limits of the practicable, in such a way that the public interest as a whole would be met to the greatest possible extent. The 'limits of the practicable' were the possible output at full employment and the need to pay our way abroad, which in essence means stimulating exports and keeping down imports.

In considering priorities we had to remember that exports must be a first claim on the national output. A large part of our food and raw materials must come from other countries, including the Commonwealth. We must pay for these by exporting coal and the kind of manufactured products these other countries wish to purchase and by rendering them such services as shipping and insurance. The Government still, however, had to decide whether the level of imports could be cut either by increasing home food production and prohibiting the import of luxuries or by curtailing its purchases of food and raw materials even if this involved rationing the home consumer. Within the amount available for home consumption, i.e. total home production plus imports less exports, the Government had to consider and deal fairly with the various claims. How much, for example, should be allocated for equipment, machinery, and industrial building calculated to increase future production and the productivity of labour? On the face of it one would be tempted to think that there could not be too much of such investment, yet it did mean an immediate setting aside of resources which could not show results for some years to come. But apart from the problem of limiting present consumption in the interests of the future, there was a difficulty arising from the limited capacity of our own industry to produce the kind of things wanted by our customers abroad. Much capital equipment would be engineering products, and there was a considerable export market for machinery of various sorts which would contribute immediately and directly to the easing of the balance of payments situation and enable us to pay for necessary imports. This is a good example of the conflict between valid arguments, and it illustrates how, if we had left things to take their own course, we should inevitably have drifted into trouble. In the end we made such allocation as we could for the re-equipment of British industry. For the reasons indicated, we were compelled, but with regret, to favour exports of machinery (at the partial expense of investment for productivity) beyond what we would have done had it not been for the seriousness of the balance of payments problem.

There were many claims on the output of the building industry. Factories, houses, schools, and hospitals were all in considerable demand. Factories were needed to replace those that had been bombed or there were repairs and extensions to be made. The demand for housing was enormous, partly because of the bombing, partly because no houses had been built for six years, partly because of the increased number of families, and partly because of the natural desire of the people to remove from out-of-date to better accommodation. Many schools had been destroyed or damaged by bombing, and in any case a substantial proportion of them were out of date. The elementary schools where I was educated are still going strong though they probably ought not to be. The welcome increase in the birth-rate faced local education authorities with great difficulties; and there was the raising of the school-leaving age from 14 to 15, and the acceptance of the principle of secondary education for all. The hospitals were claiming to be allowed to catch up with much-needed improvements and extensions, and the establishment of the National Health Service revealed deficiencies and stimulated this demand. Factories, housing, schools, hospitals—each had a strong case. Each of the Ministers concerned made a persuasive and indeed—if only one could have forgotten the others—an unanswerable case. But the fact had to be faced that they could not all have what they wanted. So we were faced with the reconciliation of the irreconcilable.

There were the claims of the various social services, of the Navy, the Army, and the Air Force, of agriculture, of the scientific establishments, of the local government services, and so on. These services had to be examined and limits set to their claims upon the economic resources.

The needs and standards of the consumers had to be provided for: food, clothing, household requirements, &c., and this was not easy. There was a world shortage of certain foods and in any case we could not increase our imports more rapidly than the rate at which we could increase the exports necessary to pay for them. And so supplies of many foods and items in general demand had to be kept below the demand at the prices then reigning. If we had prematurely abolished rationing by the ration-book, rationing by the purse would have taken its place, and social injustice and discontent would have spread. Additional wage demands would have been stimulated, leading in all probability to further increases in prices.

There were other allocations which had to be considered and made, both of a general and of a more detailed character, but I have written enough to illustrate the problem. Had there been no allocation system and no controls the situation would have been generally chaotic and would almost certainly have led to inflation and rising prices, with those who were prepared to pay most getting the resources irrespective of the Government's economic and social responsibilities to the community.

Having ascertained the resources available and the claims upon them, we found that the claims in general were in excess of the resources. We attempted, therefore, on the one hand, to stimulate production and the productivity of labour in order to make more goods available, and, on the other, to scale down the claims as fairly as possible within the limits set by production. In addition to direct controls, we limited purchasing power partly by taxation and partly by public appeals to all sections of society for restraint in seeking increases in personal incomes whether by way of wages, salaries, or dividends. We owed much to public understanding of the difficulties and to the co-operation we received from a large proportion of the public, including the Trade Union leaders.

One other general point. There is an important difference in the character of the control which any British Government can exercise over internal consumption on the one hand, and over imports and exports on the other. The Government can make decisions about the former with a high degree of assurance that they can be carried out, e.g. by a rationing system for food and by a system of licences for building. But the level and kind of exports are very much affected by the ideas and demands of other countries and by changes in world prices over which we have little or no control. The plans of the Labour Government were considerably affected by the convertibility crisis of 1947, by the need to devalue in 1949, and by the rise in world prices following the outbreak of the Korean War—yet none of these major economic events could be said to be within our control. The implication of all this for British economic planning is not to seek complete internal self-sufficiency (which would be impossible except at a bare subsistence level of living or with a much smaller population), but to pursue an economic policy which is flexible and adaptable.

Powers

If the Government were to be able to carry out its obligations to the country in this difficult situation it had to be given the necessary statutory powers by Parliament and have good machinery for reaching and administering informed decisions.

Some of the important powers necessary for carrying out an effective economic policy have been available to successive Governments for very many years, though they may not have been used for that purpose. This is true of the indirect controls, exercised primarily through taxation. With us taxation became a major weapon of economic planning. It was maintained at a high level as compared with pre-war, not only to pay for the developing social services, including education and housing and social insurance, but also to limit purchasing power to avoid 'too much money chasing too few goods', and to provide for necessary public capital investment. It was also needed to limit the consumption of particular goods. For example, despite the considerable increase in the generation of electricity, public demand was overreaching supply with most inconvenient results, so we reduced the purchase of domestic electrical appliances by increasing purchase tax on them.

But taxation alone could not ensure that the resources available were used in the best possible way, and the direct controls which had been established during the war were continued and adapted to the peace-time economy. Rationing of many foodstuffs had to be continued because it was necessary to control and cut down imports, especially from dollar areas. For a time it was necessary even to ration bread. In order to develop an export trade sufficient to pay for essential imports we had to require manufacturers to sell abroad things that people were only too anxious to buy at home: textiles and clothing materials had been important exports before the war, so clothes-rationing was retained until production could expand sufficiently to meet both home and export demand. Motor-cars were an outstanding example of successful encouragement of exports by controls and taxation. Controls over building through the issue of building licences helped to ensure that the most urgent needs of reconstruction were satisfied first and an impossible strain was not put upon the building industry. The problem of controlling investment in plant and machinery was a very difficult one. There was close consultation with the nationalized industries, all of which had large investment programmes. But in the sector of private industry it was very doubtful whether the Government had enough detailed knowledge to have justified the maintenance of machinery licensing. New factories were dealt with through the control of building licences, but apart from this, the main influence was the fixing of export targets in agreement with the manufacturers of industrial equipment.

Prices and wages presented difficulties. We extensively controlled prices but some increases could not be avoided. We could not, for example, control the price of imported commodities which rose noticeably. Under full employment the workers and the Trade Unions were naturally in a strong position as regards wages, and when there were increases of prices it was almost inevitable that there should be increases in wages also. There was understanding and a fair response to our appeals for restraint in wages claims, and we had reason for gratitude in particular to the Trade Union leaders, who did their best to restrain wages applications. We on our part made it more easy for them to do so by a policy of food subsidies, which prevented a marked increase in the cost of living and helped to keep our export prices down. We also asked companies to limit dividends and we continued the taxation on profits.

Prolongation of War-time Controls

Powers to exercise these 'controls' had originally been conferred on Ministers by the two Emergency Powers (Defence) Acts of 1939 and 1940. They were 'skeleton' Acts conferring extensive powers on Ministers to make Defence Regulations roughly for any purpose connected with the successful prosecution of the war. As Secretary of State for the Home Department and Minister of Home Security, I was among the principal Ministers concerned with the administration of Defence Regulations, and as Home Secretary it was my special duty to keep an eye on their constitutional correctness, though I was not responsible for the administration of the general body of economic and industrial Regulations.

Under the Acts numerous and important Regulations were made affecting economic matters. Perhaps the most important of these was Defence Regulation 55, which ran into well over five pages and had the title 'General Control of Industry'. Among other things the Regulation provided:

for regulating or prohibiting the production, treatment, keeping, storage, movement, transport, distribution, disposal, acquisition, use or consumption of articles of any description;

for regulating the carrying on of any undertaking engaged in essential work;

for any incidental and supplementary matters for which the competent authority thinks it expedient for the purposes of the order to provide.

Further, the control of any concern could be taken over and an authorized controller appointed to exercise such functions of control as might be provided by the order.

There was a special Regulation enabling the Minister of Fuel and Power to take control of all coal-mining undertakings. Under another Regulation the Board of Trade was given powers over the location of industry. There were extensive powers enabling the Government to control the prices of goods and services and building operations. The Minister of Labour and National Service was given powers for the control of employment and the avoidance of strikes and lock-outs and also for the safety and welfare of factory workers, miners and quarrymen, and for the provision of canteens for civilian workers, seamen, and fishermen. The Home Secretary secured by Regulation amendment of the Shops (Hours of Closing) Act, 1928, providing for the earlier closing of shops, which benefited shop-assistants, saved fuel, and encouraged people to get home before the night bombing. The examples I have given are not exhaustive, but give some indication of the field covered.

As the war neared its close it was necessary to consider what, if any, Regulation-making powers should be preserved in peacetime. During the War Coalition I prepared a Supplies and Services (Transitional Powers) Bill, which, subject to certain amendments notably in respect of the period of its operation, became the Labour Government's Supplies and Services (Transitional Powers) Act, 1945. Broadly speaking, the Act enabled the Regulations then in existence[1] to be continued, amended, or revoked. Once revoked they could not be renewed except by legislation. It also introduced additional parliamentary checks for orders and other instruments made under the Regulations. Later the Supplies and Services (Extended Purposes) Act, 1947, was passed to clarify the Government's powers on certain matters. There was an exciting debate about this. It was alleged that the Bill extended existing powers and even that it would

[1] Nearly all those which could be held to affect civil liberty had already been revoked.

enable the Government to achieve a socialist revolution by Defence Regulation. It was not so used, nor do I think it could have been.

The Emergency Powers (Defence) Acts which had been passed for war purposes contained very little definition and limitation of the field within which Ministers could make Defence Regulations. Although some very broad indication of the field was set out in the Supplies and Services (Transitional Powers) Act, 1945, the powers still remained both wide and vague. The Act of 1945 provided that it should come to an end within five years (the War Coalition Bill did not go beyond two years), but after that it could be renewed from year to year by an affirmative resolution passed by both Houses of Parliament. If, however, legislation enabling the Government to control the economic system was to be made permanent then it was clearly necessary that materially different legislation should be introduced which would enable Parliament itself to determine, in reasonable detail, the scope within which and the purposes for which such Regulations could be made. I was authorized, with the aid of a Cabinet Committee, to prepare such a draft Bill and did so. In the draft Bill for permanent legislation, therefore, we set out to state in detail the limits within which Regulations could be made. While it was true that the Bill, if passed, would have enabled Regulations to be made and operated, Parliament would already have decided in fair detail the limits within which Ministers could act. And as the Bill would have had to go through Committee and Report Stages in both Houses (the Committee Stage in such a case being taken on the Floor of the House of Commons), Parliament would have had ample opportunity to define the limits of the powers for the first time. We had already in the 1945 Act improved the parliamentary checks, but this aspect also was to be examined again. If one believes, as I do, that, to enable the community to deal with changing and often difficult economic circumstances, Governments should have power to act by Regulation in peace-time, then it clearly becomes desirable that the legislative authority should be adequately set out, that this authority should be determined in sufficient detail by Parliament after proper consideration and debate, and that the power to challenge Statutory Instruments in Parliament should be adequate.

With the assent of Mr. Attlee, the Prime Minister, I announced in a speech at the Labour Party Conference of 1949 that we intended to introduce permanent legislation of the character described. The announcement met with considerable criticism in non-Labour quarters, so it was reasonably clear that the Bill would have aroused controversy, although, had the text been made available, possibly this would have proved less than the critics anticipated.

We could not proceed with the Bill before the General Election of 1950 as final revision had not been completed. In the Parliament of 1950–1 we could not proceed with what would probably have been a controversial measure because our majority had been reduced to six. However, the draft Bill is in the archives as a basis of consideration by Ministers at any time.

In the meantime I was anxious immediately to see that Regulations which were clearly of such a nature that they would be permanently required should be made 'respectable' by embodying them in Acts of Parliament as and when opportunity offered, thus giving Parliament to that extent the opportunity to decide the limits within which Ministers could act, and to transform the powers from a Defence Regulation to a statutory basis. Some Regulations have been so dealt with and thereupon revoked. In general, however, the problem during the period of office of the Labour Party was much more to find out by experience the best way to use the quite wide existing powers, than whether these powers were adequate.

Machinery of Planning

If the organization and machinery of administration are seriously imperfect grave consequences will ensue and tempers will become frayed, for even a perfect policy will break down if there is muddle or slackness in administration. On the other hand, we have to beware of worshipping machinery for its own sake, of falling into the error of thinking that the more organization we build up, the more people we employ on the work, the more committees we establish, the more talking we do, the better. In the end it is doing the right things (and sometimes refraining from doing things) that really matters. Efficient, smooth-running organization is a vital instrument to have at our disposal. It may help us to think correctly, it may force us to face relevant facts, but it does not of itself get things done; that requires human energy, thought, initiative, and action. And thought and action must be continuous, for economic situations and factors change from time to time so that adaptation, changes, and even reversals of policy may well become desirable.

In the field of politics and government there is a special danger of elaborating machinery for its own sake. That is why we get demands from time to time for the appointment of unnecessary special Ministers for special purposes, almost on the assumption that that of itself will put things right, or for the excessive multiplication of committees within Governments. That is why within political parties there is sometimes an insistence in the name of democracy on the appointment of *ad hoc* committees, the duties of which could be better discharged by one competent person answerable to a general executive committee. There is a saying that 'another little drink won't do us any harm': well, it can. Within the field of government and politics there could be a saying that 'another little committee won't do us any harm'. And again I answer: 'Well, it can'. Democracy requires accountability: it does not require the endless multiplication of committees. Efficiency requires suitable organization and the more streamlined it is the better. But what is still more necessary are able men with clear minds and the right policy—doing things, and doing them well.

After those few cautionary words I will now say something of the actual machinery which we used to sort out the priorities which I have described earlier. We had learned a lot during the war. Not only were we experienced in war-time economic planning, but considerable official machinery existed when we came into power. There were the relevant branches of the economic Departments of State with the experience they had acquired. There was the Economic Section of the Cabinet Office[1] charged with the duty of keeping a general watch upon developments throughout the economic system as a whole, and upon events of significance abroad. There was also the Central Statistical Office which produced regular series of figures, reliable and well ordered, covering the development of our

[1] In 1953 (wrongly, as I am inclined to think) transferred to the Treasury.

national life, and published the *Monthly Digest of Statistics* as well as a series of statistical White Papers. Both those organizations were of proved utility.

Ministers, of course, had much to learn as they went along. No doubt we made mistakes; some things were not foreseen. There are critics who argue that some of them should have been foreseen in whole or in part. I do not claim that the Labour Government was perfect; nor do I think that anybody else could fairly argue that any other Government would have been perfect. Nobody could have foreseen the aggression in Korea; therefore they could not foresee its economic consequences. However, it is not part of the purpose of this book to engage in party political controversy, nor to allocate praise or blame between particular Ministers. Any Government seeking consciously and deliberately to build a better peace than that which obtained after the First World War would have had much to learn as it went along in the light of experience and changing facts. It is fair, I think, to say that what happened was that the *ad hoc* use of economic and financial controls came first, together with a limited amount of economic planning. In our first two years the main emphasis was on developing a system of co-ordination through Cabinet Committees rather than the direct economic administration by one leading economic Minister (in addition to the necessary co-ordination through Committees) which followed the appointment of Sir Stafford Cripps as Minister for Economic Affairs and the transfer of these duties to the Treasury when he became Chancellor of the Exchequer.

Before I was a victim of thrombosis at the beginning of 1947 and was out of action for about three months (during which time Sir Stafford Cripps took over my duties), the Prime Minister, Sir Stafford, and I decided that it was necessary to appoint a Chief Economic Planning Officer in the Lord President's Office. Sir Edwin Plowden, an able and public-spirited business man, who had formerly been Chief Executive in the Ministry of Aircraft Production, accepted the position. A mixed staff of business men, statisticians, and economists from outside was appointed with some civil servants to assist him. This was a notable stage in the development of economic planning. The primary task of the Planning Staff was the creation of a long-term plan for the use of the nation's resources, but its functions gradually widened. These were mainly in connexion with assessing the relative importance of the different claims on resources, present and future. This involved, for example, the assembling of much more information about investment than had previously been available. The Planning Staff also acted as a co-ordinating body in dealing with urgent current issues of economic policy, when these affected several Government Departments at the same time.

On 29 September 1947 it was announced that it had been decided to appoint a Minister for Economic Affairs, Sir Stafford Cripps being transferred to this post from the Board of Trade. The appointment of such a Minister was a new departure, for the duties of the war-time Minister of Production were by no means analogous. Sir Stafford Cripps was well fitted for the duties of the new Minister. He not only worked extremely hard, but he also manifested great moral courage in this office and at the Treasury. His loss was a very great one for the country. Mr. Attlee appointed as his successor Mr. Hugh Gaitskell, who had worked under Sir Stafford as Minister of State. Mr. Gaitskell discharged the highly responsible duties of Chancellor with extensive knowledge and ability.

Sir Stafford took over the Chief Planning Officer and the Central Planning Staff, the Economic Information Unit, and, in common with other Ministers, had the advice of the Economic Section of the Cabinet Office and the Central Statistical Office. He became Chairman of a Cabinet Committee dealing with production and related matters. When in November 1947 Sir Stafford Cripps was appointed to be Chancellor of the Exchequer he took with him his functions and the staff under him as Minister for Economic Affairs. This was an important development. It is true that it imposed upon the Chancellor of the Exchequer heavy additional duties (and the duties of the Chancellor are very heavy anyway), but it did broaden the work of the Treasury and merged economic policy and planning with financial and budgetary matters under the single control of the Chancellor of the Exchequer.

Most of the Labour Government's economic planning commenced in directions from Ministers to officials. The work was almost always carried out with the aid of official committees and working parties on which the Departments concerned were represented. In many cases these met under a Treasury Chairman, often provided by the Central Planning Staff. It was their duty to present an agreed statement of the facts, to analyse the probable consequences of alternative policies, and to present the policy issues to Ministers for decision. There were a large number of these committees. For example, there was a Raw Materials Committee, which was continuous from about 1942 right on till we left office, for allocating scarce materials, sometimes between Departments and sometimes between ultimate users. By the end of our term of office the two most important general allocation tasks were discharged by the Investment Programmes Committee and the Import Programme Committee—official bodies which produced comprehensive reports and proposals for ministerial consideration, the Ministers forming a kind of court of appeal. It was the duty of the Planning Staff and the Economic Section to see that the consequences of taking action in one field were considered in relation to our problems as a whole. For example, if on balance-of-payments grounds we had to limit the import of timber, the consequences for building and investment generally had to be investigated. During the war these problems had, of necessity, to be dealt with continually, and this experience was very valuable in the post-war period. Ministers considered the reports with their advisers and then met together as appropriate to reconcile the inevitably conflicting claims, so far as these had not already been settled at the official level. The procedure through interdepartmental committees helped to educate officials to look at problems as a whole, but even so, the claims of the various Departments were often greater than the resources available.

The quantity of imports of particular raw materials or food was usually itself a subject of controversy between the Treasury, which had to watch the balance of payments with great care, and the Department which desired to import for its own understandable reasons. It might be the Board of Trade or the Ministry of Supply or the Ministry of Health (for housing purposes) making quite a strong case for the import of raw materials, or it might be the Ministry of Food making a case for more and a greater variety of food for the people. But there we were arguing out understandable and even legitimate claims as against the overall impossibility of meeting them in full. Naturally a particular responsibility rested upon the Prime Minister, the non-departmental Ministers, and Ministers not directly concerned, to seek a settlement which as far as possible had regard to the national interest. No less was the responsibility on the Chancellor of the Exchequer and the competing economic Ministers to take heed of the facts, to consider what the general interest demanded and to conduct their part in the discussions in the spirit of give and take.

Under our system of Cabinet democracy it was neither possible nor desirable for one Minister to dictate decisions, therefore it was necessary to reach general agreement after negotiation and argument, even though the agreement was bound to be disappointing to some of the Ministers. In these discussions the Prime Minister, the Lord President, the Foreign Secretary, and the Chancellor of the Exchequer often played the part of influential arbitrators. Their ministerial duties and positions were conducive to impartiality, though now and again the Chancellor might have a particular Treasury point of view to urge. What was important if the right decisions were to be reached was that all the relevant facts should be fairly presented, and, if possible, that the facts themselves should be agreed in advance even though the deductions from the facts were disputable. This fair and clear presentation of the facts is one of the most vital elements of economic planning. The duty to be fair and clear about the facts is not only a duty resting upon the official working parties and committees: it is a duty which should always be present in the minds of all the Ministers concerned even though they are going to argue the case for their departmental interests. The facts themselves will not automatically produce a decision, but in so far as they are accepted and indisputable they will influence and limit the argument and be helpful in reaching the right conclusion.

Publicity and Persuasion

One of the excellent qualities of the British people is that, as a whole, they would wish to do the right thing by the country and that they have a sense of social responsibility greater than is to be found in most other countries. Understandably, however, there is a somewhat different psychology in peace than in war. During the war the nation was fighting for its life. Each citizen was conscious of this and realized the personal suffering and tyranny which he and his family would experience had the Nazis won. Social morale was at a very high level. Unless it appeared to be clear that the Government was wrong, official advice and even orders were accepted as necessary in the circumstances. Even the extensive direction of labour, compulsory fire-watching, and other Government orders were accepted, as a whole, in remarkably good spirit. There is, however, a natural and proper wish among our people for the maximum degree of personal freedom, though accompanied by a wide acceptance of the view that freedom should not be exercised in an anti-social spirit. When war ends and peace comes it is inevitable that a somewhat more critical view should be taken of Government directions. That is why the direction of labour was in general abandoned, though it was found necessary for a considerable time to require miners to continue mining and agricultural workers to remain on the land. The consumer had a tendency to assert his needs; he wanted to be able to buy things that he could not buy in conditions of war. However, while this is natural and desirable, there remained the danger that the citizen would not appreciate the economic problems left by the war and would therefore not be ready to play his full part in overcoming them.

Throughout, therefore, we attached the utmost importance to keeping the public informed on the economic situation, the facts about Government decisions and the reasons for them.

If the nation was to triumph over its economic difficulties it was not enough that the Government should be active in the battle: the people must be in it as well, including what are known as the two sides of industry. The general body of citizens had every right to know the economic facts and to receive from the Government the fullest possible information about the economic situation and the action necessary to keep it or to put it right. Merely to have given the people orders would have been not only undemocratic but also ineffective unless we had become dictatorial and totalitarian. We had no desire to be this, and in any case, happily, the nation would not have tolerated it. It was essential that Government and people should 'live together' as co-operators seeking the public well-being.

Each of the economic Departments possessed its information division, but they could give only departmental information. It was no less necessary that the nation should be informed and educated about the general economic situation both at home and abroad. In June 1947 an Economic Information Unit was established as part of my office. Shortly afterwards it was transferred to the newly created Minister for Economic Affairs and then in November it went with him to the Treasury. It was of fairly modest dimensions in relation to the work which had to be done. The Unit issued leaflets, wall newspapers, and news sheets for distribution and use in suitable ways to spread knowledge and guidance among the people, and was also available to newspaper men or other writers to give information or assistance on complex economic matters.[1]

I started periodical Press Conferences (continued by Sir Stafford Cripps and Mr. Hugh Gaitskell) where I, or other appropriate members of the Government, gave reports and subjected ourselves to questioning. The Press was generous and co-operative in reporting these conferences. Educational speeches by Ministers were encouraged in the country as well as in Parliament. Indeed at that time speeches dealing with the practical problems of government and our social and economic difficulties were more important from every point of view than party political speeches, even though they also had their place. Informative and well-constructed ministerial speeches are among the most useful forms of public relations. The co-operation of Employers' Organizations and Trade Unions was forthcoming in disseminating information and guidance throughout the ranks of management and workers. Information was supplied to M.P.s and to newspapers and periodicals throughout the country.

Some people questioned the necessity of all this work (at times they also cried, 'Give the nation the facts!'). But consider the magnitude and complexity of the vitally important experiment upon which we were engaged. Without reasonable information services, not only the people as a whole, but a good many industrialists and M.P.s would not have been

[1] For a full account of the work of this important branch of government see 'The Economic Information Unit' by S. C. Leslie in *Public Administration*, Spring, 1950.

adequately informed upon the programmes with which we were dealing. Unless they were all well informed there would not be forthcoming that necessary degree of understanding and willing co-operation without which Ministers could not be successful in their work.

Not long after the appointment of the Chief Planning Officer and the Economic Planning Staff I convened a meeting in July 1947 of employers' representatives, Trade Union leaders and Government officers to establish the Economic Planning Board. To this Board were submitted periodical reports on economic matters and the Board was consulted about current problems and projected policies on which they gave us valuable advice. This was another means of associating outside interests with us in our work and bringing into the official councils the views and experience of men active in the day-to-day problems of industry.

Two other joint bodies played their somewhat different but nevertheless relevant parts in collective discussions. They were the National Joint Advisory Council which met under the Chairmanship of the Minister of Labour and discussed many matters related to labour and manpower policy under wide terms of reference. The other body was called the National Production Advisory Council for Industry. The President of the Board of Trade presided over the N.P.A.C.I. which considered our production and commercial questions largely in relation to the work of the Board of Trade but was not strictly limited in its terms of reference.[1] It was sometimes argued that there were too many joint consultative bodies and that in particular the National Joint Advisory Council and the National Production Advisory Council for Industry could have been merged. Certainly one must be on one's guard against duplicating the consultative machinery which makes an undue call upon the time of busy men.

Partly for the education of the public and industry and Members of both Houses of Parliament we started the annual publication of the *Economic Survey*. The *Economic Survey* was an attempt to give a picture of our various economic problems,

[1] When responsibility for economic planning was subsequently transferred to the Treasury this body came under the jurisdiction of the Chancellor of the Exchequer.

of the probable economic resources which would be available, and the use which it was proposed to make of them. It gave reliable facts about the past, but it did not and could not pretend to be accurate in every particular in its estimates for the coming year; and because of this its publication meant that the Government was taking some risks. Even so it was worth while. It compelled us to try to ascertain the facts and the shape of things to come (which was of educational value to Ministers themselves and helped to give them that sense of realism which is necessary for the discharge of all this work). The *Survey* was read by M.P.s, industrialists, Trade Union leaders, and others, and as the Press reviewed and commented upon it, the general public not only received a good deal of education, but the discussions and arguments that ensued among them and in Parliament itself were also to the good. Most people thought of the *Economic Survey* as a plan or programme and that is how the early issues were written, but as time went on I fear that these characteristics of the *Survey* lessened.

Economic planning does not and should not involve an excessive consideration of detail. It would be foolish for Whitehall to try to satisfy itself that the number of waistcoat buttons manufactured would exactly meet the needs of the waistcoats to be made plus replacement of buttons. There has to be an internal appraisal of the larger factors in our economy; for example, the availability of labour and the stimulation of recruitment in important industries suffering from a shortage of manpower; coal, and iron and steel production; food supplies and the balance of payments. The *Economic Survey* is the outward and visible sign of such appraisals conducted within the Government organization. The *Survey*, so far as the future is concerned, cannot always work out accurately; big and disturbing events will inevitably upset its prophetic paragraphs. So it should not be regarded as a document which absolutely fixes coming events; for example, the fuel crisis of 1947 and devaluation in 1949 inevitably required substantial changes in administrative action. Throughout the year the Government has to be ready to revise estimates and policies, sometimes at short notice. Flexibility is very necessary even though we must try to get an intelligible picture of the economic situation ahead and the best way of handling it.

Conclusions

The consequences of economic planning undoubtedly caused some irritation to industrialists and private citizens. This was to be expected if people were not allowed to do what they liked. It was the more annoying when they themselves thought, as they may well have done, that it would be socially advantageous if they did the things they wished to do. Sometimes their grievances may have been well based, but it was more likely that they were unable to appreciate the wider social and economic conditions involved. Moreover, no doubt mistakes were made by the Government from time to time. As a whole, however, I would say that undoubtedly the work of economic planning and controls was in general advantageous to the nation. Without them we might have had a very limited period of boom or, because we could not pay for food and raw material imports, we might have had hunger and mass unemployment. For all this we should, as after the First World War, have paid a heavy price in human suffering and economic loss; and undoubtedly there would have been far more industrial disputes. As it was, not only did organized public expenditure on reconstruction and on the social services stimulate employment, but planning and controls also gave us a greater stability of employment and price-levels over a longer period than there would otherwise have been.

I supported the transfer of economic planning functions to the Treasury and I am still not disposed to argue that we were wrong. It should be a good thing for the Treasury to have to relate its thinking on the narrower issues of money to the wider field of economics and overall planning. It gives to the Chancellor and the Treasury a wider horizon, a more comprehensive field of related thought and action which should be of value to them. It also provides a more coherent authority in economic and financial affairs. There are, however, two considerations which give me some concern. Can one man—the Chancellor of the Exchequer—even though he may have the assistance of valuable subordinate Ministers, carry the vast burden involved? I fear that the burden helped to kill Sir Stafford Cripps just as his heavy labours at the Foreign Office may have helped to kill Ernest Bevin, an older man. One way of helping to meet the difficulty would be to transfer some of the functions of the 'old' Treasury. In the next chapter I mention the possibility of some of the Treasury's civil service functions being transferred to a non-departmental Minister. It does not seem to be necessary that either the University Grants Committee, or the Arts Council, or Parliamentary Counsel should be attached to the Treasury; these functions could be transferred to a suitable non-departmental Minister. As the University Grants Committee and the Arts Council are involved in the direct spending of public money there are surely good reasons why they should not be a Treasury responsibility. It would be a good thing to go through the functions of the Treasury in detail to see how far relief could be afforded. Some relief should be found for the Chancellor and his principal officers from their arduous labours if that be possible. It may be, however, that this relief could not be very large.

Secondly—though this rather contradicts what I have said about the advantages of making economic planning a Treasury function—we should not close our minds to the question whether this is permanently the right solution or whether we should not re-establish a Ministry for Economic Affairs. Such a Ministry would obviously greatly lighten the work of the Chancellor.

Until economic planning was absorbed into the Treasury organization it was a matter of some doubt how far the Treasury was subject to the machinery of economic co-ordination, and this in part provided the case for the transfer. But it should be considered whether the Treasury, like other Departments, should not be subjected to effective co-ordination by a Minister for Economic Affairs responsible for overall economic policies. For the 'old' Treasury was clearly an economic Department with its own interests. Moreover, though the Budget is one of the most important instruments of economic planning, other Departments have a considerable interest in its contents. It is inevitable that from time to time Treasury interests and Treasury views will conflict with those of other Departments. I am certainly not dogmatic about the re-establishment of a Ministry for Economic Affairs. We have had little or no experience, for it lasted but a few months. I put it forward merely as a possibility worthy of discussion.

Obviously, much would depend on the ability, tact, and

temperament of the Minister for Economic Affairs and the Chancellor if and when such a change were made. The Minister would need to be a man of senior rank in the Government and to possess a capacity for getting on with important colleagues (notably the Chancellor) in promoting coherent economic policies. But the Chancellor would and should remain a Minister of great importance in the Government; he should therefore be a person of real ability with a capacity to co-operate with the Minister for Economic Affairs. Unless the necessary qualities were possessed by both Ministers it would be better not to make the change. Precisely because budgetary policy is a vital element in economic affairs—just as economic and financial policy in Departments other than the Treasury can be important to the Budget—close and friendly collaboration between the two Ministers would be very important.

If the Chancellor is to carry on with the duties of the 'new' as well as the 'old' Treasury, there is a great deal to be said for the restoration of a Minister of State of adequate status under the Chancellor who would have special responsibilities in the planning field. But as so much of his work would be settling priorities between Departments, he would have to be a person of authority whose decisions were accepted on all but major issues.

Economic planning has by no means reached the stage of perfection. Indeed, it is still in its beginnings and we have much to learn. It is probable that we shall always have something to learn and a good deal of the learning will be the result of painful experience. We learnt much from the dollar crisis of 1947 and the painful thinking and processes leading up to devaluation in 1949.

Naturally we discussed what is known as wages policy among ourselves and with our Trade Union friends. It cannot be said that we reached any firm conclusions any more than our Conservative successors have done. There is, indeed, much to be said for free negotiation between the Unions and employers, with the Ministry of Labour ready to afford help and mediation if desired; that is the view of the T.U.C. and—so far as I know—of the organized employers, and in practice we accepted it. They prefer to keep wages out of politics and off the Floor of the House of Commons—and so do I. Nor do I see Ministers and the Civil Service making a success of wages determination, except through the accepted processes of arbitration. Nevertheless, both in conditions of full employment and of acute depression the level of wages must be a matter of general economic concern. Individual attacks on wages by employers or individual applications for increases by the Unions can set going, downwards or upwards, spirals with far-reaching effects. Whether general policy on such matters should be more closely discussed by the T.U.C. General Council on the one hand, and the organized employers on the other (and possibly discussed collectively from time to time), may be worthy of consideration. The State would play no fresh part, except, perhaps, to supply impartial factual economic information. However, these are large questions hardly capable of adequate exploration in this book.

Finally, let us remind ourselves that however good an individual nation may become at the business of economic planning it may well find itself in difficulties as a result of external events. In the end only world economic planning, in addition to national planning, will solve the problems. There has been a lot of talk about it in the Economic and Social Council of the United Nations, and there exist certain international agencies dealing with economic affairs. But we have not got very far: the problem is complex and it will not be easy to get the nations to agree. Just as there are conflicts between individuals and sectional interests within the national field, so there are conflicts between national interests and the well-being of the world as a whole. It is of great importance that international, regional, and world planning should proceed, and we must do everything we can to encourage it. We still have much to learn about national economic planning: we have hardly begun to learn about world economic planning.

CHAPTER XIV

Ministers and Civil Servants

To the general public the relationship between Ministers and civil servants is something of a mystery. Some people, for example, may think that a Minister is too much dominated by his civil servants—more usually referred to on such occasions by that harsh, ugly word 'officials'; I prefer 'officers'. This allegation is understandable when it is made by an ordinary citizen or a Member of Parliament who has sought unsuccessfully to get some departmental decision changed. But it is untrue as a generalization though it can be true in particular cases. Anyway, it would not be easy to be sure unless one had the chance of seeing the Minister and his civil servants in action together. Indeed, it is my general experience that if the Minister in charge knows what he wants and is intelligent in going about it, he can command the understanding co-operation and support of his civil servants. The kind of Minister who is most tiring to the officers of a Department is the Minister who does not know his own mind and cannot make it up. If the policy of a Department is hazy, vacillating, and ineffective, it is, after all, the responsibility of the Minister; it is quite as likely to be his fault as that of his civil servants.

Taking Over a New Department

Upon taking over a Government Department a Minister will be introduced to the senior civil servants of the Department either by the outgoing Minister or by the Permanent Secretary. In addition to their being introduced by name the Minister will be briefly told of their duties and he may be presented with a chart describing the organization of the Department and the distribution of functions between the different branches. By these means he will get a broad preliminary idea of the organization and work of the Department for which he has become responsible.

The Permanent Secretary and Other Officers

The Permanent Secretary of a Department is its chief civil servant. He is responsible to the Minister not only for the organization and efficiency of the Department, but also for the advice given to the Minister by the Department through the whole range of its duties, even though some of the advice reaches the Minister direct from lower down the line. Nowadays he is almost invariably the Accounting Officer of the Department. While the day-to-day work is done by the Finance Branch, whose chief officer is often called the Accountant-General, the Permanent Secretary as Accounting Officer has a personal responsibility for finance both to the Minister and to the Treasury and has to answer for the departmental accounts and estimates to the Public Accounts Committee and the Estimates Committee of the House of Commons.

Departments are divided into branches each headed by an officer of appropriate rank. All of them are answerable through the Permanent Secretary to the Minister. On many matters Under-Secretaries and Assistant Secretaries will do business direct with the Minister, but proposals of importance always come to the Minister through either the Deputy Secretary or the Permanent Secretary or both.

The Permanent Secretary is the head of the administrative hierarchy. There is usually a Deputy Secretary or Secretaries, then Under-Secretaries, Assistant Secretaries, and so down the scale of the administrative class. Many Departments have highly placed specialist officers, e.g. scientific or legal advisers. There are also the executive and clerical classes, the senior members of which may have considerable responsibilities for administration, but not for the formulation of policy. Some Departments which deal with a large volume of business not involving many policy issues are almost wholly staffed by members of the executive and clerical classes, who fill all but the highest posts in these offices and carry out a wide range of important duties.

The Permanent Secretary of an important Department carries great responsibilities, materially greater than the chief officer of any local authority, not excluding the London County Council. He has to wrestle with high and difficult matters of policy which continually arise in the course of administration.

He is not and should not be a politician, but he should know enough about politics and politicians to be on his guard against blunders and indiscretions, although it is the Minister rather than the Permanent Secretary who is paid for his political expertise and understanding of the public.

Private Secretaries

The Permanent Secretary at an early stage consults the new Minister on his wishes regarding the appointment of his Principal Private Secretary and other Private Secretaries. The Permanent Secretary will no doubt be ready with recommendations, and if the Minister is not familiar with the Department it will not be easy for him to pick and choose, though he will be wise to see the candidates proposed and to make it clear that he reserves the right to make changes later if for some reason or another he desires to do so. The Principal Private Secretary, whilst not a very senior member of the staff, is important. The post is occupied by a picked young man on his way to fill posts of higher rank in the Department. He has continuous relationships with the Minister, he has a duty to protect the Minister against unnecessary engagements or strain, and prevent papers reaching his desk with which it is not really necessary to bother him. Ideally, he should be intelligent, efficient, a good organizer, not temperamental or excitable (nor should he be dreary), and able to be long-suffering if he has to live with a temperamental or excitable Minister, with some way of his own whereby equanimity will be restored as quickly as possible. Sometimes that takes the form of the Private Secretary in the midst of a storm becoming studiously quiet, combined with a very slightly subdued and pained look which will convey to the Minister a distinct and respectful consciousness of shock, sorrow, and surprise.

The Private Secretary and his superior, the Permanent Secretary, are closely associated. The Private Secretary is the continuous link between the Minister and the Permanent Secretary, and he must see to it that both of them are informed about what is going on and are each aware of the other's feelings. Clearly, therefore, the post of Principal Private Secretary is delicate and important. He, or one of his assistants, will submit to the

Minister letters for signature or minutes for consideration, and they have to be ready to answer questions that the Minister will put to them. It is very desirable, therefore, that they should have an extensive knowledge of the work of the Department.

Ministerial and Departmental Minutes

After taking office and going through these preliminaries, the new Minister will soon have submitted to him minutes for consideration and documents and letters for signature. Minutes are departmental observations or reports with recommendations for action or, possibly, for no action. Minutes may be separately presented on sheets of paper or they may be part of a file. In either case they may deal with proposals or problems which have arisen in the higher grades of the executive class or lower grades of the administrative class, so that a number of minutes will appear, each commenting on the preceding minutes or merely recording agreement. The official minutes will terminate with one by the Permanent Secretary or one of his senior assistants according to the importance and nature of the subject in question. In a substantial number of cases there should be a minute following from the Parliamentary Secretary.

If the Minister can find time—he will not always be able to do so—it will be well for him to read all or most of the minutes. He will then have his background enriched and get to know his men better. In time he will learn what reading he can 'jump' and what he cannot. All minutes should be careful about the facts, fair in summarizing them, and clear and understandable in setting out recommendations. The comments of the more senior officers or the Minister on the minutes coming from below should be frank and even educational, but not rude. The file is seen by many people and it is not wise to roll the subordinates almost in the mud before the departmental 'public'—that is better done privately within the four walls of the superior's room. For example, it should not be recorded that the preceding minute is silly and ignorant but rather that 'As I see the facts they are. . . . It would, I think, be a mistake to . . . because. . . . The better course would appear to be. . . . In all the circumstances I recommend. . . .' The final ministerial minute should be clear and decisive unless the Minister has decided to postpone or seek further information. At times he will minute, 'Pl[ease] see me'.

If a minute badly annoys a Minister it is best for him to send for the civil servant concerned and say to him 'Look, this seems to me to be a bit unwise and foolish', or 'I really don't know what you're getting at', and indeed speak about the matter with great frankness. Even so, it is better to send a man away happy unless the matter is to be treated as one of first-class and enduring importance, or unless it is a case in which it is really necessary to be rough to teach the man a lesson. But if a Minister wants enthusiastic and willing service it is desirable for him—as in any other walk of life—to be fair and understanding so that the officer will go away and say to himself, 'Well, the Minister was pretty severe in his criticisms, but I see his point; he was fair about it and finished up with an encouraging word.' And if an officer does specially good work, it is well for the Minister (after consulting the Permanent or Deputy Secretary) to send for him and tell him so, though he should beware of causing legitimate jealousies.

A clumsy and inconsiderate Minister can easily make the Department unhappy and discouraged, whereas what he should seek to do is to make people live-minded, happy in working for him, so as to get the best out of them. Ministerial visits to the various branches of the Department, including the lower ranks, are not only educational to the Minister but rather cheering to the people down below. The good Minister as well as the good Permanent Secretary can do much to spread *esprit de corps* among the staff and that desirable feeling of pride in working for the Department and, indeed, working for John Bull. The life of the clerical officers at the base of the hierarchy is liable to be unexciting and somewhat routine. Their services are, however, valuable and they deserve notice and encouragement.

The business of minuting is sometimes held in scorn. It is said that in Government Departments the staff do nothing but send notes to each other, which go round the building (and possibly the out-buildings) to such an extent that decisions are wickedly delayed. This can happen on occasion but as a whole the criticism is exaggerated. Decisions may well tend to be slower than in a private business concern where they can well be reached even without records by the man on the spot, or as a result of a quick telephone conversation. This happens upon occasion in Government Departments just as the processes of minuting are not unknown in great private undertakings, but we have to pay some price for parliamentary democracy. One of the rights of Members of the House of Commons or the House of Lords is to put down Questions or take other action in Parliament querying or challenging any action of a Government Department, however unimportant it may be; and the Minister is, of course, responsible for all the actions of his Department whether he has specifically ordered them or not. Therefore, proper records must be kept so that it may be ascertained what decision was reached, why, and by whom. Moreover, it is also desirable to have such records for departmental reasons: in case the Minister or his civil servants should forget what decision was reached; to encourage care and responsibility in reaching decisions; and so that everybody (including the Minister) is committed and responsibility cannot well be shifted, which is only fair to everybody concerned. The minutes are, of course, for private use within the Department itself.

Formulation of Policy

The new Minister will have his own views on the policy of the Department and may well have ideas about changes in organization, though as to the latter he will be wise not to make up his mind until he has been in the Department sufficiently long to be familiar with its operation. Quite early, however, he may have a conference with the Parliamentary Secretary or Secretaries, the Permanent Secretary, the Deputy Secretary, and possibly other senior civil servants to give them a general picture of his aims in policy and possibly his tentative ideas for modifications in departmental organization. The Minister will be wise to throw the matters open for free and frank discussion and should not be resentful if dissent is voiced. Nor should the civil servants be difficult if he questions existing policies or organization. These are, in any case, preliminaries; the time for actual decision will not be reached until reports on particular matters reach the Minister for a specific decision or as a basis for papers to be taken to the Cabinet or Cabinet Committee. But such an early consultation is an advantage to everybody, for it enables the Department to have an early picture of the new Minister's aims and outlook so that they may be taken into proper account.

A great many points of policy will be initiated by civil servants, who should not be discouraged from expressing their views frankly. But in addition to being the man who decides questions put before him, the Minister should be an initiator of policy and action, for example by addressing minutes to the Permanent Secretary or the Parliamentary Secretary calling for factual information, by requiring consideration of and reports on particular questions, or by giving directions. Clearly, it is desirable that he should be intelligent, responsible, and selective and not throw paper about merely for the fun of the thing or out of a mere sense of self-importance; but also it is desirable that the Department should be conscious of the presence of a live personality at the head of its affairs, and that he is the active master of the Department and not a sleeping partner. In my experience our Civil Service generally prefers a Minister with a mind of his own to a mere rubber stamp.

Day-to-Day Administration

It should not be thought that a Department spends most of its time on legislation or even settling big issues of policy. From time to time it may be heavily engaged with a Bill, and on these and other occasions new and important policy decisions will be involved. But most of the Department's work and that of the Minister will be the day-to-day administration, and will involve discussing and settling minor headaches or big problems that are bound to arise with fair frequency. In the Ministry of Housing and Local Government, for example, the personal attention of the Minister may be required to deal with a dispute between local authorities, or between a local authority and the Department's officers on a planning scheme, or about the extension of the gas-works in the City of Oxford which caused extensive controversy and reached the correspondence columns of *The Times*. Matters such as these take the time of the Minister, but this is inevitable, for they are the kind of things that can break out into parliamentary and newspaper controversy, embarrassing to the Department. Treasury officers and their

Ministers must spend a fair amount of time on matters which in themselves are relatively small but which are worrying because of repercussions of one sort or another.

The Minister and his Advisers

In considering departmental problems or policy it is necessary for there to be frequent meetings between the Minister and his advisers. Sometimes it will be the Permanent Secretary alone or an individual civil servant lower down the line or the Private Secretary; but often the issue will be of such a character that it will be necessary for the Minister to have a gathering of quite a number of his civil servants, especially when more than one branch of the Department is involved, together with the Parliamentary Secretary. It is well to encourage at such meetings not only the presence of the civil servants below the top flight, but to encourage them to speak their mind even though they may not entirely agree with their superiors. This is good training and it enables them the better to get that understanding of the mind of the Minister which is very desirable in the interests of good administration. Indeed, the wise Permanent Secretary, as well as the Minister, will encourage subordinates to attend on suitable occasions as part of their official education and training. Moreover, it will often be the case that a subordinate has contributed much work to a paper under discussion even though it has to be altered and polished up by his superiors. It is a source of encouragement to the man below to be present when a document to which he has contributed is under consideration, whilst his loyalty to his superiors and his enthusiasm will be stimulated if he is given credit for the part he has played.

The relationship between the Minister and the civil servants should be—and usually is—that of colleagues working together in a team, co-operative partners seeking to advance the public interest and the efficiency of the Department. The Minister should not be an isolated autocrat, giving orders without hearing or considering arguments for alternative courses; nor, on the other hand, should the civil servants be able to treat him as a mere cipher. The partnership should be alive and virile, rival ideas and opinions should be fairly considered, and the relationship of all should be one of mutual respect—on the understanding, of course, that the Minister's decision is final and must be loyally and helpfully carried out, and that he requires efficient and energetic service.

We often hear in a somewhat critical sense of the 'handling' of Ministers by civil servants, but we do not so often hear of the handling of civil servants by the Minister, yet if 'handling' is at all desirable, and up to a point it is, it is necessary in both directions. Men will do their work better if a decision is given after reasonable discussion than they will if the Minister brutally raps out, 'That's the decision, you get on with it'.

I recall an experience of requiring a sharp change of policy within a week of taking up my first ministerial office, that of Minister of Transport in 1929. At County Hall and in Parliament I had led a campaign against the Bills for the co-ordination of London traffic which sought to transfer the management of London County Council tramways to Lord Ashfield's London Traffic Combine. After the 1929 Election the Bills had to have a final Third Reading in the House of Commons, and a decision was therefore necessary as to the Government's attitude. My provisional decision was that we would advise Parliament to reject the Bills, and that I would substitute a measure based on public ownership. The officers were naturally disturbed because they, Lord Ashfield's companies and the London County Council Conservative majority, had put an enormous amount of work into these Private Bills and into ending the competition between the L.C.C. tramways and the big privately owned passenger transport undertakings. And now the new Minister proposed to destroy all that work and substitute a new socialistic policy in a Parliament where the Labour Government had no majority. I invited the civil servants to put to me freely and frankly their point of view; then for some days we had keen discussions about it all. At the end I adhered to my provisional decision, said that it must operate subject to the Cabinet (who, after discussion, approved my views) and that I expected the loyal and energetic support of the Department. It is a pleasure to be able to say that that support and co-operation were at once promised and were forthcoming, and that the civil servants with whom I had argued worked very hard in furthering the policy I had decided upon.

Some American officials (even actual members of the Administration are 'officials' in the U.S.) in attendance on the

United States Government representatives at the Potsdam Conference in 1945 had an experience which to them was surprising. During the first part of the Potsdam discussions between representatives of the Governments of the United States, the Soviet Union, and the United Kingdom, the British General Election was proceeding. Some of the Americans said to some of the British: 'If there is a change of Government as a result of the election in your country there will be, we suppose, changes in your more important civil servants. So maybe we shan't see these British civil servants any more.' They were assured, though they were not wholly convinced, that this would not happen; they were genuinely surprised and could not follow it when Mr. Attlee turned up as Prime Minister and head of the British delegation in the second part of the Conference, instead of Mr. Churchill, accompanied by the same civil servants as served Mr. Churchill. Had the change in Government been the other way round the same civil servants would have appeared and a Conservative Government could have equally relied on their loyalty. The fact is, of course, that the civil servants are servants of Her Majesty, the Government—whatever the political colour of that Government may be—and of the nation as a whole.

The senior civil servants will confer freely with the Minister (unless, as rarely happens, he is unwilling to listen), and to the best of their ability place the facts before him and give such advice as they think right and proper. To discourage honest official advice—whether in national or local government—is both foolish and harmful. Advisers who are mere yes-men playing up to the Minister in the hope of advancement are just as dangerous as are obstinate and obstructive no-men. Both types are bad. Both sides to an argument should be heard and considered. At the end of the discussion it is for the Minister to come to such conclusions and give such directions as he thinks appropriate. It is then the duty of the civil servants to carry out the ministerial decision, doing their best to ensure the success of the Minister's policy, whether they have advised its adoption or not.

An Unfortunate Blunder

Occasionally, however, something may go wrong or the Minister may be badly served. If a mistake is made in a Government Department the Minister is responsible even if he knew nothing about it until, for example, a letter of complaint is received from an M.P., or there is criticism in the Press, or a Question is put down for answer in the House; even if he has no real personal responsibility whatever, the Minister is still held responsible. He will no doubt criticize whoever is responsible in the Department in mild terms if it is a small mistake and in strong terms if it is a bad one, but publicly he must accept responsibility as if the act were his own. It is, however, legitimate for him to explain that something went wrong in the Department, that he accepts responsibility and apologizes for it, and that he has taken steps to see that such a thing will not happen again.

I had one such experience when I was Home Secretary and Minister of Home Security in Mr. Churchill's War Government. It was a curious and, in a way, sad circumstance that this serious mishap occurred in the Home Office with its long traditions of constitutional rectitude, and not in the freshly created war-time Ministry of Home Security. The service concerned was the Fire Service. The use of the incendiary bomb by the enemy involved widespread fire risks. Experience showed not only that it was very difficult, if not impossible, to get a quick mobilization and concentration of the local fire brigades over a wide area on a town or district that had been subject to severe enemy attack, but also that the differing practices and the grading of the officers and men and the variations in equipment and methods of fire-fighting made it impossible adequately to blend the contingents brought together from a wide variety of local authorities of various sizes and with somewhat varying practices and traditions. They were all brave men, and I am not here arguing about the efficiency of the local organizations for their peace-time duties. But we were at war; and, though I am a local government man and did not like taking away local authority services, the nation was fighting for its life and the national interest really required that we put the situation right for the period of the war. So it was necessary to establish a National Fire Service. All the strains that fell on Ministers at that time, especially on those who, like myself, were taking a major part in resisting the enemy, made it undesirable that much parliamentary time should be spent on the consideration of what would inevitably have been a substantial and detailed Bill, quite apart from the labour involved in its preparation. I therefore decided (at first, I fear, somewhat shocking the parliamentary draftsman) that the Bill must be a short one. In substance it enabled the Secretaries of State for the Home Department and for Scotland by means of Regulations to transfer for the war period the local fire brigades to themselves and to set up a National Fire Service.

Naturally, however, the parliamentary right to challenge the Regulations was provided for. The Act accordingly stipulated that each Regulation should be laid before Parliament 'as soon as may be after it is made' and that either House could by negative resolution annul it within twenty-eight sitting days after laying. The quick merging—and it had to be quick—of the local fire brigades into the National Fire Service was a huge task which very much occupied the labours and attentions of the Home Office Fire Division and myself. Anyway, a terrible thing happened—everybody forgot to bring the Regulations before Parliament; the Department forgot, I forgot, and it was no less extraordinary that neither House of Parliament noticed that the Regulations had not been submitted. Not one M.P. or Peer spotted it. Nor did the Press.

It was not until some three years after the passing of the Act, during which we had gone right ahead in organizing and operating the National Fire Service, that somebody in the Home Office discovered that we had committed a capital parliamentary offence and that the National Fire Service was without full and proper parliamentary authority. Those concerned were most apologetic and very mortified. I was very mortified and very cross. I made my displeasure known, but, after all, I had myself forgotten, although a Minister rather expects the Department to bring such things forward. Nevertheless, I was guilty as well as the Department. And indeed the House of Commons and the House of Lords were guilty, too, for not noticing the offence. But whilst I gently mentioned the fact to the House I was careful not to 'rub it in', for it would not be human to expect the House of Commons to blame itself when it had a Minister 'on the spot' who had no alternative but to plead guilty. And it is always well to remember that in the last resort the House of Commons is the master. So I went down to the House of Commons and to its consternation explained what had happened and confessed my guilt, sincerely apologizing 'in italics' for the offence; for it was indeed a most serious offence. It was necessary to bring in an Indemnity Bill to validate the error and this gave an opportunity for further apologies. As a whole the House was generous, although quite naturally there were criticisms and some pointed observations about the dangers of delegated legislation. Although (and I do not complain) no M.P. criticized the House and its Members for not having noticed the failure, probably a number of them wished they had noticed it, for what an opportunity it would have been for a really exciting Question in the House whereby the Home Secretary could have been put in the soup. The Home Office and its Secretary of State almost went into mourning. After all, we were not a new-fangled Department like the Ministry of Supply. This serious sin against the rights of parliamentary democracy had been committed by the Home Office with its rich experience of constitutional matters; the Home Office, which was the guardian of civil liberty, the rights of the subject, and of constitutional rectitude. We certainly were ashamed of ourselves.

All this may be rather hard on a Minister from time to time, but it is right. Somebody must be held responsible to Parliament and the public. It has to be the Minister, for it is he, and neither Parliament nor the public, who has official control over his civil servants. One of the fundamentals of our system of government is that some Minister of the Crown is responsible to Parliament, and through Parliament to the public, for every act of the Executive. This is a corner-stone of our system of parliamentary government. There may, however, be an occasion on which so serious a mistake has been made that the Minister must explain the circumstances and processes which resulted in the mistake, particularly if it involves an issue of civil liberty or individual rights. Now and again the House demands to know the name of the officer responsible for the occurrence. The proper answer of the Minister is that if the House wants anybody's head it must be his head as the responsible Minister, and that it must leave him to deal with the officer concerned in the Department.

There is a circumstance in which I think a considerable degree of frankness is warranted. If a Minister has given a specific order within the Department on a matter of public interest and his instructions have not been carried out, then, if he is challenged in Parliament and if he is so minded, he has a perfect right to reveal the facts and to assure the House that he has taken suitable action. Even so he must still take the responsibility. It is, I think, legitimate in such a case that disregard of an instruction should be made known, even if it involves some humiliation for the officer concerned and his colleagues knowing that he was the one who disobeyed; for the Civil Service should at all times know that the lawful orders of Ministers must be carried out. However, such a situation is rare, though I did experience one and told the House about it.

In all these matters it is well for the Minister to be forthcoming in Parliament. Unless the matter is exceptionally serious nothing is lost by an admission of error. The House of Commons is generous to a Minister who has told the truth, admitted a mistake, and apologized; but it will come down hard on a Minister who takes the line that he will defend himself and his Department whether they are right or wrong and who shuffles about evasively rather than admit that a blunder or an innocent mistake has been made.

Transfers and Dismissals

In very rare cases a Minister may find himself markedly unhappy with his Permanent Secretary or Deputy Secretary and come to the conclusion either that the officer is unsuitable or, at any rate, that the Minister cannot well live with him. His appropriate course will be to report the matter in confidence to the Permanent Secretary to the Treasury and ask for a change. It may be that the Permanent Secretary to the Treasury will ask the Minister to let him seek ways and means of settling the difficulty without change, or it may be that he will take steps to arrange a transfer. Any change would require the approval of the Prime Minister.

Is an established civil servant ever dismissed the service? The answer is, not often. Of course, if he were guilty of such irregularities as theft, bribery, or corruption (which are rare) he would be dismissed without gratuity or pension. But the chances of dismissal on grounds of inefficiency (which is, of course, a relative term) are not great. However, some changes in what I think is the right direction have been made in recent years. For one thing, greater attempts have been made to weed out unsuitable recruits during the probation period. In recent years probation had tended to become a formality, but now it is more of a real test. Recruits to the administrative class now have to pass a Central Board conducted by the Civil Service Commissioners at the end of their probation period. Changes have also been made to facilitate dismissal or earlier retirement. Hitherto, under the civil service non-contributory pension scheme, no established civil servant could leave the Service before the age of 60 with any pension provision at all, unless he was retired on grounds of ill health, abolition of office, or declared inefficiency. Section 34 of the Superannuation Act, 1949, however, provides for paying pensions forthwith to civil servants aged 50 or over whose retirement is considered to be desirable in the interests of efficiency. (To balance this, Section 34 also makes it possible for a civil servant to retire voluntarily between 50 and 60 and still receive his pension at 60.)

There are arguments both ways about the greater use of the power to dismiss. The argument for the quality of mercy is, I think, that if dismissals on grounds of inefficiency were noticeable in numbers, or considered to be ruthless, the morale of the service might suffer and civil servants develop a habit of 'looking over their shoulders'; and that it might result in the resignation even of able people to take up appointments outside owing to a sense of insecurity. Finally, the man who is distinctly below average and, perhaps, inefficient at 55, has very likely given many years of good service in the past; and it is often by no means altogether his fault that he is no longer efficient, since he may have been kept too long on the same job or have suffered in other ways; and generally the staffs of most Departments would prefer to suffer themselves through having to work harder to carry their 'below-average colleagues' rather than see them pushed out at great personal hardship. There is an *esprit de corps* in the Service which in itself is desirable although it may lead to excessive sympathy. For dismissal it can be argued that the public service cannot afford to carry the inefficient and that ineffective work should not be tolerated; that dismissals on such grounds from time to time may provide an incentive to the staff to be on their toes. An extreme view on either side would, I think, be wrong, but I am disposed to the view that rather more dismissals on grounds of inefficiency would be good for the morale, the spirit, and the liveliness of the service. The problem is not really solved by well-meant transfers.

Top-level Appointments

The right of appointment to the top posts in a Department remains with the Minister in charge of the Department. But since 1920 the Minister has had to get the approval of the Prime Minister for appointment to and removal from posts in the top two grades in the Civil Service and in regard to posts of Finance Officer and Establishment Officer.

The reason for this arrangement was to make sure that when a vacancy in these ranks occurs in any Department, the Minister does not fill the vacancy automatically by appointing the best man in the Department irrespective of whether the Department can produce a man who is really competent to fill the job, or whether there is available in another Department a candidate who would be distinctly better than the man on the spot. The view was taken that the most suitable person to advise the Prime Minister was the Permanent Secretary to the Treasury.

When a Permanent Secretary is due to retire in a few months' time the practice is, I gather, for the succession to be discussed between the Permanent Secretary to the Treasury and the retiring departmental Secretary. It is considered right for the retiring Secretary to be consulted for he knows the Department and its men, he knows the departmental needs, and he is likely to know what his Minister wants. It may be that the Permanent Secretaries are satisfied that the right successor can be found within the Department. But such promotions are by no means automatic, and should there be doubts other names will be discussed between the two Permanent Secretaries. It may be that there is a very obvious man to fill the post, but it may also happen that he would be the best man for a number of Departments. The question then is which Department is likely to need him most. Probably other Permanent Secretaries would be consulted either because of their intimate knowledge of the various candidates under consideration or from past knowledge of the Department. In this way a broadly based judgement is built up from the views of those in the Service who have the best knowledge of the men and the needs of the Department. Usually this process results in agreement between the Secretary to the Treasury and the retiring Permanent Secretary. The matter is then discussed with the Minister concerned by one or the other or they may both talk it over with him. It is, of course, important that the departmental Minister should be properly satisfied and feel that he can work happily with the proposed new Permanent Secretary. When agreement has been reached with the Minister concerned, the Prime Minister is advised by the Permanent Secretary to the Treasury of the Minister's recommendation for the new Permanent Secretary, that the Permanent Secretary to the Treasury supports this and seeks the Prime Minister's approval, which is usually given. It is, of course, possible that either the departmental Minister and/or the Prime Minister will be unable to accept the recommendation and that difficulty may arise. I gather that this is a rare contingency, and no doubt if it occurred the matter would be the subject of friendly discussion at No. 10.

It could be argued that the principal official adviser should not be the Permanent Secretary of a particular State Department, even though that Department be the Treasury, and that the responsibility for advising the departmental Minister and the Prime Minister should be transferred to a non-departmental Minister who would be outside departmental influence. However, these are possibilities and speculations upon which I do not feel able to pronounce at this time.

The Foreign Service

In all human institutions there are imperfections, but I think that as a whole the British Foreign Service is a fine one, and that the British Foreign Secretary is generally well served. Here and there, as in the business world, are to be found some misfits. Some members of the Foreign Service may have wrong or outmoded ideas, but that can be remedied (though it may take time) by the Secretary of State if he asserts himself and, after discussion, imposes new ideas and policies on the Department; for the staff will carry out the clear directions of their ministerial chief. It may be that owing to past traditions or mistakes there are some Ambassadors in the wrong places or even Ambassadors who ought not to be Ambassadors, though I am confident that the Embassies are increasingly well staffed and served.

There is a Committee at the Foreign Office (which includes a Minister) concerned with promotions and appointments. It does good work and produces what it believes to be the best recommendations, but this matter of appointments, particularly of Ambassadors and Ministers to foreign countries, is a baffling business for any Foreign Secretary who is new to the Foreign Office and who cannot know well more than a small proportion of the men up for consideration. He can cross-examine his advisers; he may find some reason to see and talk to the 'possible' or 'possibles', but unless he is easily satisfied he cannot feel sure. The best he can do is to inspire the Committee that does the work with the right spirit and to do everything he can to be sure by cross-examining those who advise him on such matters and by personal interview. It may be that we shall find improvements of method but I am bound to confess that they are not yet obvious to me. Foreign affairs in this twentieth-century world are very different from what they were in the nineteenth century or even in the early part of this century; the old imperialism has gone and a new Communist imperialism has emerged; the 'cold war' and the propaganda and the fifth-column methods of totalitarianism create new problems; our Embassies abroad have to handle a wide variety of financial, economic, and social problems which did not concern them to any great extent years ago; the information services are of real importance. There are special and difficult problems of much importance in the Middle East and the Far East. Consequently, in the staffing of the Embassies, from the Ambassador downwards, all these considerations have to be taken into account. We are living in new times and we need some new types of men. To a substantial extent we are getting them.

The Foreign Office is conscious of these problems. It does a good deal of switching between the Embassies to prevent men getting into a rut, and a good deal of transferring from posts abroad to the Foreign Office and vice versa. This is all to the good, though in the case of some posts, notably Washington, changes should not be too frequent unless for particular reasons.

It is significant that the British Ambassador to Washington has frequently been somebody other than a career diplomat and I think this is often right. I am inclined to think that it might often be right in the case of Paris or even Rome, and, in particular circumstances related to the current tendencies of Soviet foreign policy, of Moscow. But the wholesale exclusion of regular Foreign Service men from the top position in the Embassies abroad would not be right and would have a demoralizing effect on the Foreign Service.

There is something like a Chinese wall round the Foreign Office as a result of which there are little or no temporary incursions of men from other Departments into the Foreign Office or vice versa. I agree, however, that the majority in our Foreign Service must be specially trained and spend their lives in that Service. Some secondments do take place from home Departments to the Foreign Office, but I think these transfers should be greater in number and that Foreign Office men might more often be seconded for temporary experience into the appropriate home Departments. Labour attachés, seconded from the Ministry of Labour, are of fairly recent creation and do valuable work.

Scientists in the Civil Service

In our Civil Service all sorts of scientists are employed, some permanently and some temporarily. The idea that they are all men with long hair and shuffling feet incapable of understanding the practical affairs of the everyday world is wrong. Many of them are at work on very practical matters. Even those who are in the field of fundamental or natural science rather than applied science can sometimes, because of their trained and acute minds, assist in breaking down the elements of a problem of organization and administration. So it was that scientists from the universities and from industry came to be used on a substantial scale in the two world wars, and they made a valued contribution to the scientific aspects of warlike operation and invention. Probably there was a greater use of scientists in the Second than in the First World War; but a notable development took place at the end of the First World War, namely, the establishment of the Department of Scientific and Industrial

Research. When war ended in 1945 it was inevitable that many government scientists should return to non-government work. It could have happened, though this was undesirable, that scientists would cease to play an adequate part in government.

When the Labour Government was formed in 1945 I was charged with the general oversight of scientific research and the utilization of science in the civilian field; formally the Lord President may have carried such a responsibility since the 1920's, but I think it fair to claim that we developed the work and took it more seriously than it had been hitherto. As Lord President of the Council I was in any case responsible for the work of the Department of Scientific and Industrial Research, the Medical Research Council, the Agricultural Research Council, and—later—the Nature Conservancy. It was my belief that science and the scientists had a real contribution to make to the well-being of our country in peace as well as in war. To secure that contribution it seemed to me desirable that in all appropriate cases, civil Departments—especially the production Departments—should include on their staff scientists who could take a full part in the formation of policy; and that in appropriate cases scientists from outside the Service should be used on committees.

To accomplish this I felt the need for arrangements by which I could receive continuing scientific advice at the highest possible level. My colleagues felt the need for a similar organization at the centre of government. We therefore asked the Committee on Future Scientific Policy under Sir Alan Barlow, which had been appointed in December 1945 and which had already prepared an important report on scientific manpower, to advise on this problem.

This Committee reported in the latter part of 1946. The main points of its proposals, which followed fairly closely some informal suggestions made earlier by Sir John Anderson and which were accepted by the Government, were:

(*a*) General ministerial responsibility for civil scientific policy should rest with the Lord President; departmental Ministers should remain responsible for the scientific work of their own Departments.

(*b*) The Scientific Advisory Committee of the Cabinet—a war-time body—should be dissolved and replaced by an Advisory Council on Scientific Policy with terms of reference sufficiently wide to cover not only departmental activities but also academic and industrial research in so far as these impinged on Government policy.

(*c*) The Council should be composed in equal numbers of scientists in the Government service and of eminent outside scientists; its Chairman should be chosen for his imagination, independence of judgement, and experience of the Government machine—he should not necessarily be eminent in the world of science although that would be an advantage.

(*d*) The Council should be assisted by a full-time scientific secretariat.

(*e*) In order to secure adequate liaison on scientific policy in the civil and defence fields the Chairman of the Council should be a member of the Defence Research Policy Committee which was established during 1946; the Chairman of the Defence Research Policy Committee should likewise be a member of the Council and there should be a common element in the secretariats of the two bodies.

The Council was established in January 1947. Its terms of reference were 'To advise the Lord President in the exercise of his responsibilities for the formulation and execution of Government scientific policy'. Its first Chairman was Sir Henry Tizard who was also Chairman of the Defence Research Policy Committee. He rendered outstanding service to the Council in its formative years. We were fortunate to have a Chairman who combined those qualities of imagination, independence of judgement, and experience of government postulated by the Barlow Committee, together with eminence in the world of science.

During 1946 a small scientific secretariat had been set up in the Cabinet Office to serve the various committees dealing with scientific matters. In 1947 it was transferred to the Lord President's Office. The secretariat served the Advisory Council and any sub-committees it might appoint, but in accordance with the Barlow Committee's recommendation one of its members remained in the Ministry of Defence as joint secretary of the Defence Research Policy Committee. The secretariat was of especial importance in the new organization for it was much more than a committee secretariat in the normal sense. It carried out investigations for the Council and its sub-committees; with the Chairman it was responsible for keeping under review all developments in the field of civil science and where necessary raising issues with the Council; it kept in close touch with the Central Economic Planning Staff and with the Economic Section of the Cabinet Office, and fulfilled many functions in the scientific field similar to those undertaken by those two organizations in the economic field; its head reported to me through the Secretary of the Lord President's Office, and was responsible for maintaining liaison between the Lord President's Office, the three Research Councils and the Advisory Council. A friendly and useful contact was maintained with the recognized scientific societies. Co-operation was effected with many Commonwealth and foreign Governments.

In using scientists in government there is much to be said for moving them about, for if they stay too long on the same work it is liable to become monotonous and they may become stale. Indeed, where practicable and in accordance with the public interest, there is a case for the transfer of scientists to and fro between Government and the universities, and Government and private industry. The bodies engaged in research, or their 'clients', will frequently discover new problems or subjects for research, and these projects should be considered on their merits, but unless something else is done the result may be a steady and not essential increase in expenditure, reaching enormous figures. Not only do the suggested new projects require examination, therefore, but existing subjects of research should be reviewed from time to time, for it may be that the research is continuing out of sheer habit and without likely significant results. More than once, therefore, I said to the scientists, 'If you want to spend all this new money you must look round to save some of your present expenditure.' It would be foolish to starve the scientists of necessary resources for work which is, or may well be, remunerative for the community, but in the kind of work which has been discussed in this section it is reasonable to require that science and the scientists shall, as a whole, earn their keep.

Economic and Industrial Questions

In recent years economic and industrial questions have occupied the attention of Government and Parliament to an increasing extent. It is, therefore, more than ever necessary that civil servants, certainly in the Departments that deal with these matters, should have a good knowledge of the industrial and business world and Trade Union organization and policy. There are some practical difficulties about it, but if we can avoid undue intimacy at the time or after their return to the Civil Service there is much to be said for a certain number of civil servants being temporarily seconded to private business and industrial concerns, the nationalized industries and, if Trade Unions were agreeable, to certain studies and work within the Trade Union Movement. They would not be seconded for long periods; only for a time long enough to enable them to learn the language of industry and acquire some general knowledge about its practical problems. This should improve relationships between the Departments and industry and diminish the occasions on which it could legitimately be complained that there was undue bureaucracy and red tape in governmental relations with industry.

An objection to the temporary secondment of civil servants to private industry is possible favouritism, but I am not at all sure that this objection is insuperable. In any case there should be little objection, if any, to such temporary secondments to public corporations, for they are public concerns which must have intimate and fairly continuous relationships with their parent Departments. It would be a good thing if some of the responsible civil servants in the Departments concerned were familiar with the inside working and problems of the public corporations. Indeed, there is much to be said also for the temporary secondment of certain officers of public corporations to the appropriate Government Department in order that they can see and understand the working of the governmental aspect of their affairs. Similar mutual transfers might well also be considered as between central and local government.

One of the big changes inaugurated by the Labour Governments of 1945–51 was economic planning. It had been believed by some people that the Civil Service would not give a Labour

Government adequate or sufficiently genuine service on such a big departure in peace-time policy. I would say that the Civil Service worked with great intensity over long hours and served us well. No doubt there were some sticky ones here and there, and perhaps some Departments were quicker on the uptake than others. There was, of course, some lack of experience, and in a number of quarters a lack of technique. Not only civil servants but also Ministers were largely finding their way in these matters for the first time during peace. In the limited time when as Lord President I was responsible for economic co-ordination, I sought to remedy this by bringing to the Planning Staff a few men of appropriate experience and ability from the business world, and economists and statisticians from the universities, mixing them with the civil servants. With the departure of Sir Edwin Plowden in 1953, the Planning Staff were all members of the Civil Service. I think this was a pity. There are difficulties about it, but I prefer in this organization blending with the Civil Service a suitable proportion of public-spirited men from outside. It is fair to add that the Treasury sees to it that the civil servants are largely seconded from appropriate Departments.

Tribute to the British Civil Service

From a long and varied experience of the British Civil Service in home Departments and in the Foreign Office and as a co-ordinating Minister, I have in general formed a high opinion of the energy, ability, resourcefulness and incorruptibility of our Civil Service. The belief among some of the public and even some Members of Parliament that civil servants do not work in harmony with Ministers I have hardly ever found to be justified. Mistakes may occur in interpreting the Ministerial mind—indeed such mistakes are now and again to be expected; obduracy may be met with here and there. Very large numbers of letters which the Minister has not seen go out commencing 'I am directed by the Minister of So-and-so to acknowledge your letter of . . . and to say. . . .' It is impossible for the Minister to see all these letters and the civil servants are in general really brilliant in knowing what the Minister would wish them to say. Naturally, important letters or letters on doubtful issues of policy go up to the Minister in draft for approval, but for the rest established policy has to be followed and the Ministerial mind correctly interpreted.

Many years ago there was a Labour Minister without previous ministerial experience who suddenly discovered that enormous numbers of letters were going out commencing 'I am directed by the Minister, &c.', which he had not seen. The Minister was very indignant and said, 'Why do you send out letters saying that I have directed you to say so-and-so when I have done nothing of the kind?' It was politely explained that life would be impossible for him if he were to see every one of these letters in draft. But he was insistent that he would not permit his name to be taken in vain and gave direct instructions that all such letters should be submitted to him for approval. Within a few days his room was impossibly crowded with files and draft letters. The Minister learnt his lesson and had to give way. In view of the enormous number of communications of this character which leave Departments, the fact that very few subsequently prove to be contrary to the Minister's ideas is in itself an eloquent tribute not only to the loyalty of civil servants but also to their ability in stating what the Minister would wish them to say.

The higher civil servants in Government Departments in most cases work very hard over long hours, frequently taking papers home with them to study and minute. It is a nice point to consider which is the most injurious to the public interest: an overworked Minister or an overworked civil servant. Both are dangerous and undesirable, though frequently unavoidable, especially when Governments are driving themselves and the machine hard, as we were in the Labour Governments of 1945–51. If I had to make a choice I would be inclined to say that it is perhaps more dangerous for the higher civil servants to be overworked, for they have to do the detailed planning and thinking and drafting, and if they do make bad mistakes it is possible that the Minister may not notice them, and then serious trouble may ensue. What the reader can be sure of is that the British Civil Service is loyal to the Government of the day. The worst that can be said of them is that sometimes they are not quick enough in accustoming themselves to new ideas, but then it is up to the Minister to educate them. The greatest danger in the running of a Government Department is a Minister who does not know how to handle civil servants; who does not possess a mind of his own; or who is lazy and finds life easier and pleasanter by blindly taking the advice of his civil servants without considering and criticizing it.

APPENDIX A: SUMMARY OF SESSIONAL TIME-TABLES FOR PARLIAMENTS OF 1945–50 AND 1950–1

Business	1945–6	1946–7	1947–8	1948 short session	1948–9	1950	1950–1
	Days 212	*Days 164*	*Days 171*	*Days 10*	*Days 208*	*Days 104*	*Days 153 (incl. 2 two-day sittings)**
Election of Speaker and Swearing-in	3	0	0	0	0	3	0
VJ Day: Thanksgiving Service, &c..	1	0	0	0	0	0	0
Address	4	6½	6½	4	7	6	6
Budgets and Finance Bills	1st 9 2nd 11½	13	1st 7 2nd 14	0	11½	14	15½ (incl. 2 two-day sittings)*
Supply	29½ (incl. four Fridays)	29½	26	0	26	26	26½
Consolidated Fund and Appropriation Bills	6	4	4	0	4	4	4
Government Legislation	101½	83½	88½	2	112	23	62¼
Special Debates, &c. (Debates on Government, Opposition, and Back-bench Motions, on the Adjournment and on Orders and Regulations)	41	22½	19	2	32½	19	14¾
Private Members' Time†	0	0	0	0	10 (*Bills*)	5 (*Motions*)	19 (*Motions* = 10 *Bills* = 9)
Adjournments at Recesses	4½	4	4	1	4	3	4
Adjournments as Tributes	0	0	1	0	0	0	0
Prorogation	1	1	1	1	1	1	1
	212	164	171	10	208	104	153

* On two occasions the sitting lasted beyond the normal hour of sitting on the following day.

† There was a gradual restoration of Private Members' rights and privileges following the war years and the years 1945–8. The Labour Government in Session 1948–9 had a heavy programme but felt that the time had come when some Private Members' facilities should be restored and decided upon ten Fridays for Bills rather than giving any time at all for Private Members' Motions. In 1950 the General Election occurred in February and it was not possible for the new Parliament to meet before 1 March. In this Session it was felt best to give five days for Private Members' Motions—no more time could be given because of the lateness in starting the Session. Indeed, for the same reason if facilities had been given for Private Members' Bills they could not have been completed in both Houses by the end of July.

APPENDIX B

ALLOCATION OF TIME ORDERS (GUILLOTINES)

1. *Labour Government's Iron and Steel Bill, 1948–49*

THURSDAY, 25TH NOVEMBER, 1948

Ordered, That the proceedings on the Committee stage, Report stage, and Third Reading of the Iron and Steel Bill shall be proceeded with as follows:

(1) *Committee Stage*

(*a*) The Standing Committee to which the Bill is referred shall report the Bill to the House on or before the seventeenth day of March next.

(*b*) At a Sitting at which any proceedings are to be brought to a conclusion under a resolution of the Business Sub-Committee as agreed to by the Standing Committee, the Chairman shall not adjourn the Committee under any Order relating to the Sittings of the Committee until the proceedings have been brought to a conclusion.

(*c*) At a Sitting at which any proceedings are to be brought to a conclusion under such a Resolution, no Motion relating to the Sittings of the Committee, no dilatory Motion with respect to proceedings on the Bill or the Adjournment of the Committee, nor Motion to postpone a Clause, shall be moved except by the Government, and the Question on any such Motion (other than a Motion relating to the Sittings of the Committee), if moved by the Government, shall be put forthwith without any debate.

(*d*) On the conclusion of the Committee stage of the Bill the Chairman shall report the Bill to the House without Question put.

(2) *Report Stage and Third Reading*

(*a*) Four allotted days shall be given to the Report stage (including any proceedings on the re-committal of the Bill).

(*b*) One allotted day shall be given to the Third Reading, and the proceedings thereon shall, if not previously brought to a conclusion, be brought to a conclusion at 9.30 p.m. on that day.

(*c*) Any day other than a Friday on which the Bill is put down as the first Order of the day shall be considered an allotted day for the purposes of this Order.

(*d*) Any Private Business which has been set down for consideration at 7 p.m. and any Motion for Adjournment under Standing Order No. 9 (Adjournment on a definite matter of urgent public importance) on an allotted day shall on that day, instead of being taken as provided by the Standing Orders, be taken at the conclusion of the proceedings on the Bill or under this Order for that day, and any Private Business or Motion for Adjournment so taken may be proceeded with, though opposed, notwithstanding any Standing Order relating to the Sittings of the House.

(*e*) On a day on which any proceedings are to be brought to a conclusion under any Resolution of the Business Committee as agreed to by the House or under this Order, those proceedings shall not be interrupted under the provisions of any Standing Order relating to the Sittings of the House.

(*f*) On a day on which any proceedings are to be brought to a conclusion under any Resolution of the Business Committee as agreed to by the House or under this Order, no dilatory Motion with respect to proceedings on the Bill or under this Order, nor Motion to re-commit the Bill, shall be moved unless moved by the Government, and the Question on any such Motion, if moved by the Government, shall be put forthwith without any debate.

(3) *General*

(*a*) For the purpose of bringing to a conclusion any proceedings which are to be brought to a conclusion at a time appointed by a Resolution of the Business Sub-Committee, as agreed to by the Standing Committee, or by a Resolution of the Business Committee, as agreed to by the House, or by this Order, and which have not previously been brought to a conclusion, the Chairman or Mr. Speaker shall, at the time so appointed, put forthwith the Question on any Amendment or Motion already proposed from the Chair, and, in the case of a new Clause which has been read a second time, also the Question that the Clause be added to the Bill, and shall next proceed to put forthwith the Questions on any Amendments, new Clauses or new Schedules moved by the Government of which notice has been given (but no other Amendments, new Clauses or new Schedules), and any Question necessary for the disposal of the

Business to be concluded, and, in the case of Government Amendments or Government new Clauses or Government new Schedules, he shall put only the Questions that the Amendments be made or that the Clauses or Schedules be added to the Bill, as the case may be.

(*b*) Nothing in this Order or in a Resolution of the Business Sub-Committee or Business Committee shall—

(i) prevent any proceedings which thereunder are to be concluded on any particular day or at any particular Sitting being concluded on an earlier day or at an earlier Sitting, or necessitate any particular day or Sitting or part of a particular day or Sitting being given to any such proceedings if those proceedings have been otherwise disposed of; or

(ii) prevent any other business being proceeded with on a particular day, or part of a particular day, in accordance with the Standing Orders of this House, if any proceedings to be concluded on that particular day, or part of a particular day, have been disposed of.

(*c*) In this Order the expressions 'Business Committee' and 'Business Sub-Committee' respectively mean the Committee appointed under Standing Order No. 41 (Business Committee), and the Sub-Committee appointed under Standing Order No. 64 (Business Sub-Committee) of the Standing Committee to which the Bill is referred.

TUESDAY, 7TH DECEMBER, 1948

Resolution *reported* from the Business Sub-Committee of Standing Committee C as follows:

That, except so far as may hereafter be otherwise provided by a resolution of this Sub-Committee as agreed to by the Standing Committee,

(*a*) thirty-five Sittings shall be allotted to the consideration of the Iron and Steel Bill by the Standing Committee;

(*b*) the proceedings to be taken at the Sittings specified in the first column of the table at the end of this resolution shall be as shown in the second column of that table;

(*c*) the proceedings which, under that table, are to be taken at any Sitting or group of Sittings shall, if not previously brought to a conclusion, be brought to a conclusion two and a quarter hours after the time appointed for the commencement of that Sitting or, as the case may be, of the last of those Sittings.

TABLE

Sitting	Proceedings
First	Clauses 1 to 4
Second	
Third	
Fourth	
Fifth	
Sixth	
Seventh	
Eighth . . .	Clauses 5 to 10
Ninth	
Tenth. . . .	Clauses 11 to 13
Eleventh	
Twelfth	
Thirteenth . . .	Clauses 14 to 16
Fourteenth	
Fifteenth	
Sixteenth	
Seventeenth . .	Clauses 17 and 18
Eighteenth . . .	Clauses 19 to 26
Nineteenth	
Twentieth	
Twenty-first	
Twenty-second	
Twenty-third . .	Clauses 27 and 28
Twenty-fourth . .	Clauses 29 to 34
Twenty-fifth . .	Clauses 35 and 36
Twenty-sixth . .	Clauses 37 to 40
Twenty-seventh	
Twenty-eighth	
Twenty-ninth . .	Clauses 41 to 58
Thirtieth	
Thirty-first	
Thirty-second . .	Postponed Clauses, New Clauses, Schedules and New Schedules, and any other Proceedings necessary to bring the Committee stage to a conclusion
Thirty-third	
Thirty-fourth	
Thirty-fifth	

THURSDAY, 7TH APRIL, 1949

Recommendation *reported* from the Business Committee:

That,

(*a*) the Proceedings on the Report Stage of the Iron and Steel Bill shall be divided into the parts specified in the second column of the table set out below;

(*b*) the four days which, under the Order [25 November], are given to the Report Stage of the said Bill, and portions of those days, shall be allotted in the manner shown in that table; and

(*c*) each part of the Proceedings shall, if not previously brought to a conclusion, be brought to a conclusion at the time specified in the third column of that table.

TABLE

Allotted day	*Proceedings*	*Time for conclusion of Proceedings*
		p.m.
First day . .	New Clauses and Clause 1	8.0
	Clauses 2, 3, and 4	10.0
Second day . .	Clauses 5 to 10	5.30
	Clauses 11 to 19	10.0
Third day . .	Clauses 20 to 28	5.30
	Clauses 29 to 32	10.0
Fourth day . .	Clauses 33 to 42	6.0
	Clauses 43 to 60, New Schedules, Schedules 1 to 8, and any other Proceedings necessary to bring the Report Stage to a conclusion	10.0

2. *Conservative Government's Transport Bill, 1952–53*

MONDAY, 24TH NOVEMBER, 1952

Ordered, That the following provisions shall apply to the remaining Proceedings on the Transport Bill—

1. The Proceedings in Committee shall be completed in seven allotted days.

2. The Proceedings on Consideration shall be completed in two [changed to 'three' by amendment of 21st January, 1953] allotted days.

3. The Proceedings on Third Reading shall be completed in one allotted day and shall be brought to a conclusion at half-past Ten o'clock on that day.

4. The Business Committee shall report their Recommendations to the House—

(*a*) as to the Proceedings in Committee, not later than Monday 1st December;

(*b*) as to the Proceedings on Consideration, not later than the fourth day on which the House sits in 1953 [changed to 'Wednesday 28th January' by amendment of 21st January, 1953].

5. No Motion shall be made to postpone any Clause, Schedule, new Clause or new Schedule, but the Recommendations of the Business Committee may include alterations in the order in which the Clauses, new Clauses, Schedules and new Schedules are to be taken in Committee.

6. On an allotted day—

(*a*) Standing Order No. 1 (Sittings of the House) and paragraph (2) of Standing Order No. 9 (Adjournment on definite matter of urgent public importance) shall have effect with the substitution of references to half-past Ten of the clock for references to Ten of the clock;

(*b*) Proceedings which under this Order or the Resolution of the Business Committee are to be brought to a conclusion on that day shall not be interrupted under the provisions of the said Standing Order No. 1.

7. If, on an allotted day, Proceedings on the Bill are interrupted by a Motion for the Adjournment of the House under Standing Order No. 9 (Adjournment on definite matter of urgent public importance), the bringing to a conclusion of any Proceedings on the Bill which, under this Order or under the Resolution of the Business Committee, are to be brought to a conclusion on that day after Seven o'clock shall be deferred for a period equal to the duration of the Proceedings upon that Motion.

8. If, at Seven o'clock on an allotted day, any Proceedings on the Bill which, under the Resolution of the Business Committee, are to be brought to a conclusion at or before that time have not been concluded, any Motion for the Adjournment of the House under Standing Order No. 9 (Adjournment on definite matter of urgent public importance) which, apart from this Order, would stand over to that time, shall stand over until those Proceedings have been concluded.

9. Any Private Business which has been set down for consideration at Seven o'clock on an allotted day shall, instead of being considered as provided by the Standing Orders, be considered at the conclusion of the Proceedings on the Bill on that day, and may be proceeded with, though opposed, notwithstanding anything in Standing Order No. 1 (Sittings of the House).

10. Standing Order No. 12 (Motions for leave to bring in Bills and nomination of Select Committees at commencement of Public Business) shall not apply to any allotted day.

11. On an allotted day no dilatory Motion with respect to Proceedings on the Bill shall be made except by a member of the Government, and the Question on any such Motion shall be put forthwith without any debate.

12. When the order of the day is read for the House to resolve itself into Committee on the Bill, Mr. Speaker shall leave the Chair without putting any Question, notwithstanding that notice of an Instruction has been given.

13. On the conclusion of the Proceedings in any Committee on the Bill, including a Committee to which the Bill has been re-committed (whether as a whole or otherwise), the Chairman shall report the Bill to the House without putting any Question.

14. For the purpose of bringing to a conclusion any Proceedings on the Bill which, under this Order or the Resolution of the Business Committee are to be brought to a conclusion at a particular time and have not previously been concluded, the Chairman or Mr. Speaker shall, at that time, put forthwith the Question on any Amendment or Motion already proposed from the Chair, and, in the case of a new Clause which has been read a second time, also the question that the Clause be added to the Bill, and subject thereto shall proceed to put forthwith the Question on any Amendments, new Clauses or new Schedules moved by a member of the Government of which notice has been given (but no other Amendments, new Clauses or new Schedules) and any Question necessary for the disposal of the Business to be concluded and, in the case of any Amendments, new Clauses or new Schedules moved by a Member of the Government he shall put only the Question that the Amendment be made or that the Clause or Schedule be added to the Bill.

15. The Proceedings on any Motion moved by a member of the Government for varying or supplementing this Order or a Resolution of the Business Committee shall, if not previously concluded, be brought to a conclusion two hours after they have been commenced, and the last preceding paragraph of this Order shall, so far as applicable, apply as if the Proceedings were Proceedings on the Bill:

Provided that if the Proceedings are interrupted by a Motion for the Adjournment of the House under Standing Order No. 9 (Adjournment on definite matter of urgent public importance), the time at which they are to be brought to a conclusion shall be deferred for a period equal to the duration of the Proceedings upon the Motion for the Adjournment.

If any Motion moved by a member of the Government for varying or supplementing this Order or the Resolution of the Business Committee is under consideration at Seven o'clock on a day on which any Private Business has been set down for consideration at Seven o'clock, the Private Business shall stand over and be considered when the Proceedings on the Motion have been concluded.

16. Nothing in this Order or in the Resolution of the Business Committee shall—

(*a*) prevent any Proceedings to which the Order or Resolution applies from being taken or completed earlier than is required by the Order or Resolution; or

(*b*) prevent any Business (whether on the Bill or not) from being proceeded with on any day, in accordance with the Standing Orders, if the Proceedings which under this Order or the Resolution are to be completed on that day have already been completed.

17. In this Order, 'allotted day' means any day (other than a Friday) on which the Bill is put down as the first Government order of the day, 'the Resolution of the Business Committee' means the Resolution of the Business Committee as agreed to by the House, and references to the Proceedings on Consideration or the Proceedings on Third Reading include references to any Proceedings at those stages respectively, for, on or in consequence of re-committal.

THURSDAY, 27TH NOVEMBER, 1952

Recommendation *reported* from the Business Committee:

That—

(*a*) the Proceedings in Committee [of the Whole House] shall be divided into the parts specified in the second column of the table set out below;

(*b*) the seven days which, under the Order [24th November] are given to the Proceedings in Committee, and portions of those days, shall be allotted in the manner shown in that table; and

(*c*) subject to the provision of paragraph 7 of the Order [24th November], each part of the Proceedings shall, if not previously brought to a conclusion, be brought to a conclusion at the time specified in the third column of that table.

TABLE

Allotted day	*Proceedings*	*Time for conclusion of Proceedings*
		p.m.
First day . .	Clause 1	8.0
	Clause 2	10.30
Second day . .	Clause 3	6.30
	Clause 4	9.0
	Clause 5	10.30
Third day . .	Clauses 6 and 7 and the First Schedule .	5.30
	Clauses 8 and 9	7.30
	Clause 16	10.30
Fourth day . .	Clause 10, the Second Schedule and Clause 11	7.30
	Clauses 12 and 13	10.30
Fifth day . .	Clauses 14, 15, and 17	10.30
Sixth day . .	Clauses 18 and 19	7.0
	Clauses 20 to 23	10.30
Seventh day . .	Clauses 27 and 26	7.0
	Clauses 24 and 25	8.30
	Clauses 28 to 35, the Third Schedule, New Clauses, New Schedules and any other Proceedings necessary to bring the Committee Stage to a conclusion . .	10.30

TUESDAY, 27TH JANUARY, 1953

Recommendation *reported* from the Business Committee:—

That—

(*a*) the Proceedings on Consideration shall be divided into the parts specified in the second column of the table set out below;

(*b*) the three days which, under the Order [24th November], as amended by the Order [21st January], are given to the Proceedings on Consideration, and portions of those days, shall be allotted in the manner shown in that table; and

(*c*) subject to the provisions of paragraph 7 of the Order [24th November], each part of the Proceedings shall, if not previously brought to a conclusion, be brought to a conclusion at the time specified in the third column of that table.

TABLE

Allotted day	*Proceedings*	*Time for conclusion of Proceedings*
		p.m.
First day . .	Re-committal, if any, and new Clauses .	5.0
	Clauses 1 to 3	10.30
Second day . .	Clauses 4 and 5	5.30
	Clauses 6 to 13	8.30
	Clauses 14 and 15	10.30
Third day . .	Clauses 16 and 17	5.30
	Clauses 18 to 23	7.30
	Clauses 24 to 28	9.30
	Clauses 29 to 35, new Schedules, Schedules and any other Proceedings necessary to bring the Proceedings on Consideration to a conclusion	10.30

MONDAY, 27TH APRIL, 1953

Ordered, That the Order [24th November] be supplemented as follows:

1. The proceedings on consideration of the Lords Amendments shall be completed at this day's sitting.

2. If, on expiration of four hours from the time when the Order of the day for the consideration of those Amendments is read, or at half-past Ten o'clock, whichever is the later, those proceedings have not been completed, Mr. Speaker shall forthwith put, as a single question, the question that the Lords Amendments, so far as not already agreed to or disagreed to, and (if it has not been already disposed of) the Amendment to the Bill (Schedule 4, page 50, leave out lines 22 and 23) standing on the notice paper in the name of Mr. Lennox-Boyd, be agreed to:

Provided that if at this day's sitting the said proceedings are interrupted by a Motion for the Adjournment of the House under Standing Order No. 9 (Adjournment on definite matter of urgent public importance) the time at which Mr. Speaker is to put that question shall be deferred for a period equal to the duration of the Proceedings upon the Motion for the Adjournment.

Index

PRINTED IN
GREAT BRITAIN
AT THE
UNIVERSITY PRESS
OXFORD
BY
CHARLES BATEY
PRINTER
TO THE
UNIVERSITY